VISCOUNTESS RHONDDA, EQUALITARIAN FEMINIST

Margaret Haig Thomas Mackworth, Viscountess Rhondda. Courtesy of the Mansell Collection Ltd., London.

VISCOUNTESS RHONDDA, EQUALITARIAN FEMINIST

Shirley M. Eoff

OHIO STATE UNIVERSITY PRESS: Columbus

Library of Congress Cataloging-in-Publication Data

Eoff, Shirley M. (Shirley Marie), 1954–
Viscountess Rhondda : equalitarian feminist / Shirley M. Eoff.
p. cm.
Includes bibliographical references and index.
ISBN 0–8142–0539–9
1. Mackworth, Margaret Haig Thomas, Viscountess Rhondda, b. 1883. 2. Feminists –
Great Britain – Biography. 3. Feminism – Great Britain – History – 20th century. I. Title.
HQ1593.M28E54 1991
305.42′092 – dc20
[B]

90–22439
CIP

The paper in this book meets the guidelines for permanence and
durability of the Committee on Production Guidelines for Book
Longevity of the Council on Library Resources.

Printed in the U.S.A.

9 8 7 6 5 4 3 2 1

CONTENTS

Preface vii
Acknowledgments xi

1 · Formative Influences: Family and School 1
2 · Loosening the Bonds 19
3 · Entry into a Man's World 34
4 · Independent Businesswoman 53
5 · Equalitarian Feminist 64
6 · The Private Margaret 100
7 · Publisher and Editor 117

Conclusion 147
Notes 153
Bibliography 173
Index 181

PREFACE

Despite a reputation as one of the leading feminists of the interwar years and one of Britain's most acclaimed businesswomen and political journalists, Margaret Haig Thomas Mackworth, Viscountess Rhondda, has received only limited attention from students of the feminist movement. This significant omission is probably due to a combination of factors. Few personal papers exist to help reconstruct her private life. Several large boxes of private records and mementos were stored in the basement of the *Time and Tide* offices shortly after her death, but they were apparently destroyed when the basement flooded a few months later. This lack of personal papers and Lady Rhondda's intensely private nature leave a perceptible gap in scholars' understanding of her private emotions and relationships. In addition, her varied interests make it difficult to fit her career into any easily definable category. Heavily involved in business, feminism, and journalism while on the fringes of significant literary, social, and political circles, Lady Rhondda defies simple categorization.

Much of the writing in women's studies has focused on the prewar suffrage movement, in which Lady Rhondda was only a very marginal character, and has until recently neglected the interwar period, in which she was a dominant force. Many of those who have attempted to correct this oversight still have not done full justice to Lady Rhondda. They often dismiss her as a peripheral figure who deserves brief mention for her suffragette activities and her battle for equality in the 1920s and 1930s but who cannot be forgiven for (supposedly) abandoning her commitment to feminism in later years.

Likewise, the weekly review she edited, *Time and Tide,* has found itself generally neglected in discussions of interwar policy and culture. Considering that the journal had a peak circulation of approximately 40,000 and was regarded by prominent publishers like Lord Camrose and Kingsley Martin as one of the leading journals of opinion in the 1930s and 1940s, this omission is rather curious. The other major journals, the *New Statesman and Nation,* the *Spectator,* and the *Economist* are frequently cited in both general works and studies of the press and public opinion. Even the less influential *Truth* and *Tribune* receive more comment than *Time and Tide.* The major factors contributing to this neglect are the journal's availability and dichotomous perceptions of its intent and content. Only two full sets of the journal exist – one held privately by the Trust House Forte Company, the other deposited in the British Newspaper Library at Colindale. Because *Time and Tide* is not indexed, few researchers have given it the attention it deserves, especially since the journal's reputation has suffered from oversimplifications. Many, aware of the strong feminist orientation and demands for equalitarianism in the first decade of its existence, have labeled *Time and Tide* a feminist polemic, which obviates in the minds of some any need to search for significant comment in realms outside the struggle for women's rights. But feminists, while recognizing the review's contributions to the cause in those early years, deplore its decline into "eminent respectability" and think of it as nothing more than a literary review after 1930.

Yet a study of the existing records of Lady Rhondda's life and a survey of the complete span of *Time and Tide*'s coverage of events between its first issue in 1920 and its proprietor's death in 1958 contradict such simplistic and dichotomous views. There emerges instead an underlying unity – a deep commitment to continuing the struggle for equality and social justice in the midst of the immense challenges and broadening opportunities of a rapidly changing world. Born in the heyday of late Victorianism, reaching maturity in the freer Edwardian era, and living through an age dominated by two world wars, Lady Rhondda found herself plunged into a new world and confronted with new opportunities and responsibilities for which her training and education had left her unprepared. Watching an old world die, she uneasily sought to find her place in the modern one, and despite a stellar career as a feminist, businesswoman, and journalist, never quite succeeded in adapting. The words of Matthew Arnold in his "Stanzas from the Grande Chartreuse" seem particularly fitting for Lady Rhondda:

> Wandering between two worlds, one dead,
> The other powerless to be born,
> With nowhere yet to rest my head. . .

Though she fought to break the bonds of her past, and succeeded in the public realm, late Victorian mores continued to influence her private thoughts and emotions. The one constant in her life was her commitment to the ideals of equality, individualism, and justice. While many details may be missing regarding various aspects of her life, Lady Rhondda's long record of public service and committed feminism deserve much more attention than has yet been given them.

The intent here is not to present a complete biography, but to illuminate Lady Rhondda's struggle for equal rights and social justice in modern Britain. As a young woman from a privileged background, she was recruited into the militant suffragette movement at the age of twenty-five and then committed the rest of her life to the feminist struggle. As businesswoman, prominent member of British and international feminist organizations, and publisher and editor of *Time and Tide,* she was part of a determined minority which kept the struggle for women's rights alive in the inhospitable climate of the post–World War I years. Her feminist activity is the central issue of the study, but it is necessary to examine her work in the closely related realms of domestic reform and peace activism, which stemmed at least in part from her feminism. Where possible, Lady Rhondda's personal experiences have been considered against the backdrop of women's changing political, social, and economic status.

ACKNOWLEDGMENTS

In attempting to reconstruct the experiences of Lady Rhondda, I have incurred debts too numerous to recount. Librarians and archivists throughout England, Wales, Canada, and the United States provided material and direction which made the research phase of this project a thoroughly enjoyable and rewarding experience. Brian L. Blakeley, of Texas Tech University, who introduced me to the topic, offered invaluable assistance and support. His careful reading and trenchant criticism sharpened my focus, and his encouragement provided an incentive to complete the project. Jim Brink, Jacquelin Collins, Jim Harper, Joseph King, Otto Nelson, and Walt McDonald, all of Texas Tech University, read the whole or parts of the draft and offered perceptive comments which strengthened the finished product immeasurably. Thanks are also due my colleagues at Angelo State University, who have provided support and advice throughout the project, to the reviewers for the Ohio State University Press who pointed out some of its weaknesses, suggested valuable secondary sources, and helped me to clarify my arguments, and to Alex Holzman for his encouragement and his patience. And finally, to my mother, who has been a constant source of financial and emotional support, I owe a special debt which can never be repaid.

1 · FORMATIVE INFLUENCES: FAMILY AND SCHOOL

Margaret Haig Thomas, the only child of David Alfred Thomas and his wife Sybil, was born in London on 12 June 1883. The Thomases, who had been married just over a year, had anxiously awaited the arrival of this child, who would firmly cement their union. Their marriage was an interesting mix of the landed and industrial capitalist worlds, and they had worked hard to mold the best of their two spheres into a loving and secure home for the children they anticipated. The blend they had created was distinctive, combining elements of conventional gentility and modern competitiveness, and it provided their daughter with a firm foundation throughout her life and prepared her for the challenges of a rapidly changing world.

Sybil Margaret, fourth daughter of George Augustus and Anne Eliza Haig of Pen Ithon, Radnorshire, was descended from an ancient Scottish border family, the Haigs of Bemersyde, to which the World War I commander General Sir Douglas Haig belonged. With her five brothers and four sisters, she grew up in a clannish atmosphere where family ties and responsibilities were emphasized and outsiders viewed with suspicion. Her father had unsuccessfully stood for Parliament three times, once as a Conservative and twice as an Independent, before devoting his full attention to the estate. He was a kind and loving man, but also something of an authoritarian. He expected his children to be tough, virtuous, and obedient. Any strong strain of unconventionality in the Haig women was firmly suppressed. One sister, Charlotte, had wanted to be a doctor or a businesswoman. Both occupations were vetoed by her father, and as the only unmarried daughter, she had to settle for assuming the task of family housekeeper.[1] This unconventional spirit was largely lacking in Sybil but it came out later in her daughter.

Unlike her sister, Sybil was content to cultivate the "womanly virtues." She was groomed for a life of service – to her father's family and
later to her own. By the time she married David Alfred Thomas in
1882, she had become a quiet, virtuous, and very proper young woman.
Sybil embodied the Victorian ideal of the cultured lady of leisure and
devoted wife and mother. Prepared from childhood for a life of service
and self-sacrifice, she willingly placed her husband's interests above her
own. She was widely known for the comfort and hospitality of her home
and for her many charitable acts. Acquaintances reported that she had
a rare gift for putting people at ease, and few recognized that she entertained only because it was expected of someone in her position. Sybil
was never comfortable outside her own family circle and would have
much preferred to spend her time gardening or painting miniatures.[2]

Her husband came from a much different background. The third surviving child of Samuel and Rachel Thomas of Ysgyborwen in Wales
(twelve of seventeen children died in infancy), David Alfred Thomas
was born at a time when his parents' fortunes were rather low. His father, a grocer in Merthyr Tydfil, had a tendency to gamble away hard-
earned money in risky speculative ventures. At the time of D.A.'s birth
on 26 March 1856, Samuel's latest dabbling in colliery speculations had
left the family in desperate straits. He greeted the birth of his son with
the solemn words: "Well, I see nothing for him but the workhouse."[3]
Samuel Thomas was by all accounts grim, unsociable, and a strict dis-
ciplinarian. Rachel was much younger, popular, outgoing, and slightly
extravagant. She was an independent and spirited woman for her day.
To punish her for extravagance, her husband once burned an expensive
fur coat purchased without his permission. She simply went out, bought
a new one, and informed him that she would not be intimidated by his
bullying tactics. Her granddaughter Margaret would later relate this incident, commenting that it showed "a very proper spirit."[4]

D. A. Thomas seems to have inherited more of his mother's disposition than his father's. He too rebelled against paternal authority and
was notable as a youth for his high spirits and natural charm. By the
time he reached school age, his father's fortunes had recovered sufficiently for D.A. to attend private schools, where his natural mathem-
atical abilities won him a scholarship to Cambridge (which he forfeited
because he preferred boxing, swimming, and rowing to studying). Upon
graduation, he returned to south Wales, began a long and profitable association with the Cambrian collieries in the Rhondda Valley, and entered
into a happy marriage with Sybil Haig. His financial acumen, personal

ambition, and skill in dealing with people combined to make the boy his father had feared doomed to the workhouse into a rising power in the south Wales coalfields.

D.A.'s real interest, however, was not business, but politics. He longed to enter the halls of Westminster, to serve the public, and to bask in the spotlight. He first campaigned for Parliament in 1888 and was returned unopposed as a Gladstonian Liberal for Merthyr Tydfil. By 1891 he was considered one of the outstanding members of the new generation of "radical" Welsh politicians, along with David Lloyd George and Alfred Thomas, but he never really fulfilled his early promise.[5] Though he easily held his seat through four subsequent elections, he failed to make a favorable impression on the party leadership and was never even asked to sit on a committee. His parliamentary failure was sometimes attributed by contemporaries to his difficult personality, the dullness of his speeches, or his rivalry with David Lloyd George.[6] The rift with Lloyd George apparently stemmed from ambition, egotism, and the deep political divisions within the Welsh nation. The interests of Thomas' south Wales constituents differed greatly from those of Lloyd George's supporters in north Wales. Large-scale English immigration and major industrial development in the south had caused that region to lose much of its uniquely Welsh character and to become keenly interested in industrial development, world market issues, and protection of the working classes. In contrast, declining industry and a relatively static population led north Wales to turn inward, to glorify in its distinctive Welshness. There the major concerns were land monopoly and disestablishment.[7] In attempting to serve the disparate needs of their constituents, these two men, both considering themselves the spokesman for Welsh nationalism and both politically ambitious, were certain to clash. Ultimately Lloyd George proved to be the more skillful politician. By 1902 he had emerged as the premier Welsh parliamentarian. D. A. Thomas remained in the House of Commons until 1910, but he became less involved each year. Frustrated at being continually passed over by the party leadership, he retired from politics with his desire to provide distinguished service largely unfulfilled. He returned home determined to devote all his energies to the south Wales coal industry, and in a few years he emerged as the leading colliery owner and coal broker in south Wales, earning a reputation as a shrewd and capable businessman. He used his financial acumen and organizational talents to amass a huge fortune – and seemed quite content to leave politics to the parliamentarians.

Yet five years after his resignation, the outbreak of World War I brought

D. A. Thomas back to his first love – public service. Called into service by his old rival David Lloyd George, the commercial magnate and financier proved himself an able administrator and statesman as wartime food minister. He skillfully steered food control measures through the War Cabinet over sometimes fierce objections from both the War Office and the Treasury. He interpreted policies for the press and the public and mediated potential conflicts between farmers and tradesmen, bureaucrats and businessmen, and competing government agencies. Detailed accounts left by five of the ministry's administrative staff portray his work as one of the most unqualified political successes of World War I.[8] Ironically, the committed capitalist and millionaire became most famous as the architect of an emergency socialistic experiment in food rationing during the war. He rendered excellent service to his country, earning in the process a peerage which would soon be passed on, with his fortune, to his surviving child, Margaret.

At the time of his daughter's birth in 1883, however, D. A. Thomas was just beginning to establish himself as a major businessman. Margaret was born into a happy family, firmly ensconced in the rising middle class. That her father was a self-made man who had earned his fortune in the competitive world of industrial capitalism was a source of tremendous pride to her in later years. At the time it meant a life of privileged economic and social status and physical comfort. The middle class into which Margaret was born was a product of the rise of industrial capitalism during the second half of the nineteenth century. It was still a relatively small group, but its members were very conscious of their new-found status and very committed to maintaining all the trappings and accoutrements of genteel society. The upper and middle classes together composed only 25 percent of the total population, and most of the middle class fell in the lower portion of that percentage.[9] The Thomas family, by virtue of D.A.'s entrepreneurial success and diverse business holdings, was definitely in the upper ranks of the middle class and enjoyed the benefits of that status. Margaret grew up in a family which could afford a spacious, attractive home, domestic servants, formal entertainment, and frequent travel.[10] The combination of her father's wealth and her mother's style ensured social acceptance for the family and a comfortable childhood for the young Margaret.

Few records remain to verify any but the basic facts of Margaret's childhood. The only direct information available is found in Lady Rhondda's fragmentary autobiography, written from the perspective of a mature public figure. While much is left unsaid, the autobiography paints a picture of a fairly happy, generally normal childhood. Yet her family's liberal sentiments and her status as the only child of a wealthy family gave her more personal freedom and perhaps a closer relationship and identification with her father than was typical of the average middle-class girl. The conditions of her formative years encouraged the independent thinking, assertiveness, and resistance to gender stereotyping that dominated her mature life and helped prepare her to enter and succeed in nontraditional fields.

In her autobiography Margaret portrays a picture of a stable, comfortable childhood marred only by the minor traumas and insecurities typical of a child with a sensitive nature. Her father's political aspirations meant that Margaret's early years were largely spent in London in a comfortable Westminster flat, but it is evident that she never really considered London her home. Perhaps even as a child she unconsciously associated the flat with her father's world of commerce and politics and recognized it as alien to her own "place." Instead, it was the Welsh countryside that provided the backdrop for her fondest memories and childhood pleasures. The steep, green valleys of south Wales, lined with rows of brightly painted terraced cottages, held a special charm for Margaret. Home to her was Llanwern – the old brick estate near Newport in south Wales bought by her father when she was only five. The rambling Queen Anne house and spacious grounds had an air of dignity and longevity which appealed to the introspective youngster. In winter the house could look bleak and severe from the outside, but the glowing fireplace and comfortable interior quickly dispelled the gloom. In summer, with the park full of trees, the gardens filled with flowers, and the spacious house overflowing with relatives, Llanwern was always pleasant, alive with activity, and full of sunshine. Years later, Margaret fondly remembered Llanwern as the ideal place to spend one's childhood.[11]

The days at Llanwern were generally happy ones. As a child, Margaret was encouraged to run and play, to enjoy and appreciate the beauties of nature, and to develop her body and her mind. As she was allowed more freedom than most young girls, she instinctively took advantage of her opportunities. She grew into a healthy child with fair skin, blue eyes, and a precocious smile. She was something of a tomboy and loved nothing more than climbing trees or sitting by the banks of the Severn. At home in Llanwern or within the extensive family network, she was secure, happy, and confident. But outside the family circle she was often overcome by loneliness, fears, shyness, and self-doubt.

This insecurity does not appear to have resulted from any major physical or emotional trauma but simply from the youngster's complex nature and the unsettled times in which she lived. Even as a child, Margaret possessed an inquisitive mind, an independent spirit, and a deep sensitivity to people and nature. Years later, she claimed that this sensitivity, more than anything else, created tremendous inner conflict, anxiety, and unhappiness all through her life. It caused her to dwell on supposed shortcomings, to magnify any criticism beyond proportion, and to develop unnecessarily high expectations for herself and for her intimate friends.[12] This self-doubt and anxiety are not in any way abnormal. Historians have shown that this was a dominant characteristic of the mid-Victorian middle-class ethos. The world of industrial capitalism, with its emphasis on competition and a Darwinian "survival of the fittest," necessarily created tension and anxiety that filtered down from parent to offspring. For those born in the 1880s, the rapidity of change in the economic structure and in social and sexual mores, aggravated by challenges to the Victorian consensus, forced constant adaptation and uncertainty. While it is perhaps natural for Margaret to have ascribed her anxiety and doubts to inner sensitivity, it is also beyond doubt that such feelings were common among those of her class and status.[13]

Still, for Margaret the anxiety was very personal and very real. And ironically, the source of much of her trepidation was her own loving family. In her autobiography, she writes of desperately wanting to be the perfect child but vaguely realizing that she was something of a disappointment to both her parents. Margaret feared she was neither conventional enough nor brave enough to meet her mother's expectations. Her mother believed firmly that young girls should conform to accepted traditions and cultivate "womanly" qualities. She considered independence and spirit acceptable and useful traits—as long as they did not conflict with femininity or family duties. To a youngster of Margaret's disposition, this was a stifling attitude.

Yet this same high-spirited youngster was terrified that she was too cowardly to meet the standards of her mother's relations. It was against the code of the Haig family to show fear of anything but the Almighty. For Margaret, a high-strung child with an active imagination, this proved especially difficult. While not particularly fearing the Almighty, she was terrified by dark rooms, the devil, deep water, and death. She tried to comfort herself with the knowledge that she was not afraid to climb trees or fight with the local boys, but in her heart she remained convinced that she was one of the worst cowards the Haig family had ever produced.[14]

These misgivings about her mother's side of the family troubled Margaret, but not so deeply as her father's apparent dissatisfaction. While awaiting the birth of his first child, D. A. Thomas, like many prospective fathers, had often expressed his desire for a male heir, and he could not completely conceal his disappointment at the birth of a female child. He undoubtedly loved his daughter dearly, but he was busy building his commercial empire and seemed to have little time for or interest in a baby girl. When Margaret was only a few weeks old, a dark cousin was passed off as his own fair, blue-eyed child, and her father failed to notice the difference. The family never tired of relating this prank at gatherings, and each recounting added to Margaret's miseries. Desperately lonely as an only child, Margaret earnestly prayed for a companion, but always for a little sister. Despite her father's assurances that he would not dream of trading her for a boy, she rather suspected that a little brother would push her even further from the center of her father's attention. Longing for his approval, she tried to compensate for her gender and to please her father by cultivating tomboyish ways and learning Welsh phrases to help in his parliamentary campaigns. But nothing could change the fact that she was a girl, not the boy who would carry on his name and his parliamentary and business interests. Not until much later did Margaret discover that her father was not comfortable with any young child. As she grew older and the hoped-for male heir failed to materialize, a bond of sympathy and understanding developed between the two that was rare between a father and daughter of the times.[15]

The sense of being a disappointment to the family weighed heavily at times. She came to believe that her parents and relatives loved her not because of her individual personality but because she was family.[16] Within the family circle she was assured of acceptance, but outside she would have to prove her worth. Rather than risking rejection, Margaret chose to adopt her mother's clannish attitudes and insulate herself from outsiders. She developed a shyness that could be crippling. Accompanying her mother to a neighbor's garden party was sometimes a terrifying experience, depriving her of speech and bringing tears to her eyes. This extreme shyness led the young Margaret to cultivate two habits which would plague her well into adulthood. To escape the pressures of dealing with those she felt uncomfortable with, she would withdraw into a dreamworld of exciting adventures and romantic interludes. She also learned to protect herself when feeling shy or uncertain by "playing stupid," a trick she "never quite succeeded in unlearning."[17] Habits of

reticence and withdrawal developed during childhood were never completely overcome. Even when she had become a woman of some prominence in business, feminist, and literary circles, when her home was
a frequent gathering point for important people, and her name was on
the invitation lists of the elite, she was never really comfortable in a social setting.

Nonetheless, within the family circle, Margaret found love, support,
and guidance. Because her father was frequently away on business, she
early learned of the very distinct division between the private world of
home and family and the public world of business and politics. Like
most children of the time, Margaret spent much of her childhood in
the company of her mother and various nannies or governesses. From
her mother she learned her first lessons in femininity and social expectations. This critical phase of her life receives only scant attention in
her autobiography, as Margaret seems to downplay her mother's role and
credit all the important lessons to her father. Yet it was Sybil who truly
nurtured her through those formative years.[18]

A middle-class Victorian girl learned at her mother's knee that gender
and social position were determinants in a person's life. Through the
mother's example and instruction, she learned that the home was the
proper sphere for the female species and that female needs and interests
were secondary in a male-dominated world. Woman's life was ideally
to be one of service, dependence, and self-sacrifice, and it was a woman's duty to make the home into a peaceful refuge from the masculine,
competitive, and sometimes harsh outside world. It was also her responsibility to protect the family's status by cultivating a genteel life style
and strictly adhering to the prescribed social etiquette of the day. Likewise, she must maintain the moral values of the family. The Victorian
daughter, in preparation for her later role as wife and mother, was expected to act with decorum, to cultivate the feminine skills necessary
for maintaining the home (or directing the servants, in the case of the
upper middle class), and to suppress excessive intellectual curiosity.[19]

By the 1890s, however, this notion of separate spheres had been slightly
amended. The role of the woman remained biological and spiritual. Her
duty was still defined in terms of producing and rearing children, supporting the men in her life, and guarding the family's spiritual and moral
values. This domesticity, however, was now seen in broader terms. The
late Victorian period saw a heightened awareness of international rivalry
in all its forms—economic, military, and imperial—and a concomitant
intensification of nationalistic concerns with the quantity and quality

of a nation's populace. The late Victorian generation viewed population numbers and fitness levels as indicators of relative economic and military strength. Particularly after the Boer War, concern over declining birthrates and children's health added a new dimension to the cult of domesticity and the importance of marriage and motherhood. No longer was domesticity important only as a stabilizing factor within the home and a guarantor of the standards of gentility. It now became a national duty, essential for the defense of Britain and the empire against foreign rivals.[20] New developments in female education allowed some room for personal ambition and intellectual development, but always primarily within the framework of creating a better wife and mother.

While Sybil did her best to inculcate these values through personal example, religious instruction, and social training, Margaret resisted the more confining elements of this teaching. Much later, she claimed that a girl's education in the home was designed to make her a helpmeet, entirely irresponsible and totally dependent. She also admitted, however, that while she intellectually rejected her mother's teachings and example at an early age, they influenced her temperamentally well into adulthood.[21] Many strong, intelligent women born in the 1880s and 1890s recorded in their later years a lifelong wrestling with guilt and uncertainty as they attempted to reconcile their ambition and success in nontraditional fields with the perception of femininity learned from their mother.[22] Margaret was no exception.

Her mother's efforts to mold Margaret into a proper late Victorian female succeeded only partially because of the influence of her father, who was less remote than was typical for the times. From him Margaret learned what she considered some of the most important lessons of her childhood. She once described him as a "liberal education in himself." He taught her the value of justice and fair dealing, the strength of commitment, and the merits of persistence and ambition. He encouraged her to think independently, to fulfill her own potential, and to challenge authority, and he allowed her free access to his library. While it is doubtful that he envisioned anything more for her than the role of intelligent and efficient wife and mother, he cultivated in her a strong sense of personal and public responsibility. Lacking a son, he passed on to his daughter the knowledge and wisdom that would normally have been reserved for his male heir.

Under her father's tutelage Margaret began to broaden her ambitions at a time when the average girl was being encouraged to suppress or conceal hers. At ten, she still wanted to be a mother of twelve (it would have been unthinkable to deny one's "natural" maternal instincts—an indication that her mother's teaching had more influence than she later cared to admit), but she added some more unconventional goals as well. She planned to combine motherhood with a literary and political career. She would be prime minister, and a celebrated author as well.[23] Her father's influence awakened new ambitions and encouraged minor rebellions against the prescribed formula of femininity.

The lessons of Margaret's mother and father were supplemented by a more formal education. Until the age of thirteen, Margaret was taught at home by a succession of governesses who seem to have made little impression. She later wrote that while she had learned a few trifles during that period, she could see no serious connection between her governesses and education. She undoubtedly learned to read and write, but it is impossible to determine the quality of this instruction. At thirteen she entered London's Notting Hill High School as a day student. Margaret's autobiography indicates that the decision to get a "real education" was her own and that it was prompted by the inability of her mother and governesses to go beyond "female lessons" and provide answers to such troublesome questions as the purpose of existence and the limits of reality, isolation, and the passage of time.[24] This may be somewhat self-serving. By the time she entered this school, formal education was becoming an integral part of the middle-class girl's experience and something of a status symbol in itself.[25] Given her father's wealth, his own liberal leanings, and his strong influence on his daughter's life, it seems reasonable to conclude that the decision was at least a joint one.

Margaret found Notting Hill High School disappointing. The institution was both too conventional and too restrictive for her tastes. She found the lessons boring, the teachers unimpressive, and the rules irritating. After two years she transferred to St. Leonard's School in St. Andrews, Scotland. Margaret later insisted that her choice of boarding schools was a purely personal and emotional one. She claimed that she knew only that it was located by the sea, and, most important, that girls were allowed to go out alone for walks. For Margaret, this spelled freedom. Alone, surrounded by natural beauty, she expected to find herself.[26] Again, it seems doubtful that such an important decision would have been made independently by a fifteen-year-old girl, particularly given the very weak rationale she offered. St. Leonard's, founded in 1877, was one of a new group of expensive and fashionable boarding schools deliberately designed to attract the daughters of the upper classes, and its excellent and innovative reputation would have been well known in the Thomases' social circle.[27]

At St. Leonard's Margaret was the beneficiary of mid-Victorian school reforms, which had gradually shifted the focus from small, family-style schools emphasizing social skills and superficial "accomplishments" (music, needlework, and a little French) to larger schools with organized instruction modeled on the more rigorous and competitive lines of the leading boys' schools. The new boarding schools, more closely attuned to the needs of a major industrial and imperialist power, emphasized values and skills which helped blur the traditional distinctions between private and public spheres. While they remained essentially conservative institutions dedicated to the conventions of femininity and the training of refined wives and mothers, they also emphasized public duty, physical fitness, and intellectual development. The new schools encouraged greater autonomy and individualism, and the competent, highly trained staff provided new role models in the form of the intelligent, economically independent (but single) career woman. Girls were encouraged to be less self-sacrificial and to strive for balance in fulfilling obligations to self, family, and society.[28]

St. Leonard's in particular was not content to produce decorous, idle women in the traditional nineteenth-century mold. The faculty of St. Leonard's considered it their duty to develop both character and scholarship. They were dedicated to giving each girl who passed through the school the broadest opportunity for individual development, and to turning out capable women who could make a significant contribution to their community. Hard work, critical thinking, and sound judgment formed the cornerstone of the St. Leonard's academic philosophy, while physical fitness, friendly competition, and personal honor laid the basis for daily relations.[29]

From the first day, Margaret fell in love with St. Leonard's. It seemed the perfect place for a young lady who was both a loner and a nature lover. The school was situated between the sea and the city, and the grounds offered views of the power of crashing waves and the beauty of rolling countryside, as well as the solitude of magnificent gardens.[30] Margaret was fortunate in being assigned to the house presided over by Julia Sandys, a young, attractive, sophisticated teacher known for her competitiveness and high spirits. Miss Sandys, even more than the other housemistresses, believed that a woman should never use her sex as an excuse. She expected her charges to perform well in all undertakings—studies, sports, and chores. Her standards were high, but she treated her students as equals. She allowed them greater freedom than was usual, and they responded to the trust she placed in them. She impressed them with her style and her generosity and taught them that courage, unselfishness, and self-discipline were qualities that would always bring success. She guided them to discover their talents, to develop their potential, to question authority, and to believe in themselves. Few girls passed through Miss Sandys' house without at least the opportunity to break away from restrictive conventions and thinking. Margaret was no exception. She and her housemistress developed a close relationship that lasted until Sandys' death. Over the years Miss Sandys continued to provide advice and inspiration at critical times in Margaret's life. It was she who encouraged her to publish her autobiography, and along with Margaret's father, Miss Sandys gave her support when the opportunity arose to exchange her comfortable, protected life for the challenges of the business world.[31]

Had Margaret known then what the future held, she might have been more inclined to apply herself to academic studies. At the time, however, she knew only that the freedom of action and thought at St. Leonard's impressed her much more than the academic regimen. Much later she recalled that during her school days she was "naturally lazy, naturally labor-saving, and naturally cowardly."[32] She tended to do what was expected, but no more, and saw no sense in working at subjects that seemed to have little personal application. She proved to be an indifferent student, performing well only in those subjects, literature and history, for example, which brought her pleasure. Though an avid sportswoman, she detested the required sports periods, and she despised mathematics and chapel—anything that smacked of excessive regimentation. Although intrigued by politics, she considered it unworthy of her effort, since that world was closed to her gender. She later wrote: "What was the use of taking the trouble to know and understand something in which one could have neither part nor lot? How indeed, failing the right to practice politics could one ever really hope to know them except superficially from the outside?"[33] Such tendencies did little to endear Margaret to the headmistress, Julia Grant, who found her independent ways and lack of respect for school conventions rather tiresome. In her yearly reports to parents, Mrs. Grant suggested that Margaret tended to be impatient of drudgery and needed to question less and work more.[34]

Even the tolerant Miss Sandys was occasionally exasperated by her pupil's conduct, but she allowed Margaret a great deal of freedom to pursue special interests. Under her guidance Margaret developed a fondness for history and a voracious, but not particularly selective, appetite for reading. Gradually Miss Sandys led her away from the sloppy, sentimental novels she chose for herself and toward more substantive literature. While remaining partial to the fiction of Rudyard Kipling and Anthony Hope, Margaret also developed a taste for the poetry of Browning, Tennyson, and Matthew Arnold, the treatises of John Stuart Mill, and the histories of J. A. Froude.[35] The more widely she read, the more questions arose in her mind, and the more convinced she became that the written word held a special magic and a peculiar power. The Sunday evening reading hour, disparagingly referred to as "Stale" by fellow classmates, became a highlight of Margaret's week.

St. Leonard's gave Margaret and others like her much more than a balanced education. It gave them the distance to develop as individuals, outside the role of dutiful daughter. It gave them their first real opportunities to form friendships beyond the circle of relatives and family acquaintances. As Martha Vicinus has compellingly argued, the increased emphasis on self-control and public duty in the late nineteenth century boarding school led girls to seek refuge in close personal friendships with girls near their own age.[36] Margaret's fondest memories of her days at St. Leonard's were of early morning and late afternoon walks in the garden with her closest schoolmate and lifelong friend, Elizabeth Pridden. Here Margaret was receiving a very different type of education without being completely aware of it. In "Prid" she had found a kindred spirit, and the two roamed around the garden discussing unconventional topics, educating themselves through conversation and argument. They read Erasmus, Martin Luther, and Sir Thomas More and tried to create their own utopian plan by combining elements from all three. Their talks led them to debate the merits of autocracy versus democracy, tradition versus innovation, and Roman versus Greek civilization. They made a game of it and added interest by scaling everything down to fit their particular house or the school as a whole. It is interesting to note that they generally confined themselves to past politics; contemporary issues were clearly recognized as being outside the scope of feminine interest. Present and future politics were for men. But the reading and argument stimulated thought and helped them form definite opinions. Though neither dared say so at the time, their private thoughts often turned to the future—over which they were to have no control.[37] For Margaret, the process was both exhilarating and frustrating. At the time she did not really know why, but later years brought the problem sharply into focus. Writing in her autobiography, an older and wiser Lady Rhondda expressed the central issue:

> At St. Leonards . . . we had been educated for something more than a young lady's life. We had been given our chance to drink at St. Leonards well, and for those who thirsted the waters of freedom lay there. We had learnt a freedom of initiative, had been allowed a freedom of mental development that no young lady can safely be allowed; and in my case, of course, the freedom of thought and conversation at home had enormously reinforced school. I had been allowed – nay, I had actually been taught – to think. Instincts and desires had come alight for which the life I was to be offered allowed no scope. In the years of bored inaction that lay ahead the sense of frustration was choking. Yet neither we nor our parents had the least idea what was wrong. "Why have women, passion, intellect, moral activity – these three – and a place in society where no one of the three can be exercised?" wrote Florence Nightingale in 1852. It was still true fifty years later.[38]

This insight would have been little comfort to the young girls just beginning to think for themselves. Even between very close friends there were limits to suitable topics for discussion. History and books were safe, but adolescent doubts were too risky. In Margaret's sessions with Prid, two subjects were taboo – sex and personal religious philosophy. Being unable to talk about them increased the mystery and uncertainty about each. Like most adolescents, Margaret was intrigued by the mysteries of mating and reproduction but expected to be filled in by her parents in due time.

For Margaret, the issue of sex was not nearly so troublesome as the question of religion. Although she had attended the Anglican church with her mother almost every Sunday of her life, she had decided by the age of eleven that there was no sound reason to go (besides her mother's insistence). Throughout adolescence, she had turned the difficult question of religion over and over in her mind without receiving much comfort. By seventeen, she had concluded that since parts of the Bible were beyond belief, all of it was likely to be a myth. She was fairly sure that there was no hereafter, but the process of reaching that decision had been so painful that she did not want to say anything that would cause her friend to challenge her own unquestioning faith. Secretly she had hoped that the confirmation process during her final year at St. Leonard's would provide some measurable evidence or even some spiritual experience which would enable her to believe. Instead, it only reinforced her doubts. When she expressed these, the horrified chaplain told her to pray about it or see the bishop. Rather than expose herself to further lectures or to the ridicule of classmates, she simply put her reservations aside and went through the motions. The ceremony made little impression – years later she remembered only white dresses and the bishop's shiny black boots.[39] In this one important issue, Margaret felt that St. Leonard's had failed her. She wanted answers and evidence; she received platitudes or embarrassed silence. But she had spent five very happy years at the school and dreaded leaving its safe confines, even though she had matured during her stay and knew it was time to move on. She was certain that equally positive experiences awaited her. It was years before she was this happy again.

Upon leaving school, Margaret returned home to fulfill the only role society allowed her – that of the young lady. Though she had decided to go on to college, that was to be postponed until she fulfilled the traditional rites of passage – coming out and the London Season. Margaret never questioned this. It was the common lot of young ladies of her class, though she was unsure exactly what it entailed. As Leonore Davidoff points out in her perceptive study, *The Best Circles*, this attitude was not unusual. Even among the privileged classes few knew what purpose the ritual of coming out and having a Season served. They accepted it because it was the thing to do. The norms had become so "thoroughly internalized and legitimized" through usage that they were automatically binding on those in certain circles.[40]

For the three months from April to July, Margaret and her mother dutifully made the rounds of the Season's important events. Gradually it became clear to Margaret that the Season was an elaborate facade to solidify social, business, and political contacts among the elites and to provide a forum for finding suitable marriage partners. At the time she had no objections and enthusiastically entered into the prescribed ritual. A debutante's days were filled with paying calls, shopping, and coed excursions – all strictly chaperoned. Nights were reserved for the more formal dinners, concerts, balls, and theater engagements.[41] Hanging over these events like an ominous cloud lay the knowledge that one had at most two or three seasons to find a suitable partner.[42]

For Margaret the experience was not a pleasant one. Early anticipation of new ball gowns and finding "the right man" quickly faded in the face of simpering debutantes and her own paralyzing shyness. Margaret was desperately unsuited for the role she was expected to play. She despised the small talk, the vanity of her fellow debutantes, and the strict chaperonage that inhibited natural conversation. She hated the sense of being on display. Watching the happy couples waltzing across the polished floors, Margaret felt totally out of place. Walking across the floor with a partner was sheer agony for her, and she spent most of the nights hiding in a corner and plotting her escape, waiting for the clock to strike midnight.[43] Yet for three years she dutifully made the rounds because it was expected. Years later, she marveled that she never

> consciously criticized a system which was responsible for persuading a particularly affectionate and conscientious mother (who if left to please herself would have desired to spend three-quarters of her time either painting miniatures or working in her garden and the other quarter in an old furniture shop) that she could best do her duty by martyrizing herself into dragging a bored and not even socially successful daughter through a series of aimless and useless functions. A system which hypnotized a perfectly intelligent, though perhaps rather a naive young woman, already anxious to investigate notions impersonally and dispassionately, into acceding without question to indulgence in this odd form of occupation, which in fact she was hating so much.[44]

When not attending the various functions associated with the Season, Margaret lived the life of a typical upper middle-class young woman. Her father's wealth made it unnecessary for her to seek employment, so she made the social rounds and performed a few small domestic tasks. The ambition of her youth and school years faded to be replaced by subconscious dissatisfaction and diminishing self-respect. A lack of any purpose and a sense of futility depressed her, but she much preferred doing nothing to the options available. The rounds of parties and mild flirtations some of her peers enjoyed so much had little appeal. She was something of a romantic, interested only in that one deep and lasting love who would miraculously appear at her doorstep. Nor was she interested in the pseudopolitical roles offered by organizations like the National Liberal Federation, or the social work opportunities offered through the Girls' Friendly Society or community service groups. She always thought those who engaged in such activities were guilty of wasting time on busywork and patronizing the recipients of their services.[45] This life was definitely not for her, but there seemed no other.

To escape the horrors of a fourth Season, Margaret acted on her earlier decision to go to college. She chose Somerville College, Oxford. For many young women, college—Somerville in particular—was a liberating experience. Numerous accounts emphasize the intellectual challenges, the college rituals, the individual friendships, and the sense of female solidarity so integral to the college experience. For them, the university was a community of united women claiming their right and their ability to mold the future.[46] For others, the experience served only to reinforce their sense of female isolation and insignificance. Because Oxford refused to admit women to full status until 1920, some felt like outsiders in a gentlemen's club.[47]

Margaret seems to have been one of those who felt isolated and insignificant. Her year at Somerville was unfruitful. This may in large part be because she chose to go to college for the wrong reasons. She was trying to escape from the drudgery of her immediate existence and perhaps even find a suitable husband. She had no intention of ever using her education, as she fully expected to become a full-time wife and mother. But she had nothing better to do, and she rather liked the idea of being a university woman at a time when there were few. Had she gone to Somerville directly upon leaving St. Leonard's, Margaret might have gained something from the experience. But three years as an idle, pampered daughter of the house had dulled the enthusiasm and the ambitions of the schoolgirl. Her autobiography gives no details of her collegiate career. There is nothing of the social life, the dormitory experience, or the friendships that are so vital a part of college life, nor is there any discussion of the curriculum or the faculty, or any recognition of the relatively progressive and enlightened conception of the whole Somerville scheme. Instead, Margaret seems to have been concerned only with the superficial aspects. She complained of the ugliness and plainness of the campus, of the way the tables were set, and of the musty smells of the buildings. After the gala ballrooms of London, the dons and the students looked dowdy, and everything about Somerville seemed pathetic. This early attitude proved embarrassing in later years, when Lady Rhondda became a staunch supporter and patron of the college. She admitted then that she was "quite unaware that I was watching the awkward adolescence of something infinitely worthwhile" and "had nothing but intolerant contempt" for the noble experiment.[48]

After her first year Margaret left the university and went home. She refused to reenter the social scene which she had found so futile and demeaning, choosing simply to continue in her role as dutiful daughter and wait patiently for self-fulfillment through marriage. By the time she left Oxford, she was convinced that a woman's worst fate was to remain single. Her childhood political and literary ambitions had been gradually repressed by the conditioning process carried on in the home and in the girls' schools. The young girl who at ten had wanted to be prime minister had fully succumbed to societal expectations, accepting the supposed limitations of her sex and seeking identity and purpose in marriage rather than through independent action.

Yet Margaret was a romantic. She was determined not to marry without being passionately in love, and when Humphrey Mackworth entered her life shortly after her return to Llanwern, she was ready to fall in love. Given her relatively limited experience with men, her advancing age (she was twenty-four by then), her insecurity, and her almost desperate desire to marry, it is not surprising that Margaret was attracted to Humphrey. The only son of Colonel Sir Arthur Mackworth, he was a close neighbor from Caerlon-upon-Usk, only three miles from Llanwern. In Humphrey Margaret found a combination of maturity and masculinity that appealed to her romantic nature. He was twelve years older than she, and he exhibited a sophistication that she found charming. Humphrey was wealthy and possessed the manners and military bearing to set him apart from the crowd. Despite his "slightly brooding" and domineering nature, Margaret easily convinced herself that she had not only made a good match but had found true love as well. After a brief courtship and engagement, they were married on 9 July 1908 at the parish church in Monmouth. At twenty-four, Margaret was certain that she had finally found fulfillment. Her "girlhood" was now over, and she looked forward to life as an adult woman with high hopes and even higher expectations.[49]

2 · LOOSENING THE BONDS

Upon her marriage to Humphrey Mackworth, Margaret found herself legally and physically transferred from the protection and authority of her father to that of her husband. All her life she had prepared for her new role as the privileged wife of a prominent man. While very few documents record her life with Humphrey, it appears that she settled in quickly and with little of the trauma often associated with the first months of marriage. Because she lived only a few miles from her parents' home, there was little or no sense of physical or emotional isolation from her beloved family. Because of Humphrey's wealth, there was no threat to her economic security or her privileged status. Instead, Margaret seems to have relished the chance to be mistress of her own home—to direct the servants, to add her own personal touches, to entertain her friends, and most important of all, to provide for Humphrey the same warm refuge from a harsh world that her mother had made for her father. She believed she had indeed found her identity and her life's work in being Mrs. Humphrey Mackworth. And she fully expected that that would be enough.

Margaret threw herself into her new duties enthusiastically. Her days were spent in a fairly typical fashion. An upper-class wife gave her orders to the servants and carefully checked to see that they were carried out. A substantial domestic staff freed her from any domestic drudgery and allowed her to spend her days in private pursuits. She puttered in the garden, cutting flowers to decorate the drawing room. In the afternoons she paid calls on her mother or close neighbors, or received visitors in her own home. Free days were generally spent in reading or keeping up with family correspondence. When her husband returned from his work, they would share a quiet dinner if there were no pressing social or familial obligations to attend to. Then they would settle in for a comfortable evening at home, he with his pipe and papers, she with her book or some kind of handiwork.

Margaret quickly became bored with this regimen. While she un-

doubtedly tried to be a good wife, she never really reconciled herself
to domesticity or subservience. She began to resent her husband's freedom. He had his work, his clubs, and his cronies, while she had little
to do outside the home – and servants to do everything in it. Many years
later, presumably drawing upon her own experiences, Margaret wrote
that there were two things wrong with the marriages of the well-to-do.
First, the wife was treated not as a human being in her own right but
as an appendage of her husband. And second, she claimed, custom decreed
that husband and wife must be invited everywhere as a couple and that
the wife's appearance and social skills were regarded as a measure of
her husband's position and success in life.[1] Given Margaret's lifelong
discomfort in formal social settings, visiting as a couple must have been
a constant source of anxiety.

Gradually, over the first three years of her marriage, Margaret's resentment turned from domestic routine to her husband himself and to some
extent to the institution of marriage. The age difference, sophistication,
and formality that had seemed so romantic in Humphrey during their
engagement proved less appealing within the confines of marriage.
Differences in outlook and personality that had been submerged during
courtship became glaringly apparent. While Humphrey the suitor had
been exciting, solicitous, and romantic, Humphrey the husband seemed
dull, predictable, and emotionally detached. The domineering manner
that Margaret had taken as a measure of strength she now saw as a sign
of masculine arrogance and weakness. The very proper, very conservative Mackworth family seemed daunting and even oppressive to the
less conventional, more spontaneous daughter-in-law. The couple's incompatibility could not be masked. Whereas she loved literature and
conversation, he cared only for his hounds and the hunt – a sport she
found both cruel and indefensible.

As their differences became increasingly apparent, Margaret began to
rebel against her subordinate position within the marriage. She had expected her marriage to be a partnership of equals and her home to be
a forum for intelligent discussion modeled along the lines of her own
parents' relationship. Instead, she became a dependent in the worst sense
of the word. While expecting protection and financial support from her
spouse, she had not bargained for his domination. Humphrey treated
her well and provided for all her material needs, but she needed more.
She craved emotional support, intellectual stimulation, and a sense of
purpose that were not available in her marriage. She desperately longed
for a child, believing that motherhood would fill the emptiness in her

life. She wanted nothing more than to bear sons who would protect the empire and daughters who would guard the nation's moral values.[2]

Yet it was neither child nor marriage that brought Margaret personal satisfaction and allowed her to escape her self-doubt and boredom. Instead, the militant suffragette movement provided the first major turning point of her life and gave her for the first time in her adult life a sense of purpose and of some control over her destiny. She was at last involved in an activity where she thought *her* actions, not those of her father or husband, counted. Her entry into the movement shortly after her marriage reawakened dormant ambitions and brought latent talents to the surface. As her commitment to the movement became stronger and as she found satisfaction outside the domestic realm, she grew increasingly dissatisfied with her marriage and began to move psychologically and physically away from her husband's world. Had she become firmly committed to the cause a little earlier, the marriage might never have taken place.

Despite the fact that her father was a Liberal member of Parliament, Margaret had been almost unaware of the movement that eventually changed her life, but this was not all that unusual. Though the demand for women's suffrage had been slowly gaining ground since the 1850s, press coverage was limited, and past gains had introduced a strong element of complacency into the upper and middle classes. That women had gained entry into the professions and the universities, the right to vote in some municipal elections, and the right to serve as school board members and poor-law guardians sometimes obscured the fact that women were not much closer to receiving the parliamentary vote in the early 1900s than they had been forty years earlier. The women's suffrage issue continued to face resistance from diehard antisuffragists, who based their opposition on supposed feminine inferiority, sentimentality, and lack of political acumen or experience, as well as from politicians of all parties and large numbers of relatively satisfied women. The major impediment was the entanglement of the suffrage issue with broader political questions of adult suffrage in general, the redistribution of Irish constituencies, and the difficulties of the Liberal Party.[3]

But British feminists in increasing numbers continued to challenge the status quo on an ever-broader basis. By the early twentieth century, feminists were attacking the notion of separate domestic and public spheres. They were demanding not merely an entry into a supposedly masculine political sphere but a voice in redefining that sphere in accordance with female values and needs. The demand for the vote became part of a broader strategy designed to bring women's special skills and attributes to bear on issues of community well-being. Emphasizing the nurturant rather than the regulatory functions of the state, British feminists argued that female participation was vital in fulfilling the social mission of the state precisely because of their nurturing experience in the home.[4] Using this reasoning, suffragists in the early 1900s worked not only to convince the public of the rightness of their cause, but, more important, to convince the Liberal government that support for passage could be found and that the issue was just as compelling as competing concerns, particularly Irish home rule and national health insurance.[5]

By 1903, two distinct wings of the suffrage movement had developed. The Constitutionalists, led by the National Union of Women's Suffrage Societies (NUWSS), focused on marshaling support within the House of Commons and educating men and women about inequalities. Since this group was dominated by women Liberals, they had no desire to embarrass the existing government. They wanted only to force Liberal members of Parliament to consider suffrage in their broad reforming tradition and to try to organize cross-party support. These suffragists worked patiently within the system, hoping to get a private members' bill on the parliamentary agenda.[6] Under the tactful leadership of Millicent Garrett Fawcett, the suffragists commanded respect from large numbers of men and women, but their gains on the local level were overshadowed by their failure to win the vote. The patient arguments and legal claims of the respectable suffragists were not being heard, and dissatisfaction with their cautious measures grew.

The second wing, the militant camp, was led by the Women's Social and Political Union. Formed in 1903 by Emmeline Pankhurst and her daughter Christabel, the WSPU initially drew its strength from Independent Labour Party affiliations. By 1906, however, the WSPU had begun to dissociate itself from Labour because of that party's limited parliamentary strength, its failure to incorporate suffrage into the party platform, and the general lack of sympathy for working-class politics of the WSPU's more elite supporters.[7] In the beginning the militant suffragettes focused on demonstrating the urgency of and broad popular support for women's enfranchisement through massive, but peaceful, demonstrations. By 1905 the WSPU was stressing direct action to force the government to grant its wishes. It demanded "deeds not words" from the politicians and vowed to pursue a policy of confrontation to publicize the cause and force compliance. Though always in a minority, the suffragettes constituted a vocal and highly visible pressure group.[8] They embarked on a policy of harassment designed to intimidate members of the government and dramatize the issue of women's suffrage. They interrupted speeches by Liberal speakers and occasionally subjected them to minor physical abuse. From 1908 on, they embarked on a series of calculated, limited threats to public order.[9] Public demonstrations escalated into violent confrontations and premeditated acts of civil disobedience, eventually leading to prison terms and hunger strikes. The militant vanguard, at least in the early stages, revitalized the suffrage campaign and prompted women to choose between alternative strategies. The movement politicized thousands of idealistic young women impatient with their restricted lives.[10]

Among these newly politicized women was Margaret Mackworth, and it was the militant campaign, with its promise of activity and excitement, that she found most appealing. Margaret became associated with the movement relatively late and was therefore involved in the more aggressive phase. She was introduced to the movement only a few weeks before her marriage by a cousin, Florence Haig, who was herself an active member of the WSPU. Initially Margaret appears to have been interested in affiliating with the militants less because of their feminist program or their particular mode of campaigning than because of her cousin's excitement and sense of mission.[11] Margaret was intrigued by her passion for the cause, just a bit jealous of her sense of purpose, and slightly suspicious of the whole enterprise. She agreed to attend a huge suffrage rally with Florence to judge for herself.

Margaret's initial encounter with the feminist movement was a fortuitous one. She took part in the massive prosuffrage demonstration held on 21 July 1908 in Hyde Park.[12] Marching through the city to the music of "La Marseillaise," thousands of women of all ages became caught up in the emotions of the organizers. Upon reaching the park, they heard speakers express ideas till then only half-formed in the minds of most. They were told of the injustices of women's being deprived of a voice in the government that expected them to pay taxes, of the inequality of women before the law in such matters as divorce and child custody, and of gender discrimination in working conditions and pay. More important, they were challenged to commit themselves to changing this deplorable situation. On Margaret, comfortably ensconced in the upper middle class and preoccupied with her impending marriage, the arguments made little impression.[13] She was inspired not by the nobility of the cause but by the spirit of the movement and the emotional release of pent-up energies and frustrations. She was "instinctively thrilled with this chance for action, . . . totally ignorant of, and unconcerned with, the arguments for our cause. It was a temperamental, not in any sense an intellectual conversion."[14] Only after this first flush of excitement faded did she begin to sift through the complexities of the issue in order to justify her commitment on a more rational basis.

Margaret left the Hyde Park meeting determined to join the WSPU, but her formal affiliation was delayed for several months by her father's objections. Though long a supporter of women's rights, he regarded militant activity as unconstitutional. Always a firm believer in the parliamentary process, he thought women should continue to work through, not outside, the system to bring about the desired changes.[15] Respect for her father's convictions and his position as a Liberal member of Parliament led Margaret to reconsider, but still on an emotional rather than an intellectual level. Her autobiography reveals no sense of internal anguish, no attempt to sway her father by the issues—only a sense of missing out on a great adventure. In the end, she determined to join anyway, justifying her rebellion on grounds typical of more committed suffragettes. Because he was a man, no matter how tolerant, liberal, or well-meaning, her father's judgment on women's matters was necessarily suspect.[16] According to Margaret's own record, which is generally very sympathetic to her father, he resigned himself to the decision but gave little actual encouragement or support.[17] He had given his advice, and it had been rejected. Having frequently urged his daughter to think and act independently, he now had to accept the consequences. In the months between the Hyde Park rally and her joining the WSPU, however, Margaret had married into the very proper, very Conservative Mackworth family. Her husband had no sympathies with the movement and must have resented her willingness to consider her father's objections without apparently seeking out his own position. Humphrey was primarily concerned with any potential embarrassment to his family or disruption to his own household. He did allow her to join, but with one proviso— she had to promise not to go to prison for the cause.[18] In the early days, this promise seemed a minor concession. Women fully expected to gain the vote within a few months, so Margaret agreed to the condition without argument. When she joined the "voluntary army," the only requirements were paying a nominal membership fee of at least one shilling a year, signing a pledge endorsing the objects and methods of the WSPU, and severing all political connections until the vote was granted to women. Members were expected to work diligently and unquestioningly for the cause. Loyalty became the keynote of the movement—loyalty first to the cause, then to the leaders, and finally to fellow suffragettes. Only slightly less important was courage – physical courage to take to the streets, risking bodily harm, imprisonment, and even death in breaching this traditionally male territory, and emotional courage to risk ridicule, censure, and loss of respectability.[19]

For a few, the movement meant martyrdom; for Margaret and many like her, it meant excitement and freedom. Yet whether they realized it or not, it was a curious type of freedom, one that demanded a new form of subordination. The WSPU was an autocratic body ruled by Christabel and Emmeline Pankhurst, and in the early years by Fred and Emmeline Pethick-Lawrence. Fearful that democratic decision making would slow momentum and possibly dissipate energies, the foursome jealously guarded their prerogatives and marshaled a subservient cadre of loyal lieutenants and a mass of submissive enlistees. The rank-and-file membership had no more control, no more part in the decision making process than they had previously exercised in their own lives. Still, the very act of enlisting appears to have fostered a feeling of independence and control.

For Margaret this type of movement, demanding total loyalty, total obedience, and total commitment to a cause, may well have been the only type of activity which could have awakened her dormant talents and desires. Describing her youth in her autobiography, Margaret said that she was naturally lazy, naturally cowardly, and inclined to give only what was expected of her.[20] Further, she wrote: "I had to be given an uncommonly good reason before I was prepared to work sooner than idle. I had a perfect horror of being busy for no reason. The end had to be absolutely worthwhile before I would bestir myself to work at the means."[21]

In the militant suffragette movement, she found both a cause to fight for and leaders who expected much. But just as important, she found a strong sense of belonging to a sisterhood and immediate acceptance into a new network of friends and supporters. For an only child trapped in an unhappy marriage, the sense of belonging was especially gratifying.

Once she was brought into the movement, Margaret quickly became passionately active. Unfortunately, the only records of her activity are those she left in her autobiographical writings. Her experiences, however, seem consistent with those of other small branches far from the London headquarters. Her first task was to help organize a local WSPU branch at Newport, south Wales. The branch was fairly typical, drawing most of its support from young women of various backgrounds and including smaller numbers of older women and a few men sympathizers.[22] Between 1908 and 1910, Margaret was initiated into a number of activities that were supposedly alien to a woman's nature. She was called on at first for relatively simple — but highly visible — tasks: selling the paper *Votes for Women* on street corners, walking in processions clad in sandwich boards propagandizing the cause, and door-to-door canvassing. Such activities caused embarrassment to many converts. Kitty Marion, a young suffragette, wrote of her experience selling the paper: "What a lesson in self-denial, self-abnegation, self-disciplin! [*sic*] The first time I took my place on the 'Island' in Picadilly Circus, near the flower seller, I felt as if every eye that looked at me was a dagger piercing me through and I wished the ground would open and swallow me."[23]

One would expect a person of Margaret's natural shyness to have been victimized by the same emotions, but — at least in retrospect — she thoroughly enjoyed these tasks. She later wrote that they satisfied her "natural appetite . . . for colour and incident"[24] and provided an outlet for suppressed energies. As a member of the group, she could justify actions that would have been unacceptable even to herself as an individual. It was a liberating experience.

Her enthusiasm and her success at these basic assignments led to increased responsibilities in the movement. She was called on to write articles and letters for local papers and to organize suffrage meetings. Her first attempts were not always fruitful. Only a short time after joining the WSPU she reports being asked by some of her father's constituents at Merthyr Tydfil to speak at the local Liberal Club. Uncertain of how to proceed and wanting company in her misery, Margaret wrote to Annie Kenney, one of the Pankhursts' chief lieutenants, to join her. When the two arrived at the meeting place, they were greeted by a rowdy crowd armed with tomatoes, herrings, and noisy gongs. It was impossible to be heard, but in the true militant spirit, they spoke for an hour each rather than give the impression of defeat.[25]

This experience led Margaret to reconsider her primarily emotional commitment to the suffrage movement. She realized that the "obvious rightness of its ideals"[26] was not readily apparent to the crowds she had to face or the public which would read her articles. She needed to be able to justify her commitment on a rational, intellectual basis before she could answer hecklers and capture converts. She had to be able to defend her position against obstinate, unreasonable opponents and to convince the undecided. To do this, she needed to know much more about the issues involved in the suffrage question. Margaret began reading everything she could find on the history of women, prominent women of the past, and social, political, and economic inequalities in the modern world. Her studies reinforced her emotional commitment to the movement and strengthened her resolve to see the fight through to the end. Three works particularly impressed her: John Stuart Mill's *Subjection of Women* (1869), Olive Schreiner's *Woman and Labour* (1911), and Cicely Hamilton's *Marriage as a Trade* (1909).[27] In Mill she found a humanist approach, emphasizing the common characteristics of men and women and the consequent injustice of unequal treatment. In Schreiner she read that middle-class women had lost their social usefulness and become parasites, while working-class women were consigned to economic drudgery and low pay. In Schreiner's view, the right of all women, married or single, to work was central to women's health and happiness. In Hamilton she read that marriage was a form of sex slavery, a trade in which a woman exchanged her body for subsistence. Such ideas combined with her personal experiences to bring Margaret to a deep philosophical and intellectual commitment to feminism for the first time. Her studies gave her new insights into the interests and needs of women, the importance of bringing a feminine perspective into the political realm, and the existing inequalities facing women. She became convinced that women must have political power as a first step to improving the conditions under which they lived, and that waiting for men to grant power without a fight would be futile. The militant way seemed to her the only way.

The new-found commitment encouraged Margaret to branch out in her suffrage activities. She wanted to use her knowledge to spread the word, but she was not a natural public speaker. The shyness and reticence that had plagued her as an adolescent threatened to limit her effectiveness, but she was determined to try to overcome this disability for the good of the cause. With her former schoolmate, Elizabeth Pridden, she decided to practice her speaking and try to convert a new district to militancy. They chose Devonshire, an area which had been relatively untouched by the suffragette movement. At Barnstaple Margaret tried her hand at open-air speaking for the first time and again was not particularly successful. Her pleasure at the audience's laughter quickly evaporated when she realized it continued long after her jokes ended. Searching for the source of amusement, she spied a large placard inscribed with the slogan "Blokes for Women."[28]

Such incidents were not atypical. Rather than attempting to discredit the suffragettes' arguments, many antisuffragists concentrated on attacking

the suffragettes themselves. It was not unusual to find suffragettes portrayed as physically unattractive, sexually repressed women who needed
only to find a man to ease their frustrations. Margaret herself was victimized by these innuendos. Several years later, Vera Brittain recounted
her surprise on first meeting Margaret. She had not expected her to be
physically attractive and was shocked at Margaret's comely appearance
and shy, diffident smile.[29]

Margaret quickly became accustomed to the taunts and jeers of the
crowd and learned to use their negative emotions to fuel her own responses.
Rowdy street-corner meetings and impromptu speeches from the back
of an old cart in remote parts of Wales brought out the best in her. She
was a failure at formal speaking, but when aroused she could become
almost eloquent. Each meeting inspired her and renewed her spirits,
and each brought local recognition and increased responsibilities. She
became secretary of the Newport branch of the WSPU and faithfully filed
weekly (later monthly) reports for *The Suffragette*. Unsuspected organizational abilities surfaced as the demands increased. She was called on
to arrange demonstrations, open-air meetings, and social functions.
Fund-raising events and interviews with local politicians, physicians,
and women's groups required extensive planning, preliminary research,
and the development of conversational skills. Margaret found that she
enjoyed the new demands and that she was no longer afraid to try new
avenues of activity.

Because she lived in south Wales, however, away from the centers of
political activity and near her father's constituents, Margaret's activities
were limited. There were few chances to participate in deputations to
Parliament or to interrupt meetings. It was a fundamental commitment
of the suffragettes not to allow any minister to speak without being reminded of women's unsatisfied demands. In Margaret's entire militant
career, she succeeded in confronting only one cabinet minister, but it
was the prime minister, Herbert Asquith. During the general election
of December 1910, Margaret journeyed to Scotland to take her turn at
heckling government ministers. Asquith was scheduled to address a
meeting at the town hall in St. Andrews. Women had been barred, ostensibly on the grounds that the hall was too small, but the suffragettes
were not deterred. Margaret slipped through the police guards, jumped
onto the running board of Asquith's car, and leaned into the open window. The only problem was that in her excitement, she could never
remember if she had said anything to him. Within moments she was

pulled off and chased away by the crowds.[30] She had done her duty and expected to return to calmer activities in Wales.

Throughout the country, however, the campaign was intensifying, and suffragettes were called on to perform more difficult and more militant activities. Earlier tactics had failed to win the authorities over, and the momentum was slipping away. Members increasingly channeled their frustrations into new activities designed to force a confrontation. They moved from mass campaigning and heckling of ministers to confrontation with police and destruction of property. In the name of votes for women, respectable ladies cheerfully smashed windows and sabotaged men's clubs and golf courses, hoping to be caught and sentenced to jail for the cause. The escalation became self-perpetuating. According to Martin Pugh, militant activity became "less a method forced upon them by political obstructionists than a necessary prop to the WSPU itself."[31]

From smashing windows it was only a short step to arson. The militants no longer sought to change opinion but to do damage, hoping that property owners and insurance companies would pressure the government to give in and grant the vote to women. As the campaign intensified and militant tactics increasingly led to jail sentences, new demands were made on the more privileged of the members. A jail sentence would impose unnecessary hardship on the working-class members; therefore, "the ladies" were expected to take up the slack.[32] For the first time, Margaret began to resent the restraints placed on her activity by her husband. Her early promise not to go to prison became more and more frustrating. It seemed to handcuff her and prevent her from doing her share while others were doing so much.[33] Finally she decided that the cause was much more important than either her word or her comfort.

Ironically, Margaret's decision to commit arson and risk going to jail involved her in the one militant activity that she could not wholly support. She had a revulsion for destroying other people's property, especially their letters. The thought of people expecting mail and not receiving it caused her to question policy for the first time. Reluctantly she decided that the activity was warranted because the cause was just. She soothed her conscience by reminding herself that it was the government's obstinacy that had forced the suffragettes into this unsavory activity. If they wanted the arson stopped, all they had to do was give women the vote.

With the rationalization process complete, Margaret resolved to carry out her instructions. She would set the example for the south Wales suffragettes, showing them how easy and how safe the latest task was.

On 21 June 1913, Margaret was supposed to place an explosive substance in the letterbox on Risca Road in Newport. She was so nervous that she made herself very conspicuous. Describing the incident, Margaret wrote: "My heart was beating like a steam engine, my throat was dry, and my nerve went so badly that I made the mistake of walking several times backwards and forwards past the letter box before I found courage to push the packets in. Then as they were rather bulky, I had to force them a bit before they would drop in."[34]

Relieved that her duty was done, Margaret returned home to await her fate. At the end of a week, just as she was beginning to relax and feel safe, she was arrested and charged with arson. For four hours she was held in the Newport jail in a dark, dirty cell. Released on bail, Margaret returned home to face the barely contained displeasure of her husband and in-laws. As she nervously awaited her trial, she contemplated the next step. She was torn between her fear of dark places and isolation and her commitment to the movement. The thought of jail horrified her, but so did the thought of taking the coward's way out and letting her fellow suffragettes down. The decision tormented her until the day of sentencing. Despite the severity of the crime, the sentence was light, probably because of her status within the community. Fined £10 plus an additional £10 court costs, Margaret refused to pay and elected to go to prison for a month.[35]

Certainty that the decision was correct bolstered her courage as she entered the county prison at Usk. The physical aspects of the prison were a welcome surprise after the short stay in the Newport jail. The cell was clean and well lighted, and it looked out into the inner courtyard. Previous suffragettes had won for their successors the right to wear their own clothes and take their own books, but these comforts could not compensate for the loneliness and the sense of being locked in. As the heavy iron doors clanged shut and the footsteps receded, silence descended on the tiny cell. Margaret was alone, with only her few books and her thoughts to keep her company. To one accustomed to activity, it required an almost superhuman effort to sit still and do nothing. The walls closed in, and the month's sentence stretched endlessly before her. Freedom seemed an eternity away, and Margaret, like many of her fellow prisoners, was human enough to have misgivings but devoted enough to the cause to withstand the doubts. She determined to join other suffragettes in a hunger strike to hasten her release and to bring attention to the cause. The daily fight against hunger and thirst weakened her body and increased her tension, but Margaret suffered less than many of her fellow suffragettes. At the end of only five days she was released, though others were allowed to go without food for longer periods. Margaret attributed her early release to the fact that she lived close by, but the prominence of her family surely played a part as well. Because she was imprisoned under the infamous Cat and Mouse Act, she should have been rearrested as soon as she recovered. Just before she was due to return to prison, however, her fine was paid anonymously. She raised no protest. She had done her duty by going to jail. Once was enough.[36]

Other suffragettes were not so lucky. It is instructive to contrast Margaret's treatment with that of Helen Gordon. Convicted of throwing a stone through the post office window in Manchester, Miss Gordon was sentenced to a month's imprisonment in Strangeways Prison, Manchester. She, too, went on a hunger strike, but she was not released. Instead, she was fed by force. Food was forced into the stomach through a rubber hose placed in the prisoner's mouth. The process was both painful and humiliating. Gordon wrote that after feeding, one became "a little more desperate than before," but "her sense of justice [had] been violated and she must rebel . . . her spirit [soared] triumphantly in spite of the injustice."[37]

Had Margaret been forced to undergo this indignity, her resolve might well have been strengthened, too. As it was, she felt vindicated. She had given all the movement had asked and could now channel her energies into new directions that were opening before her, particularly in relation to her father's business interests. Within a year, the outbreak of fighting in Europe brought an end to the militant campaign and absorbed women's energies in the nation's war effort. Any form of sex war was deemed inappropriate while the nation engaged in a life-and-death struggle. The vote temporarily receded into the background.

The abrupt demise of the militant campaign before victory was achieved has led to a tremendous debate over the movement's impact. Accounts of participants and of some later feminist writers attempt to imbue the movement with a heroic strain, insisting that the martyrdom of the suffragettes had brought the fight to the brink of victory by the time war broke out.[38] More balanced accounts, however, see the movement as having a dual effect. On the positive side, militancy brought the issue of women's suffrage before the public and forced women to choose between alternative strategies. Many women who could not support the militant methods were prompted to join one of the milder organizations. Until about 1910, the two wings of the suffrage movement, the WSPU and the NUWSS, complemented each other. The militants received the publicity, while the Constitutionalists kept up a steady stream of argument and persuasion. After 1910, however, militancy became counterproductive. The suffragettes, caught up in the emotions and violence of their sex war, lost sight of the goal. The constantly increasing violence worked to alienate more people than it convinced, leaving the militants in disarray by 1912 and turning lukewarm supporters into antagonists. Even active suffragette supporters, most notably the Pethick-Lawrences, were alienated by the extremism which was gradually obscuring the original purpose.[39] Large numbers of women, particularly of the working class, withdrew their support, not so much because of the violence but because of "the double shuffle between revolution and injured innocence, the playing for effect and not for results."[40] Sandra Holton has shown recently that another current was at work within the WSPU (and the NUWSS as well). She identified a "democratic suffragist" element, which was attempting to ally the women's suffrage cause with broader reform agitation and more specifically with the Labour Party in an attempt to secure a more democratized Britain.[41] By the time war broke out, the WSPU was no longer functional. The combined physical strain from hunger striking, the political strain from defections, and the difficulties in operating as a quasi-legal underground organization had spent its energies. The militants had become increasingly out of touch, and were now millstones around the neck of the broader suffrage movement.[42]

For Margaret, however, the true measure of militancy was not its failure to win the vote but its impact on the individual suffragettes. She regarded the vote as a symbol of deeper changes in the status of women and the gradual erosion of sexist customs and prejudices within British society, not as an end in itself. The militant strategy had altered its participants' opinions of themselves, giving them self-confidence and self-respect. Margaret never expressed any regrets about her participation.[43] She had loved the excitement, the adventure, and the sense of power that her involvement had provided. Looking back on her experiences years later, Margaret wrote:

> The knowledge of it had come like a draught of fresh air into our padded, stifled lives. It gave us release of energy, it gave us that sense of being of some use in the scheme of things, without which no human being can live at peace. It made us feel that we were part of life, not just outside watching it. It made us feel that we had a real purpose and use apart from having children. . . . It gave us freedom and power

and opportunity. It gave us scope at last, and it gave us what normal healthy youth craves—adventure and excitement.[44]

As a suffragette, Margaret underwent a process that modern feminists would call consciousness-raising. She had experienced the exhilaration of breaking away from restrictive conventions and the excitement of challenging discriminatory practices and ideas. She had been forced to use her mind to consider feminist alternatives to male-oriented and male-directed laws and customs. In the process, she had gained new insight into the needs and interests of women in general and into her own worth. The recognition that she was not some appendage of the males in her life but a person in her own right gave her a new sense of self-confidence and self-respect.[45] This attitude allowed her to shed the role of self-effacing housewife for that of self-assured businesswoman and carried her psychologically further away from her husband's world.

3 · ENTRY INTO A MAN'S WORLD

The militant suffragette movement had given Margaret new confidence and courage to act independently. It had allowed her to develop previously uncultivated organizational and public relations skills and had instilled in her a desire to escape the life of "unoccupied faculties and petty futility"[1] which had been her lot since leaving boarding school. During her brief prison stay, she had come face to face with her own fears and her own inner strength. Yet it appears that Margaret was moving away from the militant movement even before she went to prison. She remained committed to their goals, but began to question their methods. She was no longer prepared to give her absolute loyalty to the WSPU (as evidenced by her acceptance of her anonymous benefactor's payment of her fine), nor was she prepared to return to her former life of social duties and of overseeing the household. Fortunately, her parents provided Margaret with the opportunity to branch out into the world of business, a step which drastically altered her personal life and opened new avenues for activity and self-fulfillment. During the final year of militant activity, Margaret was "invading male space" on very different terms.

Many years later Margaret wrote that had she not had a rich and famous father "devoid of the usual inhibitions about using female material if it happened to come handy,"[2] she would never have been heard of outside her own locality. But in fact she owed her original chance more to her mother. Her father's business interests had grown to the point where he needed an assistant to help manage the vast Thomas coal empire as he prepared to diversify his commercial investments. He wanted a confidential secretary and administrative assistant whom he could trust to learn the intricacies of the business and to put the family fortunes first — someone to fill the place a son might have taken. His wife suggested that he try Margaret, reminding him that no one had more respect for his judgment, more faith in his decisions, or more reason to protect the family's financial status. Though he had apparently never given a thought to bringing a woman into the business, D.A. respected his wife's opinions enough to give the matter careful consideration. He had taught his daughter to think and had discussed the problems facing the Thomas industrial concerns with her since her teenage years. Father and daughter were bound by sympathy, mutual admiration, and similar temperaments. Upon consideration, it seemed only natural that his heir, regardless of gender, should occupy the place beside him.[3]

Margaret was flattered by her father's confidence but frightened that she might disappoint him and uncertain about the risks involved. Her husband and his family were not supportive. They considered it unfeminine to work in public, particularly if one did not have to, and probably resented her willingness to place her father's wishes over her husband's. Ultimately Margaret minded much more what her father thought. She knew her training had not prepared her for the challenges of business but desperately wanted to make him proud of her. Convinced that her father would back her financially and give her emotional support, Margaret gratefully accepted the opportunity to prove herself in her father's eyes.[4]

The responsibilities were heavy for both father and daughter. D.A.'s action was, if not revolutionary, at least unorthodox. Business was a man's world, and colleagues must have questioned this apparent sentimentality in a man of Thomas' stature. Typically, junior positions went to university trained males, and the idea of a female, particularly a *married* one, would have undoubtedly caused consternation among partners and investors. By appointing his daughter his personal assistant, he laid himself open to criticism and put his reputation as an astute businessman on the line. Both father and daughter had an important stake in the experiment. He had to prove it was an intelligent business decision. She had to prove that she, a woman, was capable of working in the field of business and industry. The fact that both had so much to lose probably caused each to take special pains to make their new venture a success.

D.A. took his daughter under his wing. While using her for minor secretarial and messenger services, he also began to instruct her in the management of the Thomas fortune. He taught her not only the basics of the coal industry and the intricacies of corporate financing but also the tactics of negotiation, the value of fair dealing, and the art of bluffing. Building on her years of listening to his ruminations during long country walks, Margaret quickly caught on and was rewarded with increased responsibilities and a salary of £1,000 a year. She began to draft her father's confidential letters and memoranda and to do background research on special projects. With each new task she gained confidence

and insight into men and business, and her father gained respect for
her abilities and her instincts. By mid-1914, he had turned over the
Thomas newspaper interests to Margaret, giving her complete control
over a relatively minor but potentially important part of his business
empire.[5]

Margaret was absorbed by the new challenges and barely had time
to notice the ominous events leading to the outbreak of the First World
War. The invasion of Belgium on 3 August 1914, the unprovoked attack
on a small, neutral state by a coguarantor of its neutrality, horrified liberal
Edwardians and provided the occasion for a declaration of war against
the German aggressor. Buoyed by the conviction that their cause was
just and right, the British people serenely went about their business,
confident that an Allied victory would be achieved by Christmas. While
the men were enlisting for service, the nation as a whole – and women
in particular – were advised to continue with business as usual.

But almost immediately the suffrage movement turned at least partially from its normal activity in response to the declaration of war. The
NUWSS continued to exert pressure for women's inclusion in any franchise reform, but the central leadership encouraged their members to
support the war effort. This caused internal troubles: the true pacifists
within the movement resented being asked to work for what they considered an immoral cause. Nonetheless, many of the suffragists engaged
in volunteer work for charitable or relief agencies, raised funds for hospital units at the front, or took jobs in order to release men for military
duty. The WSPU's support took the form of more dramatic gestures. The
leadership declared a halt to the sex war and became visible symbols
of patriotism and cooperation in the government's recruiting campaigns.
They also promoted xenophobic fears of possible German influence in
the government and the military. And, of course, they confronted males
in civilian clothing with the white feather of cowardice.[6] Ironically,
Margaret's experiences conform more closely to those of the mainstream
Constitutionalists than to her militant sisters'.

In its early stages the war had no significant impact on Margaret's
life. It caused a slight inconvenience for the Thomas commercial interests, as travel and communication difficulties threatened to impair
business contacts in Canada and the United States. To speed up inquiries
into a number of projected schemes, D. A. Thomas planned a business
trip for the spring of 1915.[7] Margaret accompanied him, taking notes
and drafting memoranda about Pennsylvania coal mines, a potential barge
service on the Mississippi, and railway routes and mineral rights in north-

ern Canada.[8] As these projects were generally outside Margaret's area of expertise, the excursion was more of a holiday than a business trip for her. When her secretarial duties were completed, Margaret retreated to New York for a round of dinner parties, theater engagements, and shopping sprees. She learned less about business on this journey than she learned about herself. In New York, for the first time in her life, Margaret enjoyed the social scene and considered herself something of a social success. The freer atmosphere in the States and the warm hospitality she received helped her to overcome her shyness and begin to look forward to meeting new people and entering fully into the social activities available to a woman of her status.[9]

But the return voyage to London had the more profound impact on Margaret's life and brought the first personal realization of the horrors of war. On 1 May 1915, Margaret and her father boarded the *Lusitania* despite warnings from the German embassy and widespread rumors of an impending submarine attack. They were fully conscious of the risks involved, but Margaret later claimed that her father wanted to be back in Llanwern for the glorious mid-May weather and that she herself secretly hoped for an adventure without truly expecting anything to happen. Six days into the journey, just off the southwest coast of Ireland, the *Lusitania* was torpedoed. In the chaos that followed, over a thousand passengers went down with the ship. Her father, who was on the opposite side of the ship from Margaret, found a place in a lifeboat and quickly reached safety only to experience hours of anxiety as the fate of his daughter remained unknown. Margaret, buoyed by a life jacket, floated in the ocean, terror and discomfort mounting both in and around her, before she mercifully lost consciousness. Three hours after the attack she was picked up by the *Bluebell,* a small patrol steamer. The crew at first thought she was dead, but a passing sailor noted her shallow breathing and summoned medical attention. Weakened by the struggle and severely bruised, Margaret emerged from the blackness happy to be alive but facing a three-month battle with bronchial pneumonia.[10]

Looking back on the *Lusitania* incident, Margaret referred to the experience as the apex of the bridge between her youth and mature adulthood.[11] The timid young lady had been forced to face her apprehensions and learned that she could control her worst fears. Her confidence soared, and the fear of death which had overwhelmed her as a child receded. She wrote: "When Death is as close as he was then, the sharp agony of fear is not there; the thing is too overwhelming and stunning for that. One has the sense of something taking care of one—I don't mean in the

sense of protecting one from death; rather of death itself being a be-
nignant power."[12]

She emerged from the experience with her faith in British efficiency
and in humanity slightly tarnished. She was convinced that the chaotic
situation had been worsened by the inadequate preparation, disorganization, and panic of passengers and crew. But even more she was confronted as never before with "what German brutality meant," and with
many others determined that she would "not rest till they had paid the
debt they owed."[13] The death of the twenty-nine children on the *Lusitania* affected her as the death of countless soldiers on European soil
could not. The fact that the passengers had been warned and that the
two nations were at war did not, in her mind, excuse the inhumanity
of the act.

She recovered from the ordeal prepared to do her part for the war effort,
but once again found the opportunities available rather limited. It was
still a man's war, and women's abilities were not deemed important enough
to make any significant contribution to the war effort. Until the summer
of 1915, women were called on only for minor tasks. Working-class women
suffered a slight setback at the beginning of the war as jobs in the traditional women's trades of food, textiles, and clothing were threatened by
the patriotic upsurge of instant economy measures, but wartime demands
for uniforms and provisions brought those jobs back within eight months.
Middle- and upper-class women generally had to be content with the
type of voluntary activities Margaret had never had much use for—knit-
ting socks, helping Belgian refugees get settled, making sandbags, and
encouraging the menfolk to do their duty.[14] Margaret's participation in
this phase of war work was limited to some very minor assistance in
the Belgian refugee schemes and to encouraging Humphrey, who was
stationed with the Remounts at Bristol. Like many of the women of Britain, she would have liked to do more, but the present scheme did not
offer many possibilities.[15]

As the war continued and more men were needed on the battlefronts,
opportunities for women began to open up. The substitution of women
for men in such traditional male occupations as those of bus and tram
conductors, drivers, ticket collectors, and police officers became acceptable as a means of releasing more men for the armed services. Success
in these ventures and critical munitions shortages combined to lead to
a further acceptance of women war workers. In May 1915, David Lloyd
George was appointed minister of munitions. He was prepared to tap
the only large potential labor source available in order to solve the prob-

lem of weapons supply without taking men away from their military duties. The widespread publicity given to the critical shell shortage allowed him to force concessions from the trade unions and temporarily break down gender barriers in the munitions industry.[16] But still, for women of Margaret's class and status, these broader opportunities meant little. The only "suitable" occupations for women like her were secretarial or administrative jobs, and there were as yet few openings in those areas.[17]

But Lloyd George's appointment did allow Margaret to play a peripheral role in the early war effort and indirectly gave her an opportunity to hone her business skills. Lloyd George asked his old rival D. A. Thomas to travel to America to arrange for the purchase of weapons and ammunition. This vital mission gave the Allies a breathing space and earned D. A. Thomas a baronetcy in 1916. The mission was possible in part because he felt safe leaving his business affairs in the hands of his daughter. He gave her power of attorney and turned over complete control of all his private business for the duration of his stay in America. She did not take his place on the boards of directors, but she did manage his finances and keep him informed about all business dealings.[18]

Shortly after his return to London, Lord Rhondda was appointed president of the Local Government Board and later succeeded Lord Davenport as food minister in 1917. Lord Rhondda's ministerial appointments again made great demands on his time and energies and forced him to turn over larger business responsibilities to his daughter. At her father's urging, the other board members elected Margaret to fill the vacancies, and she spent the next two years traveling between London and Cardiff to attend board meetings. Despite the technicalities, Margaret acted as her father's proxy and was the liaison between him and his business colleagues. They accepted her only because she was his daughter and because they expected the arrangement, which relieved them of responsibility and kept them in touch with Lord Rhondda's wishes and his acute business sense, to be temporary.[19]

Had it not been for the war and for Lord Rhondda's standing within the business community, Margaret's position would probably have horrified the more conservative directors. But circumstances had provided her with a unique opportunity, and the mantle of her father's trust guaranteed that she would at least be given a chance to prove herself. She became director of more than twenty companies, entering the boardroom with some trepidation. For the most part Margaret was content to remain in the background. She spoke very little, but listened intently and learned much about the workings of big business and the blind spots of her male counterparts. She enjoyed the board meetings and dutifully reported to her father, discussing proposed mergers and labor difficulties with new insight and increasing appreciation.[20]

This apprenticeship served Margaret well in the future, but it came to a temporary halt when she was called on to play a more active role in the war effort. During the dark days of 1917, the demand for more effective mobilization of the nation's manpower led to the creation of a National Service Department with a special Women's Section under May Tennant and Violet Markham. The section was charged with recruiting volunteers and allocating materials needed for the war effort. The broad-ranging duties of the department necessitated a decentralization of the work load through the establishment of seven provincial centers — five for England, one for Scotland, and one for Wales. By virtue of her stature in the Welsh community, Margaret was appointed to fill the position of commissioner of Women's National Service in Wales. As commissioner she was responsible for recruiting women for agriculture, for collecting woolen, cotton, and paper goods, and for organizing provincial selection boards for the Women's Army Auxiliary Corps (WAAC). In addition, she acted as an unofficial intelligence officer for the Women's Section, reporting on female morale, responses, and needs.[21]

Margaret entered into these new duties enthusiastically. Her days as a local organizer for the WSPU had trained her well. From her headquarters in Cardiff, she directed advertising campaigns, organized recruiting programs, and filed detailed monthly reports. She also traveled extensively within Wales, distributing enrollment forms, answering questions, and exhorting Welsh women to rise to "the best traditions in this hour of the nation's need."[22] Touring the major cities, Margaret used her commercial and press contacts to lay the foundation for strong propaganda campaigns throughout the Welsh provinces. Her monthly reports to the London office consistently emphasized the special problems of recruiting in Wales. She was critical of the discrepancies in pay between London and Welsh workers, pointing out that the higher rates paid in London were siphoning off much of the labor pool needed for local jobs. She further stressed that recruiting in a largely agricultural area required a lengthier time period for successful completion than a similar campaign in an industrial area.[23]

Her understanding of conditions in Wales helped to make Margaret's recruiting activities relatively successful. Large numbers were recruited for WAAC service in France, and significant progress was made toward convincing Welsh farmers to hire women for agricultural work. Margaret's efforts drew praise from both the director of her own division and representatives of related departments. The traveling inspector for the South Wales Division of the Women's Branch of the Board of Agriculture and Fisheries singled Margaret out for her invaluable services in organizing meetings with farmers and potential women land workers.[24] This commendation caused Violet Markham, assistant director of the Women's Section of the National Service Department, to write an encouraging note, which stated in part: "If you can convert the farmers and persuade them to take the women, you will indeed be rendering true National Service. It is everything to make a beginning, and the converted farmer is indeed himself the best of all possible recruiting officers."[25]

Despite these successes, Margaret's activities, and those of the department as a whole, were hindered from the very beginning by bureaucratic jealousies, conflicting instructions, and unnecessary delays. For the regional commissioners, delays in getting printed forms, contradictory reports of the number of job openings, and widespread rumors of neglect of the enlistees' welfare presented obstacles to effective recruitment.[26] For the department as a whole, poorly timed press releases and lukewarm support from the War Office and the Ministry of Labour handicapped the operation throughout its tenure. The Treasury's refusal to provide funding for paid subcommissioners and difficulties with the recruits' being promptly placed by the employment exchanges also contributed to the relative ineffectiveness and early demise of the original section. On 25 June 1917, May Tennant and Violet Markham resigned from their positions, and the department was dismantled, leaving the problem of women's recruiting unsolved.[27]

Continuing difficulties led to another shift in policy and further opportunities for Margaret. In November 1917, the War Cabinet placed responsibility for recruitment in the hands of Sir Aukland Geddes' Ministry of National Service. One month later, a small Women's Section was created, supposedly with complete control over the recruiting of all women for work of national importance. Colonel A. Corsellis was appointed to head the section, with Margaret as the Chief Controller of Women's Recruiting.[28] Margaret was thrilled. For the first time, she had been given a substantive task in an important ministry. She threw herself into her new job, temporarily suspending all business activity to devote her energies to the immediate task.

In the early stages Margaret found the appointment exhilarating and the prospects potentially rewarding. Her primary responsibilities included helping devise and coordinate a plan for the systematic recruitment of

women for the various corps and departments open to them and serving
as the official liaison between the ministry and the various women's
groups (the Voluntary Aid Detachment, the Women's Legion, the Women's
Land Army, and so on) involved in the war effort. As chief controller,
she held conferences with other departments and women's organizations
to discuss the most efficient means of utilizing women in industry,
agriculture, and military auxiliaries, as well as ways to make such service more appealing to potential recruits.[29]

The insight she gained from these meetings and her experience in
business and the earlier Women's Section helped Margaret plan the general scheme for women's recruiting outlined in her "Memorandum on
Woman Power" for Lord Milner, the secretary of state for war. This
memorandum provides the first written statement of the ideas that had
long been forming in Margaret's mind and would become the foundation for her later business and editorial philosophy. The document emphasizes efficiency, economy, coordination, and communication while
criticizing redundancy, extravagance, and interdepartmental feuding.
Margaret suggested that the War Cabinet must take charge and direct
the ministries of National Service and Labour to put aside petty differences and concentrate on the very real problem at hand—the adequate
mobilization of the nation's womanpower. She also proposed that the
employment exchanges be reinforced and popularized by the addition
of local recruiting and selection committees, which would inspire public
confidence and stimulate participation. Closer coordination of the military
branches was recommended as a means of eliminating waste and duplication. The memorandum called for periodic meetings of the heads of
the three women's services to discuss matters of mutual interest and to
secure a fairer allocation of available recruits. The same centralization
process was advocated for the nonmilitary services. Margaret suggested
that the Ministry of National Service create a small and carefully chosen
Woman Power Council to oversee the selection process and direct each
recruit into the area best suited to her abilities and the nation's needs.[30]

While the ideas set forth in this memorandum showed a solid grasp
of the problems and gave definite suggestions for improving conditions,
Margaret soon found herself confronted by the same problems that had
so frustrated Tennant and Markham. Lack of cooperation and resentment from other government departments, most notably the Ministry
of Labour, and significant opposition from the leaders of other women's
organizations, most notably Lady Londonderry, director of the Women's

Legion, combined to weaken the effectiveness of the department.[31] Margaret found the constant bickering, backbiting, and raising of obstacles very disappointing. It often seemed that while her suggestions were solicited to obtain a woman's response to certain problems, they were rejected out of hand by other ministries because they represented a narrow "woman's view," and by other women's groups because they were not representative of their particular beliefs. Caught between these two conflicting perceptions of her work, Margaret found her effectiveness greatly reduced. The Women's Section which she headed was admittedly able to do only "useful scraps of work here and there, but not much more"[32] before it closed in October 1918.

Most of the positive aspects of Margaret's work at the Ministry of National Service concerned gathering and processing information in several critical areas. When Margaret accepted the position, accusations of dissension, mistreatment, and immorality in the training camps hindered women's recruiting. Concern mounted for several months but became acute when Miss Phillipa Strachey, head of the Women's Service Bureau, a voluntary organization which recruited women for various types of government service, announced that conditions in the camps were so bad that the bureau would no longer supply volunteers. Such public criticism prompted Sir Aukland Geddes to request that Margaret prepare a report on the welfare of women in camps operated by the various government departments. Margaret's study of nine camps found satisfactory conditions in those run by Queen Mary's Army Auxiliary Corps and the Women's Royal Naval Service, but it was highly critical of those of the Women's Royal Air Force (WRAF). Her report warned that the disorganization, inefficiency, and lack of discipline in the WRAF camps could destroy confidence in all the women's corps, because the public tended to ignore or blur the differences between the separate branches. Pointing to several recent resignations of senior officers and general malaise among recruits, Margaret insisted that drastic reorganization be carried out quickly if the WRAF were to be an addition to, rather than a drain on, the nation's war effort. Impressed with her conclusions, Sir Aukland Geddes suggested that Margaret present the data to Lord Weir, secretary of state for the Royal Air Force, with a recommendation that the WRAF be completely reorganized and staffed with new personnel. Upon apprising Lord Weir of the unsatisfactory state of affairs, Margaret found him already familiar with the problems and prepared to discuss the recommendations with the heads of the other two women's services. After discussion and careful consideration, the process of re-organization was begun with the removal of Miss Violet Douglas-Pennant as commandant of the WRAF.[33]

This action precipitated something of a crisis at the end of the war. Unhappy at her untimely dismissal, Miss Douglas-Pennant asked for a parliamentary inquiry, hinting at collusion and conspiracy to discredit her and prevent her from reporting scandalous behavior on the part of male officers charged with giving overnight leaves to female recruits to enable them to participate in all-night drinking and sex sprees. She also charged that she was being removed so that Geddes could appoint a relative, Mrs. Alexandra Chalmers-Watson, to the position.[34] These accusations were never proven, but the charges and inquiries are significant as an indication of Margaret's tendency to rely heavily on the advice of others and of her developing showmanship.

In the original accusations of collusion, Margaret's name does not appear,[35] but as the controversy heightened her name surfaced frequently. It appears that much of the information Margaret included in her report was based on hearsay, garnered from talks with personal friends rather than with the actual participants. She neither sought full corroboration of the incriminating evidence nor confronted Miss Douglas-Pennant with the serious accusations. While later inquiries invalidated Miss Douglas-Pennant's charges, the lack of thoroughness in the original report did lead to some legitimate concerns. These concerns were magnified when Lord Weir admitted under cross-examination that he had wished to appoint Margaret to fill the vacancy created and when copies of her letters about the incident were "lost," or disappeared, from the files of both the Air and National Service ministries.[36]

Such incidents created some suspicion, and Margaret took the stand at a parliamentary inquiry to explain her actions. Her confidence in the propriety of her conduct combined with her wit and indignation to lend credence to her testimony and humor to an otherwise monotonous proceeding. Margaret's showmanship delighted the *Times* correspondent, who treated his audience to a number of crisp exchanges. Asked if her dealings with Miss Douglas-Pennant had been straightforward, Margaret replied in the affirmative and defiantly retorted, "I object to the insinuation." When Lord Wrenbury referred to the 1 April birthdate of the WRAF, Margaret quipped, "I really never could understand why they chose that date."[37]

Aside from the Douglas-Pennant incident, Margaret's tenure at the Ministry of National Service was generally free from controversy. Several schemes for recruiting and raising morale were developed, but they fell prey to bureaucratic delay. Margaret was able, however, to use her position to gain support for a personal project, the Win the War Centres. While these centers had the approval of the Food, Food Production, and National Service departments, they do not appear to have been officially sanctioned by the government. It appears, instead, that the plan was developed, organized, and promoted by Margaret personally in response to an acute need she observed while performing her duties. In the course of her work, Margaret became increasingly concerned with the confusion, misinformation, waste, and inefficiency among the general public. To alleviate the problems, Win the War Centres were developed to provide local facilities for the dissemination of accurate, up-to-date information on home front problems. The centers advised interested citizens on the economical use of food and fuel and the production and preservation of foodstuffs. They also attempted to promote such patriotic principles as self-denial, voluntary rationing of scarce items, and the purchase of war bonds. The scheme received strong endorsement from the *Times* and from prominent politicians. The centers' General Council boasted such leading figures as David Lloyd George, Andrew Bonar Law, Lord Robert Cecil, and the Lord Mayor of London.[38]

Margaret also used her position to strike a small blow for women's equality. As the fourth anniversary of the war approached, Margaret was asked by the Ministry of Information to contribute an article on women's share in the war for an anniversary edition of *Overseas*, the journal of the Overseas Club and Patriotic League of Britons.[39] Male contributors paid tribute to women's contribution to the war effort in glowing terms. Articles abounded with hyperbole – "magnificent service," "splendid achievement," "gallant daughters of Britain."[40] Margaret might have been expected to make the same type of glowing report. Instead, she pointed out the impertinence of praising women's war work as if it were some aberration. British women, like British men, were simply doing their duty and doing it well. To treat them as the exception rather than the rule was to obscure their abilities, willingness, and initiative.[41] This simple statement did more to legitimize women's war work than all the exaggerated and condescending praise, no matter how well-intentioned.

Her straightforward manner and workmanlike attitude and performance brought Margaret personal prestige and broadened responsibilities in the latter stages of the war. In April 1918, concern over bureaucratic growth and inefficiency in the Ministry of Munitions led to the appointment of a Staff Investigating Committee charged with determining proper methods and procedures for promoting economy and efficiency in the ministry's clerical and administrative departments. As the sole female member of the committee, Margaret consistently worked to ensure that the contribution and special problems of the women staff workers be given adequate consideration. She proposed that a panel of women volunteers be established as an ad hoc subcommittee to undertake investigations and provide independent reports on the status of women workers. Margaret accepted the responsibility for coordinating the subcommittee, consolidating its findings, and reporting to the official committee. The efforts paid off in a special report on the conditions of women employees which was appended to the Staff Investigating Committee's final report. While the appendix was in general harmony with the overall conclusions of the final report in recommending less duplication, better training, and more effective coordination of duties, it differed slightly in emphasizing that many of the problems were created by the temporary employment of women in large numbers and the lack of training opportunities available to them before the war.[42]

Margaret's knowledge of and concern for women workers also led to her appointment to the Women's Advisory Council of the Ministry of Reconstruction. As the war drew to a close, the ministry sought practical advice from prominent men and women on the most effective and least disruptive means of demobilizing women war workers as well as enhancing postwar employment prospects for women. Subcommittees were established to consider the future role of women in the civil service, domestic service, and the health services. Margaret was originally targeted to chair the Civil Service Subcommittee but withdrew her name from consideration to avoid a conflict of interests when she was asked to give evidence before the Treasury Department's Committee on Recruitment for the Civil Service chaired by Viscount Gladstone.[43] Instead, she was appointed as chairperson of the Subcommittee on Health and Kindred Services. This body was given responsibility for outlining an ideal scheme for postwar health and social services, with particular attention to the role of the voluntary worker. It was apparently expected that most women war workers would return to traditional female occupations or to voluntary employment at war's end.

This expectation also led the Women's Advisory Committee into a study of the domestic service problem. New opportunities for employment during the war and the generally low pay and low status of domestic workers had severely drained the available labor supply for domestic service during the war years and had created much anxiety over the future of the industry.[44] In the subcommittee debates on the issue, Margaret consistently expressed concern over the practical problems of excessive hours and lack of recreation for servants and advocated a thirteen-hour day, with three of those hours set aside for leisure and two more for meals.[45] These hours were apparently too lenient for other members of the committee to support, and the final report concluded only that definite hours should be established, that affordable training facilities be developed, and that the status of domestic work be raised to make it a more appealing alternative for young women entering the labor market.[46]

In all their various wartime positions, Margaret and the women of Britain had fulfilled their duties conscientiously and well. They had made mistakes, but often as a result of inadequate training and experience, which could have been expected with an influx of an additional 1,345,000 women workers into engineering, banking, clerical work, civil service, transport, nursing, and agriculture between July 1914 and July 1918. These women workers were greatly appreciated in the dark days of the war, but advances were not as significant as they might first have appeared.

While it is true that women employees received high praise in the press, they were often met with hostility and resentment in the factories and on the farms. Their success was threatening because it demonstrated that women with limited training could perform tasks that had previously been considered the domain of skilled males. New types of occupations were opened to women, but for the most part this expansion was a temporary phenomenon which did not outlast the war. Higher wages were paid in specialized trades, but in the occupations held by the majority of women the rise in wages was small, and the decline in purchasing power was considerable. Though more women were working, the number of women in the higher professions and in executive positions did not notably increase during the war years, and traditional notions of men's and women's work and discrepancies in pay continued well into the postwar years.[47] In fact, the immediate postwar years saw a revival of opposition to married women's employment outside the home. The 1919 report of the Women's Employment Committee of the Ministry of Reconstruction actually recommended against the continued employment of married women, while a number of local school boards instituted new regulations requiring women teachers to resign on marriage. Likewise, those women who were reluctant to leave their industrial jobs found themselves assailed as greedy, ungrateful interlopers by the same journalists who had recently hailed their entry into those jobs.[48] Still, the war experience did give women new confidence in the range of tasks they could perform and created higher expectations and a slightly higher standard of living, particularly among working-class women.[49]

As the war brought limited economic changes for the women of Britain, it accelerated social changes that both enhanced and destabilized the lives of the female population. Significant gains were made in civilian health matters because of improvements in health care administration and nutrition. Female and infant mortality rates declined significantly. The entire nation benefited, but these developments were most notable among the working classes. They were partially offset, however, by the escalation of respiratory diseases among former munitions workers and a general deterioration in British housing.[50] Women as a whole tasted a fleeting freedom during World War I. They were encouraged to act independently rather than through the family. Greater mobility and enforced separation from husbands or fathers contributed to a loosening of community controls, an emphasis on personal development and personal satisfaction, and for some the shedding of old inhibitions. But along with this freedom came a sense of confusion and ambivalence for many. The old rules no longer seemed to apply, but new standards had yet to emerge, leaving women in the postwar years uncertain about what was expected of them.[51] Many women, having once tasted independence, found it impossible to revert to their prewar lives.

The impact of the war on women's suffrage is still a matter of controversy. Undoubtedly the war illuminated discrepancies in the electoral registers and made wholesale franchise reform palatable, and women's war work had undermined the legitimacy of the separate-spheres ideology. In the course of the conflict, women had taken on almost every "male" task other than battlefront action and parliamentary service. Their performance had cast doubts on the old antisuffragist arguments of inferiority and emotional instability, but it is unlikely that those notions were entirely dispelled. Nor had it lessened politicians' fear of the possible disruption that might be caused by a broadened franchise.[52] Sandra Holton argues convincingly that the war may actually have delayed women's suffrage, since the prewar democratic-suffragist alliance with Labour had already ensured that women would have to be included in any franchise bill. In her view, war work may have played a role in altering some opponents' views and in providing a device to allow more vocal adversaries to save face when switching positions.[53] David Sweet, taking a different position, argues that politicians recognized that it would have been politically unthinkable to call a general election without recognizing the voteless fighting men and the contribution of women war workers.[54]

Regardless of the exact motivation for including females in the wartime franchise extension, politicians had no intention of allowing the female majority to dominate the electoral process or of rewarding the young and unpredictable munitionettes and land girls for their wartime service. The Representation of the People Act of 1918, which Sweet calls "the true inauguration of democratic politics in twentieth century Britain,"[55] was not all the suffrage supporters had hoped for. While introducing universal manhood suffrage for males over the age of twenty-one, it restricted the vote for females to those over thirty who could meet the occupancy requirements for local elections or who had served in one of the auxiliary services. A large number of female war workers in areas like industry, agriculture, and nursing, regardless of age, remained unrepresented in the newly expanded electorate.

For all of Britain the war had wrought tremendous physical and emotional changes. For Margaret personally, the war years had been "a dark jungle of tension, and anxiety, and excitement,"[56] punctuated by both deep personal loss and a sense of freedom. During the war Lord Rhondda's health began to fail under the strains and pressures of his work at the Food Ministry. As his condition deteriorated, George V elevated Baron Rhondda to a viscountcy on 19 June 1918 as a reward for his wartime service. The peerage carried with it a special remainder allowing the title to pass to his female heir upon his death. Lloyd George wrote that George V had agreed to such departures from precedent only "in cases where the service rendered to the State is very conspicuous."[57] Lord Rhondda was not able to enjoy the prestige or benefits of his new status, but the knowledge that the privileges would pass to his daughter comforted him in the final days of his life. On 3 July 1918, David Alfred Thomas died. Margaret's grief was acute. She had lost a parent, a friend, and a mentor, but she inherited his title, his business concerns, and a considerable fortune.[58]

This newfound economic freedom and elevated personal status probably contributed to the growing strains in Margaret's marriage to Sir Humphrey Mackworth. Very little evidence exists regarding their thirteen-year union or subsequent divorce. In her autobiography Margaret passes over her failed marriage quickly. Her explanation attacks neither her husband nor the institution of marriage. Instead, it emphasizes the personal incompatibility of the partners (in very general terms) and the social conditions of prewar days, which encouraged protected females to marry without really knowing either themselves or their prospective husbands. She does, however, tend to take the lion's share of the blame for herself, commenting that she, in particular, was "unfit" for the role. Whether this is simply the typical self-effacement of an Edwardian woman or an expression of a deeper feeling that her failure as a wife was the result of some sort of personal disability cannot be proven from the existing records. What is clear is that the two parted on fairly good terms. Margaret states simply that the war had made her incompatibility with Humphrey more evident than before, and the couple decided "not to drag an uncomfortable life-sentence to its weary end."[59] Writing to her friend Elizabeth Robins in December 1921, Margaret reemphasized this point. She wrote: "I expect its [sic] best in the long run to own up to a failure but the process is beastly—I think it both our faults—or perhaps neither—we simply never fitted—though we tried to pretend we did for thirteen years."[60]

Despite Margaret's reticence about this chapter in her personal life, she undoubtedly gave the matter very serious thought. Though its incidence had risen significantly in the aftermath of the war, divorce continued to carry a heavy social stigma, particularly among the upper and upper middle classes.[61] For most women, divorce would be unthinkable because they would risk losing their home, their children, their financial security, and their reputation. Margaret, however, was virtually free from such concerns. Upon her father's death, the financial and social security previously held through her husband were superseded by her own status. She was now a woman of independent means and a peeress in her own right. Being childless and having a secure role outside the home surely made the break easier for her.

Nonetheless, the marriage did continue for three years after the war. The pair had begun to grow apart before the war, but Humphrey's extended absences for military service and Margaret's frustration at not conceiving a child widened the breach. After the war Margaret's business interests kept her in London much of the time, while Humphrey remained in the Welsh country house. They occasionally traveled together but maintained two separate households and spent less and less time together.

Contemporary reports of the divorce proceedings published in the *Western Mail* and the *Times* provide a general account which neither party publicly challenged. In December 1922, Margaret sued for divorce on the grounds of Humphrey's statutory desertion and adultery. The evidence she provided in this uncontested suit indicated that the break came on her return to England from a holiday in France in October 1921. While overseas, she testified, she had constantly written her husband but received no replies. Arriving home, she found a letter stating in part, "The present position is impossible. We cannot go on as we are,"[62] and suggesting an indefinite separation. Margaret claimed she appealed to Humphrey to reconsider, but he refused. Margaret's lawyers then produced the register of the Midlands Grand Hotel for 5 July 1922, which was signed Humphrey and Margaret Mackworth. Employees of the hotel verified that the woman in bed with Humphrey the next morning was not his wife, and the divorce was granted on 21 December 1922.[63] Six months later Humphrey remarried. He continued to live on the Mackworth estate until his death on 2 May 1948.

It is difficult to ascertain whether this evidence caused the divorce or was manufactured to facilitate it. Both Margaret and Humphrey were by this time unhappy in the marriage, but the only acceptable ground for divorce at the time was adultery. Ruth Adam suggests that it was still traditional for the gentleman to take the blame (or credit) in divorce suits "since the seducer . . . cut a better figure than the cuckold."[64]

The day after the divorce was granted, Margaret departed for France in the company of a party including an unattached male, sparking rumors of an impending marriage of her own.[65] Margaret never remarried, nor does there appear to have been any further contact between her and Humphrey. Theodora Bosanquet, Lady Rhondda's closest confidante, recorded in her diary that Margaret did not even comment on his death. Any feeling which had existed between the two had long since vanished.[66] Whether or not Margaret regretted the decision to divorce in later years is uncertain. She remained a firm believer in the institution of marriage throughout her life and wrote rather wistfully to her dear friend Winifred Holtby in December 1933 (eleven years after her divorce) that "Mistressship is no use really—eternal vows are the only thing even if they do interfere a bit with the pattern of one's own life."[67]

The war years and her divorce had drastically altered Margaret's life. Like many of her generation, she approached the new era with contradictory emotions. On the one hand was a strong sense of loss and disillusionment brought on by wartime casualties and dislocations, and on the other a sense of pride in a job well done and a commitment to making the new world a better place than the old one. Looking back to the postwar mood, Margaret wrote: "We found ourselves in an utterly changed world. Across that gulf of chaos whose memory we needed above all else to wash away, the frontiers of 1914 were already dimmed and half-forgotten. We could not even had we wished, join this new comparatively sane world on the jagged edges of the one that had broken off five years before — this new one was quite a different place."[68]

4 · INDEPENDENT BUSINESSWOMAN

Lady Rhondda emerged from the First World War with a new determination to preserve and extend the two concerns which had come to mean the most to her—the feminist struggle and her father's legacy, reputation, and business holdings. In the years immediately following the war, the viscountess found herself torn between the two. She longed to continue the active fight for women's rights, to revive the old camaraderie of the suffragette movement, and to see the battle through to its end; but the responsibility of carrying on her father's work and seeing his projects completed weighed heavily on her mind. She quickly came to realize that the two desires were not necessarily incompatible. Success in business could fulfill her responsibilities to her father's estate and at the same time strike a blow for women's rights. Business activity could open doors and establish new contacts which could be exploited in the continuing struggle for true equality. With this long-range goal in mind, Lady Rhondda embarked on a solo business career, determined to succeed for herself, for her father, and for all women. For the next decade she made a concentrated effort to administer her commercial responsibilities, and she established herself as Britain's leading businesswoman.

Despite her admirable reputation, it is difficult to evaluate both the nature and the success of Lady Rhondda's business career. Contemporary accolades were many, but the paucity of personal records makes it impossible to provide more than an outline of her holdings and a sketch of her influence in the companies she directed. Since few women in Britain were as wealthy in their own right, and since serious barriers to women's participation in business existed, Lady Rhondda's experiences cannot be accurately judged according to any existing model, but only by the limited knowledge of her activities, the testimony of her contemporaries, and the extent to which her business activities served the purpose she desired.[1]

Upon her father's death, Lady Rhondda inherited vast commercial interests in such diverse areas as coal, shipping, publishing, and insurance. The *Directory of Directors* for 1919 listed Lady Rhondda as a director of thirty-three companies (twenty-eight of them inherited from her father) and chairman or vice chairman of sixteen of those. Among the more prominent companies were the Cambrian Collieries, the British Fire Insurance Company, the *Cambrian News,* and the South Wales Printing and Publishing Company. With such diverse holdings, it is not surprising that Lady Rhondda had no clear, coherent business philosophy in the early years. She simply committed herself to carrying on her father's policies and continuing his support for existing research programs, particularly in regard to the development of more efficient fuel sources and the application of scientific management techniques to small collieries. She was determined to carry on her father's work and to prove that women were capable of an independent business career.

She would need every bit of that determination. By the early twentieth century, many doors into the public realm of commerce and business had been forced open for women, but the world of business and industry remained a lonely place for them. Restrictive notions of woman's proper role, continued barriers to full participation, and double standards for male and female performance made life in the business world a risky venture.[2] While Margaret had entered business before the war as her father's apprentice, his death left her in a very vulnerable position. She had inherited his holdings and his wealth, but she had lost the protective mantle of his support. Embarking on a solo career in the upper ranks of a masculine profession provided a major challenge, for which Lady Rhondda had been poorly prepared. Men who had accepted her as D.A.'s proxy during the war now had to be convinced that she was capable of standing and acting on her own. And perhaps more important, Lady Rhondda needed to prove to herself that she could survive in the world of business without paternal protection and guidance. Having come to her enviable position through family connections, she was not truly comfortable with her good fortune and often doubted her own abilities.

In attempting to prove herself, Lady Rhondda faced a number of disabilities common to any woman entering the professions. Unlike many women who had carved out careers for themselves in the "womanly" areas of nursing, teaching, or social work, Margaret, by force of circumstance, was carving her career out in a decidedly nonfeminine sphere. Big business was a male preserve, and she had few role models to look to. As in other areas, women who tried to gain a foothold in masculine power centers were met in the 1920s with either defeat or only partial acceptance.[3] The few women who dared venture into the lion's den found themselves objects of curiosity, jealousy, and resentment. Lady Rhondda was somewhat surprised to see that her associates were very conscious of and resentful at her altered status. She was no longer D.A.'s daughter, holding the fort until he could return. She was now a woman seeking to enter their chosen field on equal terms. Her mere presence was threatening; her possible success was menacing. Women's competition was still too recent a phenomenon for men to accept readily. If the bastions of the male professions could be so easily breached by a largely untrained female, they asked themselves, would it not detract from the entire profession? Thus, Lady Rhondda found herself the victim of subtle discrimination and condescension even from men like Seymour Berry and D. R. Llewellyn, who had previously been her strongest supporters. As long as she agreed with her male colleagues, she was wise, an *exceptional* woman. When she disagreed, she was *only* a woman, not to be taken seriously.[4]

Lady Rhondda found herself suspect not only because of her gender but also because of her appearance. Newspaper reporters expressed surprise that a young, attractive, and "to all outward appearances purely feminine" individual like Lady Rhondda could be a success at business, commenting that she was "curiously unlike the type associated with great affairs and enterprises."[5] This sentiment was most likely shared by a number of her associates, and such prejudices made it difficult for any woman to be taken seriously in the businessman's world.

While her gender and appearance should not have been regarded as serious disabilities, there were more pressing, and less subjective, reasons to be skeptical about Lady Rhondda's business abilities. Critics were quick to point out that her training had been inadequate in comparison with that of most of the businessmen with whom she would be expected to deal. Admittedly, the intensive crash course she had completed at her father's side and the wartime responsibilities she had fulfilled helped to overcome the worst defects in her training, but her competitors had been developing and honing their skills since early adolescence.

No one was more aware of this drawback than Margaret herself. Throughout her business career, she expressed regret that she had not been trained, educated, or equipped for the role she had been called on to play. Through childhood and adolescence, young ladies were protected and encouraged to develop the "feminine traits" of modesty, docility, and submissiveness. They were taught to distrust their own instincts, to defer to the judgment of others, and to regard ambition as a vice rather than a virtue.[6] Despite her own relatively positive experiences, Lady Rhondda always regarded such defects in her education as the major drawback to a truly successful career. She blamed many of her difficulties on the fact that she had been brought up according to the appropriate pattern for a girl and only by force of circumstance been compelled to enter the predominantly masculine commercial world, without the proper tools or mental toughness.[7] She strongly resented the fact that male colleagues failed to recognize that many of their female counterparts' limitations were a result of inadequate education and training rather than some inherent sex trait. She often railed at businessmen who used the mistakes of an individual businesswoman to condemn all businesswomen as an inherently inferior group, while consigning successful women to the "Exceptional Woman" category – and thereby dismissing their achievements.[8] Over the years, experience and diligence helped overcome some of the specific difficulties, but Margaret never overcame the insecurity. Looking back on what many contemporaries considered a stellar career, Lady Rhondda admitted that "the struggle between early training in diffidence and later acquired knowledge and confidence never totally ceases."[9] Carol Dyhouse's study of other prominent women born in the 1880s who stepped outside the traditional feminine role indicates that this sentiment was not an unusual one. She found that women who had carved out successful careers for themselves constantly battled with their own ambitions, well aware that society regarded their pursuit of an occupation outside the home as unseemly in a female.[10]

Such insecurities were present in part because all women in business were outsiders, cut off from the informal channels and contacts which their male colleagues relied on for inside information. The men's clubs, where the nuances of proposed mergers, precarious deals, and economic prospects were thoroughly discussed, were, of course, closed to the female invader. Many an important business deal was concluded over lunch at the clubs, and the exclusion of females served to limit the scope of their professional activities. Lady Rhondda often complained that this enforced segregation prevented her from fully participating in her chosen profession. Business success, she suggested, depended on a thorough understanding of intelligent professional gossip. For a woman, the avenues to the inside tips were automatically off-limits.[11] She was, and would always remain, something of an outsider. This feeling of being an outsider later plagued her editorial career as well. Writing to Virginia Woolf, whose *Three Guineas* had briefly highlighted the outsider theme, she claimed that no woman editor of a weekly review could remain unaware of how much an outsider she was or of how exclusion from the inside gossip could effectively circumscribe a career.[12] Even in the 1930s, when her journal *Time and Tide* was one of the most influential weekly journals in the nation, she still felt that "If we were men, the task of securing the advertisements or subsidies we need would not be half so difficult. All the way round our difficulties are increased because we are women."[13]

Despite the numerous drawbacks, Lady Rhondda did emerge as perhaps the most successful businesswoman in England during the interwar years. While later financial setbacks and apparently unsound business decisions cast a shadow over her overall business reputation, there is no doubt that she achieved the respect and admiration of her peers during the first phase of her commercial venture, earning such accolades as Britain's "Queen of Commerce" and "the feminine Cecil Rhodes."[14]

Her early success undoubtedly was due in part to the good condition of the concerns she inherited and to her own early dedication and persistence. Sandra Winston, in *The Entrepreneurial Woman* (1979), identified six basic characteristics conducive to a successful business career. Winston claimed that a feeling of displacement, a history of attempting to exert control over one's destiny, and a sense of independence placed an individual in the proper frame of mind for embarking on a solo business career. If combined with the proper role models, a willingness to take risks, and adequate financial resources and contacts, these characteristics would ensure success.[15] While developed two decades after her death, this model fits Lady Rhondda's career fairly accurately. The experiences of World War I, the death of her father, and the strains of her faltering marriage had engendered a sense of dislocation in Margaret's life. The war, too, had fostered a limited sense of independence and had reinforced the desire to control her own destiny earlier evinced in her decision to go to jail despite her husband's disapproval. In her father she had a positive role model, and he had provided her with the financial means, the early experience, and the contacts to enable her to begin her solo career with all the assets prerequisite for success. It was now up to her to use and develop those assets.

In the first five years after the war, Lady Rhondda devoted much of her time to mastering basic business skills and to soothing the fears of her male colleagues. She listened and learned from those with more experience as she gradually developed her own talents. This educational process was made easier, Lady Rhondda suggested, because women in the upper ranks of British commerce were so rare that their presence was not particularly threatening. Men at the top, she believed, were less susceptible to exaggerated fears of female competition than were rank-and-file workers. Because they had risen through the ranks on their individual abilities, they were more confident and secure in their positions. They might be jealous of an individual woman, but they were not actually afraid of competition from women per se, as was often the case in the lower ranks of business and industry.[16] This statement appears rather naive in view of the fact that most members of the business elite, like Lady Rhondda, gained their positions through family wealth and prestige rather than individual merit.[17] Perhaps it was simply effective diplomacy to put her male counterparts at ease.

Margaret knew that hers was in some ways a path-breaking experiment and that it was bound to create some tension and hostility. During the early years, she deliberately downplayed her femaleness to convince her business partners that her presence need not disturb their normal routine. To put the men at ease, she took up pipe smoking and dressed conservatively, choosing stern, utilitarian suits and low heels and avoiding short skirts, flashy jewelry, and distracting colors.[18] She wanted to be respected as a colleague and believed that being as unobtrusive and "masculine" as possible would achieve the desired result.

This assumed masculinity probably did less to endear Margaret to her associates than did her sensitivity and her developing professionalism. Recognizing that some jealousy and resentment was natural, Lady Rhondda generally avoided displays of righteous indignation or injured innocence, which would only have increased existing tension or antagonism. She avoided political machinations and so-called feminine wiles and relied instead on long hours and stubborn persistence. Contemporary reporters praised her business acumen, her common sense, her shrewd practicality, her persuasive tongue, her uncompromising realism, her capable performance in a formerly masculine stronghold, her knack for making people feel comfortable, and her sensitivity to the feelings of those around her.[19] Winifred Holtby, who worked closely with Lady Rhondda on *Time and Tide*, advised Vera Brittain to consider Lady Rhondda's formula for success should she ever become an eminent personality. She wrote that Brittain should "treat the little worms nicely. They like it."[20]

Unfortunately, no consistent statement of Lady Rhondda's business philosophy exists. Her press comments on the subject reveal a naive idealism. She frequently insisted that the true meaning of life came only from the knowledge of work well done and that monetary gains were relatively unimportant in business decisions. She was a firm believer in the work ethic, in efficient management, and in encouraging young talent. But most important, she stressed that businessmen must provide a true service to the public and not become too bogged down in "insignificant" financial details.[21] At first glance, this seems totally unrealistic, but recent research indicates that this attitude may have been fairly typical among gentrified industrial capitalists. The intellectual historian Martin Wiener attributes the economic decline of Great Britain in the twentieth century at least partially to such attitudes. He argues that commercial and industrial leaders "accommodated themselves to an elite culture blended of preindustrial aristocratic and religious values that inhibited their quest for expansion, productivity, and profit."[22] For Lady Rhondda, such attitudes did at times prove financially costly. When asked about possible conflicts between the financial interests of a millionaire businesswoman and the editor of a political review, she responded: "I never allow my pocketbook to joggle or deviate my pen. When Lady Rhondda, stockholder and director in a commercial company, stands in the way of Lady Rhondda, editor of *Time and Tide,* I divest myself of my business, stock, and directional interests . . . sometimes to my financial loss."[23]

In hindsight it is evident that Lady Rhondda was not an outstanding businesswoman, perhaps because she lacked the total commitment she herself regarded as necessary to sustain a long-term business career. By the mid-1920s her financial fortunes began to decline because of a combination of personal and external factors. Lady Rhondda appears to have made some unsound business transactions of an undisclosed nature which caused her to doubt her own abilities and may have hastened her departure from business. Writing to her American friend Doris Stevens, she confided that her attempts to make *Time and Tide* a success were hindered by a significant cash-flow problem. "Practically everything I've got my money in [will] not pay and [is] not likely to pay for some years to come," she confessed. Further, she wrote, these years "are bringing the desire to live through and know what its [sic] right to do — I can only just hold on." The cash-flow problem was compounded by the costly subsidies of *Time and Tide* and by Lady Rhondda's penchant for lavish entertainment, expensive shopping sprees, and foreign travel. By 1931, falling dividends prompted her to make a realistic assessment of her financial difficulties, and she was forced to bring in some additional funds by leasing her country house.[24]

Lady Rhondda's own actions were only partially responsible for the financial troubles she faced in the 1920s and 1930s. External circumstances, including the worldwide economic depression and significant turmoil in the coal and iron and steel industries, demanded adjustments that she was not prepared to make. Declining productivity, outdated facilities, expanded production abroad, and the development of alternative fuel sources undercut the industries upon which her fortune was built.[25] The damaging effects could have been mitigated by expansion into some of the new industries. Electricity, engineering, chemicals, and construction were all areas of potential growth. Whether Lady Rhondda was opposed to diversification, preoccupied with her publishing interests, fearful of the risks involved, or blind to the changing realities of the modern world is uncertain, but whatever the reason, she missed the opportunity to secure an unquestioned reputation as an astute businesswoman. By the early 1930s, she began to disengage herself gradually from the commercial world by resigning many of her directorships and disposing of the majority of her holdings. By 1935 she served as a director of only six companies.[26] She maintained limited holdings in coal, iron and steel, and shipping, but disposed of all publishing interests outside the Time and Tide Publishing Company.

Yet during the 1920s Lady Rhondda received much praise and many awards for her business activities. In 1923 she was elected a member of the Council of the Institute of Directors, a group of England's most prominent business leaders which acts as a governing body and publicist for the institute as a whole. She was one of the first five women members of the London Chamber of Commerce and the first woman ever invited to speak at the annual meeting of the British and Latin American Chamber of Commerce.[27] In 1926 she became the first woman to be elected president of the Institute of Directors.[28] While Lady Rhondda was elated at the honor, she must have been dismayed at the manner in which the nomination was announced. Presiding at the institute's annual general meeting, Sir John A. Cockburn described her as having not only proved herself in commercial affairs, but also as having "one of the cleverest business heads in the country." He then, however, condescendingly added that "women generally were more equable and more businesslike than men, neither rising to such heights of disastrous imagination nor sinking to such depths of despair. They were," he maintained, "less speculative, and less inclined to plunge."[29] While there is no record of a response, there is little doubt that the viscountess would not have been happy at such an artificial distinction. Lady Rhondda did, however, express surprise in a subsequent interview with the *Paris*

Telegram and Continental Express correspondent at the interest aroused by her election to the position. She could not really understand why women were still regarded with suspicion in the upper ranks of commerce, or why anyone would be astonished at the thought of a woman director's being elevated to a position of leadership.[30] Since there were now some three hundred women company directors, it seemed only fitting that their collective existence be recognized.[31] Lady Rhondda's recognition provided a visible acknowledgment of women's place in modern business and helped break down some of the informal barriers to women's advancement. Her success surely provided an inspiration for future women in business, but it seems doubtful that it altered the attitudes of the business community or the general public.

While many successful women attempted to divorce themselves from women's issues, Lady Rhondda used her new-found prestige to help further the cause of women in business. She was instrumental in the formation of the Efficiency Club, an organization which functioned as a support group for professional women, a clearinghouse for inside information, and an unofficial lobby working for the admission of women into the British Chamber of Commerce and the Overseas Club.[32] With Caroline Spurgeon, a professor at Bedford College in the University of London, she was a driving force behind the formation of a Business and University Women's Association composed of equal numbers of distinguished university and business women committed to publicizing the growing number of career options available to women.[33] When the International Rotary Foundation decided to reject a petition for women's entry into that august body, she helped organize and became the first president of the Provisional Club, a service organization for women established along the same lines and with the same goals as the Rotary Club.[34] Lady Rhondda also became a major spokeswoman for women in the professions, opening bazaars, speaking at conferences, and keeping the issues of the benefits of feminine influence and the continued obstacles to full participation alive in the press. She was an ardent defender of women's right to work and to be treated and compensated equally. Yet there is no evidence that Lady Rhondda made any practical attempt to bring women into leadership positions or to provide enlightened reforms beneficial to females in the companies she directed (with the exception of the Time and Tide Publishing Company). While this might seem unusual for a staunch feminist, it was perfectly consistent with Lady Rhondda's equalitarian philosophy. Committed to an absolute legal, political, economic, social, and moral equality between the sexes, she generally believed in judging individuals on their abilities rather than their gender.

But despite all the recognition she received, the role of businesswoman was not one in which Margaret was ever totally comfortable. She enjoyed commercial affairs and loved the give-and-take of board meetings, but she never really mastered the arts of compromise and delegating authority which are so instrumental in a successful commercial career. Her autobiography provides an explanation of her success which is candid but slightly self-deprecating. While not actually apologizing for her career, she seems many times to belittle her achievements. Her commitment to and belief in the value of her work are often obscured by defensive explanations of her divergence from traditional female roles and by frequent references to her extraordinary advantages, the hereditary basis of her position, and the accidental nature of her success.[35] Emphasizing how easily it had all come, she downplayed her own hard work, abilities, and determination as well as her worthiness of such acclaim.

That an intelligent, successful career woman should feel the need to justify and excuse her accomplishments was in part a measure of the strong pressures to fulfill cultural and societal expectations. In Lady Rhondda's case, however, the problem goes deeper. She, more than her contemporaries, recognized that she was fulfilling her father's dreams, not her own. In her heart she knew that business was not the vocation she was best suited for or the most interested in.[36] This realization caused her to spread herself too thin during the 1920s. Trying to continue her father's work and the struggle for women's rights and to fulfill her own rapidly developing publishing aspirations, she ended up doing several things well, but none exceptionally.

In trying to analyze Lady Rhondda's career as a businesswoman, the primary obstacle is the lack of any agreed definition of what a successful business career entails. If success lies in the amassing of great wealth, the introduction of innovative techniques, or the creation of a commercial empire, she was a failure. There is no indication, however, that she desired great wealth or that she defined success in monetary terms. At the end of her autobiography Lady Rhondda wrote that had she been a man, she would never have gone into business, but would have chosen instead politics, law, or writing. But she added: "Being a woman, I had to grasp at any rope that would help me to climb out of the pit. Business had served its turn as a key to set me free, to give me the status of freedom, and the right of entry into the world of free men."[37] It is apparent that Lady Rhondda was less interested in money than in its fruits. In the tradition of the country gentry or the gentleman farmer of an earlier era, she saw business in terms of its political and social rather than its financial aspects. In place of great wealth she sought social status, respect, and visibility. Having no heir, she was less concerned about amassing wealth and property than about establishing her legacy to the next generation through *Time and Tide*. Judged by the standard of the political businesswoman, Lady Rhondda was successful. Business had been good to her. It had given her wealth, visibility, a solid reputation, and important contacts, all of which could be exploited for those interests which were dearer to her than business could ever be.

5 · EQUALITARIAN FEMINIST

At the same time Lady Rhondda was establishing herself as a respected business executive, she was also building a reputation as one of Britain's leading feminists. Having spent several years fighting for political equality for women, she was not prepared to accept the partial enfranchisement offered by the 1918 Representation of the People Act as a legitimate conclusion. While welcoming the legislation as a step in the right direction, she was neither naive enough nor complacent enough to expect that such a limited measure would break down the still significant barriers to full participation. Genuine political equality was far from being a reality, and unequal social legislation and barriers in the workplace threatened to undermine the progress already made and demoralize the movement. To abandon the cause because her personal fortune left her able to do so was unthinkable. The struggle was too important to leave unfinished, and she was too involved personally to expect others to continue the fight by themselves. Believing in both the principle of equality and the special contributions women could make to a better, more humane existence, Lady Rhondda could not rest until all vestiges of political and legal inequality and all insinuations of female inferiority were removed. Placing her talents, her fortune, and her influence at the disposal of the feminist cause, she embarked on a long, tiring, and sometimes lonely crusade to advance the position of the female population. To the end of her life she continued to press for justice, full participation, and the removal of economic and social barriers to women's advancement.

This continuing commitment to the feminist cause was first evident in Lady Rhondda's attempt to organize women industrial workers into a nonparty pressure group, the Women's Industrial League (WIL), in the closing days of the war. Despite their acknowledged success in wartime industries, women workers faced dismissal and reduced earning potential because of rapid demobilization and the reentry of former soldiers into the work force. Organization and leadership were necessary to safeguard working women's interests and to secure recognition of their right to justice in the workplace. During her tenure at the ministries of National Service and Reconstruction, Lady Rhondda had become well acquainted with both the problems and the prospects of women workers, and she had developed a tremendous though somewhat patronizing respect for the courage of the working-class woman. She was determined to see that those less fortunate than she would have a voice in the postwar labor settlements. She would act as their spokesperson until the workers could organize along democratic lines and elect their own leaders.

Under Lady Rhondda's guidance, the Women's Industrial League opened its doors to all women industrial workers over the age of eighteen who were willing to pay the shilling subscription fee. Membership ranged the gamut from laborers and machinists to superintendents and directors. Local committees were formed in the major industrial centers and elected representatives to a central policy-making board which was given authority to "speak with one voice in matters of common concern."[1] The WIL sought to maintain the present status of women in industry, to secure training and education programs for female employees, and to broaden the scope of employment opportunities available to women. Other primary goals included equal pay for equal work, improved working conditions, child care facilities, and adequate representation on government, industrial, and public boards to ensure women workers a voice in determining their future.[2] These aims were to be pursued through constitutional methods rather than militant activity. Having won at least partial political power, Lady Rhondda recognized that it was now time to work within the system to bring about needed change.

The WIL, with Lady Rhondda at its helm as provisional chairman, undertook a well-organized campaign designed to publicize the difficulties facing women industrial workers and to bring pressure to bear on the government to take a specific stand on the role and the rights of these individuals. A steady stream of letters to the press, memorials to the government, and deputations to Parliament focused attention, gained sympathy, and provoked a limited response. In a memorial to David Lloyd George dated 4 December 1918, Lady Rhondda presented a moderate but firm statement of the workers' needs and their determination to be regarded as useful, functioning components of British industry. While recognizing the claims of returning servicemen and highly skilled workers for special consideration, she demanded a quick end to other artificial and unjust barriers to employment of women in industry, arguing that such barriers prevented the country from fully utilizing and developing its potential. Claiming the right to equal pay for equal output, better conditions, and a stronger voice, the memorial reminded Lloyd George of the new voting power of women and asked for an explicit statement of his intentions should he be returned to power in the next general election.[3] The prime minister replied to the challenge in a document some feminists refer to as "the Charter for Industrial Liberty."[4] He endorsed the league's platform wholly and promised, if returned to power, to work to see that occupations, training and educational programs, and commission representation were opened on a more equal basis. The memorial also received endorsement from the *Times,* which printed an editorial supporting the WIL's contentions and commenting that the test of employment should not be the gender of the worker but rather the relative return to the employer and the general interests of the state.[5]

Over the next few years, the WIL continued to agitate as the expectations of fuller economic participation and industrial acceptance failed to materialize. Its leaders attacked the Pre-War Practices Act (1919) and demanded the exclusion of new industrial processes from its jurisdiction. (The act forced women back into unskilled, low-paying jobs by making it illegal to retain wartime "dilutees" in jobs formerly reserved for skilled craftsmen.) Meetings were held to encourage the organization of domestic workers, to educate women on the possible effects of pending industrial and social legislation, to demand that the needs of women workers not be overlooked in the reconversion process (the process of shifting from military to civilian production), and to stress government accountability for seeing that women not suffer disproportionately in the anticipated employment crisis. Always in the fore of the WIL agitation was Lady Rhondda, presiding over meetings, leading deputations, speaking to conferences, and writing trenchant letters. Her title and her reputation in British commerce provided the struggling women industrial workers with an entrée, which might otherwise have been denied them, into the pages of the *Times* and the appointment books of ministers.

Lady Rhondda frequently wrote to the *Times* criticizing the government's handling of the reconversion process and its apparent disregard for the concept of justice in the workplace. She protested the wholesale discharging of women workers and demanded that constructive measures (of an unspecified type) be adopted to alleviate the economic distress, and that the government take responsibility for finding jobs for women in peacetime occupations.[6] She also criticized the government's failure to take advantage of knowledgeable and experienced women in its appointments to commissions and boards, expressing particular outrage at the absence of female representation on the Industrial Fatigue Research Board.[7]

Lady Rhondda expressed these same themes in a series of speeches and deputations in the early months of 1919. Speaking to the Royal Institute of Public Health in February on the topic "Women in the Ministry of Health," she emphasized the importance of the feminine viewpoint in matters of health care policy and indicated that the time for token participation had long since passed. Women, she said, would no longer be content to accept lower positions but would now demand representation at the top policy-making levels and direct access to the ministers.[8] In deputations to Sir Robert Horne at the Ministry of Labour in March 1919 and to G. N. Barnes at the War Cabinet office in July, Lady Rhondda again demanded that women's needs and views be given fuller consideration and that women receive full representation on important delegations, both to protect their interests and to provide much-needed evidence. In speaking with Barnes about the exclusion of women delegates from the upcoming International Labour Conference, Lady Rhondda pointed out the need for women's input on critical issues in the workplace, most notably those involving maternity leaves, night work, hours, and working conditions. She also emphasized the inconsistency of excluding women on the basis of their lack of practical experience with the issues at hand while giving an all-male delegation responsibility for dealing with questions relating to childbirth, a matter wholly outside their area of expertise. The inclusion of women advisers to that delegation, while slightly better than total exclusion, was still little more than worthless patronization.[9]

Testifying before the War Cabinet Committee on Women in Industry, Lady Rhondda carried her argument a step further, suggesting a truer equality in the workplace. She advocated not only that men's industries be opened to women but that women's work also be opened to men. Artificial distinctions and the resulting wage differentials between male and female occupations, she contended, should be eliminated for the good of all workers and the more efficient mobilization of the nation's human resources. Admitting that lack of effective organization among women employees was partially responsible for the workers' plight, Lady Rhondda encouraged them to join the women's federations within the trade unions to prevent their continued use as cheap labor. But a note of uncertainty crept into her testimony when she was questioned about married women workers. Conceding that it might not be desirable for women to work after marriage, she nevertheless expressed certainty that the issue was one that only individual women could decide for themselves. Marriage alone should not prevent women from holding jobs they were otherwise qualified for and still capable of performing.[10]

Such ardent championship gave the Women's Industrial League much public exposure but did little to change conditions. While the WIL's demands seem perfectly reasonable today, the odds against the struggling organization were staggering. Without significant political power or numbers, the league lacked the weapons needed to overcome government apathy and complacency (they had, after all, given women the vote), public resentment, and isolation from sympathizers in the Labour Party and the trade unions. Even the very moderate demands for equal maintenance grants for men and women in the same training programs were denied on the grounds that men required more money to support themselves. Demands for access to better jobs met with sympathy, but the pressing obligations to returning soldiers made positive action to get jobs for women unfeasible. More radical requests for true equality and a strong voice in future decisions never even received serious consideration.[11]

Her experience with the Women's Industrial League served to strengthen Lady Rhondda's conviction that serious obstacles to women's advancement and acceptance would not be overcome easily and to crystallize her commitment to the continuing fight for absolute equality. Until all legal barriers were removed, she believed, change could not be expected in either actions or attitudes, and women would continue to be regarded as inferior beings. Only through their own responsible actions could women prove themselves capable of full citizenship and earn the respect that would gradually erode the obstacles to complete participation. The partial franchise of 1918, if properly exploited, could serve as the wedge which would gradually force open all doors. This realization prompted Lady Rhondda to channel her energies into broader feminist activity designed to help mold British women into an effective political pressure group, to remove all legal barriers to women's equality, and to educate women in the arts of politics and responsible voting. Her renewed commitment led her into a series of feminist ventures that taxed her resources, energy, and emotions for much of the rest of her life. Primary among these were the formation of an equalitarian feminist society, the Six Point Group; the establishment of a feminist periodical, *Time and Tide;* and the contesting of women's continued political exclusion through a lawsuit against the House of Lords.

Of the three ventures, *Time and Tide* was the first to be launched, an indication of the importance Lady Rhondda attached to education and the power of the written word. It offered a response to the pressing need for a publication which would give primacy to women's issues and perspectives and educate the new voters with respect to their rights and responsibilities. If women's voices were to be heard, women could not rely on the established, male-controlled press. Only an independent forum would ensure that their demands and activities would not again be cloaked in either silence or ridicule, as they had been during the militant protests. Only a periodical run by women and for a wide audience would provide the remedial political education and the feminist analysis that could weld women into an effective voting unit capable of forcing changes in British society.[12]

And only the support of a wealthy patron like Lady Rhondda made such an enterprise possible. On 14 May 1920, the first issue of *Time and Tide* appeared under the editorship of Helen Archdale. In its early years the journal exhibited a strong feminist and political orientation. In the pages of *Time and Tide* female writers and politicians openly debated the pressing political and social issues of the day, encouraged feminine consciousness and activism, and monitored the performance of parliamentarians and the status of legislation bearing on women's issues. From the beginning, Lady Rhondda was the financial backbone of the journal and played an active part in policy-making and editorial philosophy.[13]

It is not surprising, therefore, that the need for a specific program of feminist action which became the basis for the Six Point Group was first suggested in the pages of *Time and Tide*. The 19 November 1920 issue included an editorial statement emphasizing the necessity of overcoming complacency and self-satisfaction within the feminist movement and using the newly won voting power to achieve specific reforms. Three months later, on 17 February 1921, the Six Point Group was founded by Lady Rhondda and a few close friends from the suffragette days, including Rebecca West, Cicely Hamilton, and Elizabeth Robins.[14] They originally envisioned the new organization as a nonparty pressure group working to obtain a broad range of social reforms which would benefit women of all classes and move society closer to the ultimate goal of equality. Yet the predominantly middle-class base of the organization was apparent in its preoccupation with legal disabilities, married women's property rights, and professional pay differentials.[15] As its name suggests, the group focused on six closely connected issues it wished to see addressed: widows' pensions, equal guardianship for both parents, stricter child assault laws, improvements in the legal position of unmarried mothers, equal pay for teachers, and equal employment opportunities for men and women in the civil service. These six issues were chosen because of their urgency, their probable appeal to the general public, and because the final two would force the government to take the lead in establishing a precedent for equal pay and equal opportunity. The choices appear to have been well made. New members quickly signed up, and twenty-four major feminist organizations, including the British Federation of University Women, the Federation of Women Civil Servants, the National Union of Women Teachers, and the Women's Citizens Associations agreed to cooperate in the attainment of these goals.[16] Members hoped to exert direct and indirect pressure on the government by monitoring its promises and its performance, by promoting awareness among voters and public servants, and by securing the return of supportive members of Parliament.[17] Within the broad commitment to the six points, members were generally given free rein to express themselves openly in order "not to allow members to be cramped in acting quickly by too much red tape."[18]

The Six Point Group received considerable acclaim, and much was expected of it in its early years. Vera Brittain reported that in 1922 hopes for future female liberation from traditional restrictions appeared to rest with the Six Point Group and the Society for Constructive Birth Control. David Mitchell has asserted that the organization had the support of all active suffragists in the postwar era.[19] *Time and Tide* not surprisingly provided constant coverage and special supplements publicizing the group's aims, activities, and successes. The journal praised the simple and practical platform and commended the Six Point Group for concentrating on supposedly achievable goals rather than stirring false hopes with idealistic, visionary schemes.[20]

With resourceful supporters, excellent writers, a periodical backing it, and Lady Rhondda at its helm, the Six Point Group anticipated great successes. Members of the group worked tirelessly to keep the issues before the public and to press for actions instead of sympathetic but unhelpful words and gestures. Aside from necessary fund-raising events, the Six Point Group concentrated primarily on educational programs and political lobbying. Inquiries were conducted into such questions as government employment of females, child assault, and the problems of unmarried mothers. Reports were prepared, pamphlets were published, and the pages of *Time and Tide* were filled with the findings of these investigations. Weekly meetings were held in which discussions on topics ranging from female police officers to women candidates for Parliament were considered. The group also sponsored open-air meetings in Hyde Park to demand passage or rejection of pending legislation and sent representatives to the houses of Parliament to report on critical debates. Prominent members kept up a steady stream of letters to the press pointing out inconsistencies in the laws and in the government's responses to women's demands.

Once the educational process was under way, the Six Point Group turned its attention to exerting political pressure to bring about needed change. Elections in 1922, 1923, and twice in 1924 provided many opportunities to press their demands and much evidence of how little serious attention "women's issues" received. Hoping to change the prevailing attitude, the Six Point Group adopted a policy of holding the party in power responsible for its treatment of feminine concerns, a tactic which had worked well before the vote was won and was expected to be even more successful since partial enfranchisement had been accomplished. Lloyd George's coalition government was criticized for its procrastination over an amendment to the Sex Disqualification (Removal) Act and its tendency to abide by the letter, not the spirit, of the law.[21] Speaking for the group's entire membership, Lady Rhondda condemned the Conservative government of Bonar Law, suggesting that it had done "extraordinary [sic] little" for women and warning that women were aware of the differences between promise and performance.[22] Ramsay MacDonald's Labour government fared little better. Delighted at the election of a government supposedly sympathetic to feminist demands, women anticipated advances on the franchise, widows' pensions, and guardianship, and opening of the civil service.[23] Within four months, however, Lady Rhondda was expressing disappointment at the government's hypocrisy and betrayal in both legislative and administrative matters. Claiming that MacDonald had never truly been a feminist, she wrote that "never again will the non-party women hail the advent of a Labour Government with enthusiasm under the impression that a friend is assuming office."[24] The government in power, regardless of party, would not be able to deny responsibility while the Six Point Group monitored and publicized its promises and its performance.

The parties were not the only ones who received attention from Lady Rhondda and her colleagues. Just as they held the parties liable for their actions, the members of the Six Point Group held individual members of Parliament accountable. The speeches and voting records of parliamen-

tarians were monitored and analyzed to see where each member stood
on the six points. If sound on these, members of Parliament could be
counted on to be "full of generosity, imagination, wide vision, and sincer-
ity of purpose."[25]

Those who proved consistently obstructive found what they had said
excerpted in handbills and *Time and Tide*. Beginning with the general
election of 1922, the Six Point Group published Black Lists of politicians who hampered reform and White Lists of those consistently supporting women's equality. Most members of Parliament fell into the
"Drab" category, neither good enough nor bad enough to deserve mention.[26] Particularly offensive individuals could find themselves facing
organized opposition during reelection campaigns. Like the old open-
air meetings of the suffragette days, these campaigns brought out the
best in Lady Rhondda.

In *Testament of Youth* Vera Brittain told of a campaign against Dennis
Herbert, Conservative member for Watford, in the 1922 general election. Herbert had made himself persona non grata with feminists by
his continued resistance to passage of two laws they considered vital,
the Criminal Law Amendment Bill and the Matrimonial Causes Bill.
Speaking first, the young and inexperienced Vera Brittain found herself
heckled and challenged by a voice from the crowd which proved to be
that of the notorious Herbert himself. Flustered by the experience and
her own inadequate response, she sat down subdued and frustrated.
Lady Rhondda followed her to the platform and immediately turned
the tables on Herbert. With *Hansard's Parliamentary Debates* in her
hand, she flung his own statements back in his face, swinging her listen-
ers to support a resolution deploring his attitudes and utterances by a
majority of four to one.[27] They failed to unseat Herbert, but their pressure most likely caused some politicians to temper their statements, and
the Six Point Group took credit for the defeat of any blacklisted candidates.

Occasionally these tactics brought repercussions. In June 1926 the group
sent two resolutions, one calling for votes at twenty-one and the other
for the admission of peeresses to the House of Lords, to members of
Parliament. Lord Curzon, who had consistently found himself on the
Black List, sent a scathing reply:

> In view of the attitude of the Six Point Group towards myself at the
> last two General Elections I shall certainly not give the slightest con-
> sideration to any resolution which they might put forward, though as
> a matter of fact my views on many questions coincide with those of
> the Six Point Group. In all such cases where I am aware that these

views do coincide I shall endeavor to make it clear that your Organization is opposed to me, and I do not for one moment admit that your Organization is representative of the female portion of the electorate, or that it has any special right to speak for women as a whole.[28]

Since male politicians like Herbert and Lord Curzon seemed bent on hindering women's progress, the Six Point Group had no qualms about supporting female candidates or those specifically pledged to uphold feminist demands. Members were unstinting in their praise of women members of Parliament like Nancy Astor, Margaret Wintringham, and Ellen Wilkinson – and equally unstinting in their criticism of the parties' failure to support more women of such caliber. Lady Rhondda argued that female representation was becoming increasingly vital because women were becoming more politically aware, and there was no one to speak for their concerns accurately. Women's ideas, she suggested, lost their substance and intensity as they passed through the brains of male members of the Commons. Even if a man could be found to put the woman's point of view before the House, it took months to coach him in the pertinent details and rationale. Then women had to sit back and pray that the government official put up to answer him knew even less about the issue.[29]

To counter this, women were encouraged to vote as an independent bloc as women first. As long as women were excluded from the House of Lords and from equal voting privileges, and as long as marriage bars and pay differentials in government posts continued, Lady Rhondda contended, it was the duty of women to cast their votes for no particular party but against such blatant discrimination.[30] This stand did not endear the Six Point Group to political parties or to male politicians, nor did it result in widespread election of women. Candidates were too few, and their appeal was too limited. The expectation that women would see issues in primarily gender-related terms was rather naive.

Despite persistent pressure and activities, it soon became evident that some of the "achievable" goals the group had set for itself were far from attainable under the prevailing political and social attitudes. During its first years of existence, the Six Point Group concentrated on achieving passage of an enlightened amendment dealing with child assault to the Criminal Law Act. In 1922 the group was a moving force behind the adoption of an amendment which raised the age of consent from thirteen to sixteen, removed "reasonable cause to believe" that the minor was of consenting age as a defense, and increased penalties. During the debates the group had criticized the tendency to try to "protect" the sensibilities of women jurors. In assault cases, evidence was often withheld from women jurors on the grounds that they might be offended. In a letter to *The Nation*, Lady Rhondda asserted that such action not only discriminated against women; it made them worthless as jurors by depriving them of the information they needed to perform their duties and contribute to the community. Such "protection" prolonged an outdated stereotype of women shrinking from evil rather than facing and conquering it.[31] Passage of the Criminal Law Amendment buoyed the spirits of female activists and encouraged additional agitation, but their other campaigns did not bear fruit until 1925, with the passage of a guardianship law and the granting of widows' pensions. While the successful conclusion of these battles was welcomed as a significant victory, it was already clear that the courts would try to minimize the effect of the new laws.

With the passage of each piece of legislation, a new point was added to ensure that there were always six specific concerns for which the group was working. The first substitutions, political and economic equality, indicate a growing awareness that the program of social reform conceived by the founders would never happen as long as women were excluded from the councils of power by law, prejudice, or masculine prerogative. To be effective, women had to have equal opportunity in all human activities. Thus in 1926 the Six Point Group altered its constitution to reflect a new motto, "Equality First." The group's revised program replaced the timely issues of the past with broad, timeless demands for total equality in political, economic, legal, moral, social, and occupational realms.[32]

Of these, political inequality, as evidenced by continued limitations on the franchise and exclusion of peeresses from the House of Lords, was regarded as the key obstacle to advancement. To redress discrepancies between men's and women's status, rewards, responsibilities, rights, and opportunities, the group adopted a tripartite strategy involving legal activism, information, and education. Through the passage of anti-discriminatory legislation, attempts to influence public opinion in favor of women's demands, and education of a younger generation to a greater sense of social justice between the sexes, the Six Point Group hoped to achieve the full equality that would allow women to work for specific issues of interest to themselves and to society as a whole.[33]

This demand for complete equality placed Lady Rhondda and the Six Point Group in the middle of the major feminist debate of the interwar period. With the granting of partial suffrage, the simple, unifying demand "Votes for Women" had been removed. The feminist movement began a series of semantic and ideological arguments that resulted in a fragmentation and disarray threatening to undermine the limited victories and prevent progress. Fully aware that the continued existence of feminist societies depended on the development of new goals and broader activities, the National Union of Societies for Equal Citizenship (NUSEC; formerly NUWSS) sponsored a debate over the proper sphere of feminist reform, the definition of equality, and possible gains from continued agitation. The debate sparked a serious controversy between supporters of the traditional equalitarian approach and proponents of the so-called New Feminism, or social feminism, that continues to polarize the women's movement today.[34]

The equalitarian feminists, drawing their inspiration from Mary Wollstonecraft's *Vindication of the Rights of Woman* (1792) and their support from propertied and professional women, argued for a literal and absolute equality with men. Demanding "a fair field and no favor," they claimed for women the right to be regarded not as a special group but as equal human beings. They insisted that the movement should concentrate on removing all vestiges of gender differentiation (even those which appeared beneficial) and all artificial barriers to feminine advancement in British politics, economics, and society. Once such barriers were destroyed, individual men and women would be responsible for fulfilling their own potential. Given an equal chance, equalitarian feminists were convinced, women could and would take an active part in reshaping the values and priorities of the nation in a manner that would enrich the lives of both sexes. Believing that equal citizenship for women was the only truly legitimate concern for the feminist societies, the equalitarians resented talk of the unavoidable differences between men and women and believed that agitation for such specific reforms as birth control, family allowances, and gender-based protective legislation deflected attention from the vital issue and weakened the demand for true equality.[35]

These traditionalists were increasingly challenged by an alternate brand of activism led by Eleanor Rathbone and Eva Hubback of the NUSEC in the early 1920s. Calling themselves "new feminists," these social feminists drew solid support from working-class women, trade unionists, and the Labour Party, and claimed to speak for the masses of dependent women. In her presidential address to NUSEC in 1921, Eleanor Rathbone criticized her middle-class counterparts for their complacency and self-satisfaction. She called on women who wanted more from feminism than voting privileges, the right to stand for Parliament, and entry into the professions to join her in seeking a "real equality" (as opposed to the literal, absolute brand of the equalitarians) more in line with the special needs of women.[36] Rathbone encouraged women to define equality not by what men had, but by what women needed to satisfy their circumstances and fulfill their aspirations. Gender differentiation was a fact; social feminists demanded that Britain's political and economic policies acknowledge the differences and adapt, particularly in matters involving maternity rights, housing policy, and industrial protection. Instead of rejecting all protective measures on principle, social feminists advocated analyzing the laws carefully, welcoming those beneficial to women, condemning those that would limit female competition, and pressing for the extension of safety measures to include males in dangerous occupations as well. To the social feminists it seemed only natural that the women's societies should concern themselves with legislation involving family allowances, birth control, and hazardous working conditions—all of which the equalitarians considered social rather than feminist reforms. Good laws dealing with these issues, they believed, would create a better, if still unequal, society.[37]

Philosophical divisions did not prevent feminists of both persuasions from cooperating in the early 1920s to support a broader franchise, expansion of industrial, educational, and political opportunities for women, and some social reforms involving child and female welfare. But as feminist agitation shifted its focus toward economic considerations, the ideological split widened. Those who believed equality meant the right to be treated the same and those who thought it meant the right to be treated differently could no longer reconcile their differences. While the issues of birth control and family allowances had forced a bigger breach between the two branches of the feminist movement, it was the argument over protective legislation, including maternity leaves, that brought their disagreements into the open, resulting in a public split and further fragmentation in the late 1920s.

The growing breach forced feminists to reevaluate their philosophies and take sides on the ideological split over the meaning of equality. For Lady Rhondda the central issue was not whether equality or social betterment was preferable but which one deserved primacy in the feminist struggle. Because she was raised in liberal surroundings and had reached self-fulfillment through militant activism and participating in the traditionally male world of commerce, she regarded equality and social reform as inextricably intertwined. She strongly believed that women's contribution was needed to work toward solving serious social problems of the day and achieving a better balanced and more humane society. Yet *before* women could participate in reshaping societal values and priorities, she felt, they had to have equality before the law. Only when women enjoyed the same legal and political power as men would they be able to ensure that their needs and concerns were taken out of the special – and therefore marginal – category and placed in the mainstream of normal – and therefore important – issues. Only through an equal partnership could women alter society along more equitable lines and obtain the fulfillment that comes through active decision making and the exercise of personal responsibility.[38] Thus Lady Rhondda placed herself fully in the equalitarian camp as early as 1923, stating that "women have no greater contribution to make towards civilization than [the achievement of] complete and absolute freedom of opportunity to put their full weight into things."[39]

At the same time, however, she recognized that the equalitarian approach was neither the most popular nor the easiest. In a speech to representatives from America's equalitarian society, the National Woman's Party (NWP), Lady Rhondda admitted that there were more reformers than feminists in the women's movement: "The passion to decide to look after your fellow-men, and especially women, to do good to them in your way is far more common than the desire to put into everyone's hand the power to look after themselves."[40] She also recognized that the fight for absolute equality would necessarily be a long-term struggle. Past experiences had proved that female apathy, governmental inaction, and male intransigence were powerful deterrents to the radical change being demanded and that women would continue to be exploited while the battle was being waged. Thus, while steadfastly maintaining that absolute legal equality be the primary focus of feminist agitation, Lady Rhondda was willing to compromise on certain short-term, stopgap measures to protect women and correct socially determined inequalities until full equality could be achieved.[41] Protective measures and worker assistance programs, she believed, should indeed be available, but to all workers regardless of gender.

Lady Rhondda was far from wanting women to adopt the thinking or behavioral patterns of men. For her, equality was a matter of the opportunity to use one's talents and develop one's potential. Early in her journalistic career, she was extremely critical of the aggressiveness, materialism, and false pride of men. She portrayed male resistance to sharing power with women not as sexism – a rationale common to other equalitarian feminists – but as a result of ignorance and a stubborn refusal to face the facts supporting women's claim. Believing that male-dominated society had made major mistakes, even to the extent of waging a war that had shaken British society to its foundation, Lady Rhondda expressed certainty that women possessed qualities which would broaden men's outlook and lead to a more peaceful and humane world.[42] Women, she believed, should not imitate men's ways but should instead exert pressures that would counter the negative tendencies of men's characters. The years, however, tempered Lady Rhondda's original optimism and faith in intrinsic value differences between the sexes. The strongest evidence of her changing perception is her correspondence about Virginia Woolf's feminist and antifascist pamphlet entitled *Three Guineas*. Woolf had suggested that the exclusion of women from leadership positions had helped preserve their moral superiority at the same time that it had encouraged the incorporation of the masculine traits of acquisitiveness, combativeness, and belligerence into national policy. Professional women, she argued, should form a new, noncompetitive order based on the art of peace rather than eternal preparations for war.[43] After reading *Three Guineas*, Lady Rhondda wrote to the author, saying that she hoped it was true that men and women were inherently different when it came to considerations of peace, war, competition, and general combativeness. If this were true, women would really make a difference when they gained power on the national and international levels. Yet, she continued, her experience in public life caused her to doubt that such inherent differences really existed. In her own life and in those of her women associates, she had seen echoes of the same pride, vanity, and combativeness, though admittedly none of the desire to do the actual killing.[44] The difference between the sexes, it seemed, was not so great as she had once thought.

In the mid-1920s, however, Lady Rhondda had not yet developed these qualms. She optimistically expected that the removal of barriers to female participation promised significant advances in the economic and political spheres. Economic activism was still necessary because of industrial dislocations, the illusory nature of wartime advances, wage differentials, and the still formidable ideology of motherhood. The high hopes for equal employment opportunity and equal pay which had accompanied passage of the Sex Disqualification (Removal) Act, which ostensibly barred gender discrimination in political and vocational appointments, in 1919 had faded by the mid-1920s. While many professions and industries had grudgingly admitted women, discrimination in promotion and pay and the continued existence of marriage bars severely limited women's chances to play a significant role in the economic life of the nation.[45] Such prob-

lems led Lady Rhondda to launch a renewed assault on economic inequality. In addition to relying on the Six Point Group and publicity
in *Time and Tide,* Lady Rhondda joined with other prominent feminists, most notably Chrystal Macmillan, Elizabeth Abbott, and Helen
Archdale, to discuss the possibility of creating a new organization devoted exclusively to the economic emancipation of industrial and professional women. Believing that the only real protection for any class
of women lay in equal status, equal pay, and equal opportunity, these
women laid the foundations for the Open Door Council.[46] Organized
in May 1926, the new group committed itself to cooperating with other
women's societies to educate the public about the increase in gender-
biased protective legislation and the dangers of such restrictions, to oppose the passage of new restrictions, and to ensure that all women, irres-
pective of marriage or motherhood, had the right to engage in paid work.[47]

These general goals became the basis for joint Six Point Group–Open
Door Council action throughout the 1920s and 1930s. Publishing pamphlets, writing letters, and pressuring parliamentarians, the two groups
worked for justice in the marketplace by concentrating their attentions
on two of the most flagrant offenses, protective legislation and unequal
remuneration. Campaigns against the Lead Paint Bill in 1926 and the
Factories Bill in 1927 refined and reinforced their ideas on protective
legislation. Claiming "Protection is too often the description of tyranny
applied to women,"[48] the two groups demanded the removal of all protective measures because they limited earning capacity, reduced the possible fields of employment, and denied women status as responsible
adult citizens.[49] The tradition of protection, they argued, was both
obsolete and detrimental to the interests of the entire community. Before
women became citizens, it might have been acceptable to place them
alongside children in a dependent category, but the vote had changed
that. Women were now responsible for their own actions. In a letter to
the editor of the *Times* dated 11 November 1926, Lady Rhondda and
other prominent members stated: "A Bill which treats women as non-
adults, which denies them the right to judge for themselves is in essence
a retrograde matter, and we are convinced that women have nothing to
gain from a false humanitarianism supported by doubtful facts."[50] If
jobs were too hazardous for women, common sense would indicate that
they were surely unsafe for men as well. If the government truly wanted
to help women workers, they suggested, it need only provide equal
status and equal safeguards.[51]

One such safeguard, equal pay for equal work, continued to dominate the two societies' economic agitation throughout the twenties and thirties. The addition of a demand for equal pay to an already outrageous assertion of women's right to work outside the home provoked strong resistance and outright hostility in those economically disturbed times. As long as the economy was sound women were welcomed as cheap labor, but when unemployment threatened they became targets for dismissal and scapegoats for the nation's domestic woes—despite the fact that the vast majority of women workers were employed in either specifically women's work like domestic service, nursing, and teaching or in unskilled, low-paying jobs. Since women's position in the work force was marginal, it was easy for employers to pay them lower wages for comparable work. In good times low pay was justified on the grounds that women had less strength, less training, less commitment, and less ambition. Women were also looked on as unstable employees, tending to leave the workplace for marriage or motherhood. And it was claimed that they did not need as much money as men to survive. In times of depression the presence of women in the work force was often resented despite the low wages they earned.[52]

Such arguments, of course, fueled the passions of equalitarian feminists in the Six Point Group and the Open Door Council. In deputations, press releases, and public meetings, they reemphasized women's wartime experience, abilities, and integrity, and they attempted to pressure successive governments into rectifying inequalities in both pay and opportunity.

To further the cause Lady Rhondda engaged in a press debate with the Lord Privy Seal, J. H. Thomas, on the so-called pin-money controversy. Thomas, arguing that women worked only for spending money, criticized their presence in the 1930s labor force as selfish, uneconomical, unfair, and immoral. He suggested that only the awakening of women's moral responsibility—and presumably voluntary withdrawal from the workplace—could save the nation from the deepening depression. Lady Rhondda countered by claiming that women worked because they needed the money to offset rising costs and arguing that in trying times women had a special obligation to work because national prosperity demanded the efficient use of all human resources. No individual, male or female, should expect the community or another person to play the role of keeper and provider.[53] As successive governments evaded the issue, maintaining that equal pay was a matter for employers and unions, agitation intensified. Calling on the government in November 1935 to abolish women's economic slavery, Lady Rhondda joined with other prominent supporters to remind them: "Men will continue to fear and distrust women in the labour market, just as long as women are forced to undercut them. Women will suffer a feeling of resentment just as long as their work is undervalued. The State needs the best work of men and women, and this will be best secured under equitable conditions of service."[54] Again her arguments went unheeded. Politicians paid lip service to the idea of equal pay, but they took no action to ensure it in Lady Rhondda's lifetime.[55]

While economic inequities were important, equalitarian feminists generally believed that political inequality was the major obstacle to progress. Before women could truly protect their own interests and work for the betterment of society, two formidable barriers had to be removed: the continued limitations on female suffrage and the exclusion of women from the House of Lords. Both of these issues, and the broader goal of equality they symbolized, were of vital concern to Lady Rhondda, and she took an active part in working for the abolition of these legal disabilities through organizational commitments and through a lawsuit against the upper house of Parliament.

The Sex Disqualification (Removal) Act, passed in December 1919, opened with these words: "A person shall not be disqualified by sex or marriage from the exercise of any public function, or from being appointed to or holding any civil or judicial office or post, or from entering or assuming or carrying on any civil profession or vocation."[56] Women had greeted this legislative advance enthusiastically, certain that it heralded an era of true equality. Yet within eighteen months, its limits became clear. Dismissal of women on marriage continued in the civil service, teaching, and nursing, and the House of Lords continued to exclude women. Feminists prepared to challenge the application and definition of the Sex Disqualification (Removal) Act and force the government into proving its good faith. Lady Rhondda, one of only twenty peeresses in their own right to be affected by the exclusion from the upper chamber of Parliament, and a prominent woman of affairs, was the perfect test case for the legality of the refusal to allow women into the House of Lords and to determine the government's true intentions regarding gender equality.

The question of admission of women to the upper house of Parliament originally came up in 1919 shortly after admission to the House of Commons had been granted. Pointing to the fact that only one woman had been elected to the Commons in the first general election after women gained the right, the Lords argued that it was apparent that the people did not want women representing them. Besides, they suggested, such an alteration in the composition of Parliament would be inopportune, since a comprehensive reform of the House of Lords was on the agenda for future discussion. So few were involved that it did not seem worth the effort, they argued.[57] But to many women committed to the principle of complete equality and believing that women could make a difference in legislative matters, it was worth any effort it took. When, three years after the Sex Disqualification (Removal) Act was passed, there was still no progress toward the proposed reform, and women were still prevented from performing an important political function, Lady Rhondda prepared to force the issue.

On 19 October 1921, she presented a legal petition to the king requesting a writ of summons to Parliament, the same summons received by male peers eligible to sit in the House of Lords. She did this not out of any particular desire to sit in what she called "that somewhat effete Parliamentary body," but out of a desire to challenge one of the vestiges of blatant gender discrimination. If she were successful, she would have gained a useful platform for pressing women's issues, and if she failed, her failure would highlight the hypocrisy of the government's position on sexual equality and perhaps breathe new life into the feminist movement.[58] Her petition, apparently harmless and seemingly justified under the present law, sparked a long legal battle that illustrated some of the anachronistic qualities of the House of Lords that had led many of both sexes to demand comprehensive reform. As long as the hereditary chamber remained, Lady Rhondda demanded her right, and by extension the right of all women otherwise qualified, to take their rightful place and perform their rightful duties.

The first stage of the Rhondda Peerage Claim prompted little controversy. The petition was referred to the Committee of Privileges charged with evaluating such claims and recommending action to the House of Lords. The Committee of Privileges, consisting on this occasion of eight members, five with considerable legal experience, first heard the case on 2 March 1922. Lady Rhondda's attorneys, G. J. Talbot and W. A. Greene, based their case entirely on the Sex Disqualification (Removal) Act. They contended that sitting and voting in the House of Lords was a public function from which otherwise qualified individuals, holders of peerages in their own right, had been disqualified by their sex. Passage of the Sex Disqualification (Removal) Act had, they claimed, legally removed this disqualification, and peeresses should be admitted without delay. Speaking for the government, Attorney General Sir Gordon Hewart offered no objections, and the committee voted seven to one to recommend that the full house accept the claim and the summons be issued.[59]

This apparent victory was greeted enthusiastically by Lady Rhondda and her supporters. Delighted that the case had been decided in her favor, Lady Rhondda called her admission to the "last feudal assembly of Europe" a remarkable triumph for feminism.[60] This sentiment was echoed by Nancy Astor, the first female member of the House of Commons, who hailed the decision as a vindication of the principle of equality and saw Lady Rhondda's presence in the upper house as a harbinger of serious consideration for urgent reforms of interest to women.[61] Feminist groups both at home and abroad applauded the decision. At home, the NUSEC praised the victory not only for its immediate impact in giving women the opportunity to share in the legislative work of the Lords, but from the broader perspective of the precedent set for future applications of the Sex Disqualification (Removal) Act.[62] The Montreal Women's Clubs sent their congratulations, and equalitarian feminists in the United States supported Lady Rhondda's claim on the basis that barring any woman from any opportunity implied the inferiority of all women.[63] The press, too, responded favorably. *The Vote,* the organ of the Women's Freedom League, rejoiced in the removal of another hurdle to full participation but suggested that distinguished women should in future be given fuller consideration in the honors lists and should have the same chances of being raised to the peerage as men. The foreign press, as represented by *Le Figaro* and *Le Petit Parisien,* viewed the outcome as an important decision and a victory for the cause.[64] Even the *Sunday Times'* political correspondent commented that the attorney general had interpreted the law with "refreshing breadth and modernity" and wondered if such a drastic constitutional reevaluation had ever been achieved with so little difficulty.[65]

While public response was generally positive, there were those who were hostile. The duke of Rutland commented that he did not think any woman could teach the Lords anything new and that women were probably out of their depth in high politics. He further stated that the admission of women to the House of Commons had not added charm, dignity, or usefulness, and that if a female took a seat next to him, he would probably laugh.[66] The *Westminster Gazette,* while generally supportive of Lady Rhondda, nonetheless pointed out the discrepancy between this case and a simultaneous decision to exclude women medical students from a series of lectures. It stated: "The moment which sees

Woman, in robes and coronet, sweep to her rightful place in the House of Lords sees her summarily ejected from a medical lecture-room. And whereas Lady Rhondda, great tho her personal abilities undoubtedly are, inherited her place in national life, the struggling young medical student is bravely working to win one for herself."[67] Other newspapers, most notably the Cardiff *Western Mail,* attempted to denigrate and ridicule the achievement, stating:

> All conquering woman is ceasing to be a supplicant. Whenever she approaches some old citadel of masculine privilege and prerogative down comes the drawbridge, up goes the portcullis, and she marches gaily in, with a fluffy toy dog in one arm and a vanity-bag hanging from the other. She is engaged in the agreeable pastime of forcing open doors. The House of Lords, helpless before the initiative of Lady Rhondda, has now yielded to gracefully irresistible encroachments, and solemn pompous ennobled lawyers are faced with the staggering possibility of a woman someday sitting on the Woolsack as Lord Chancellor, with a pretty French maid hovering in the background and making eyes at the train-bearer.[68]

It was soon evident, however, that the petition's supporters had rejoiced too soon and that its opponents had little to fear. Rumors surfaced almost immediately that the less enlightened peers were appalled at the committee's acceptance of the petition and were gathering forces to put an end to the "silliness." Seldom particularly keen on issues involving change or reform, the hereditary peers were not going to stand by idly in the face of this latest threat to the status quo. At first supporters of the claim thought that the decision's positive press reception might temper their lordships' disapproval and prevent a reversal.[69] Those hopes were quickly dashed when the lord chancellor himself, Lord Birkenhead, came forth to lead the opposition.

The press had a field day. Cartoons, articles, and interviews followed the developing contest almost daily. Among the more apt of these was the *Sunday Chronicle*'s (London) 19 March 1922 edition, which featured a cartoon showing Lord Birkenhead as Horatius holding the bridge against the Amazons led by Lady Rhondda. The cartoon was accompanied by an article written by Robert Blatchford. Blatchford described the resistance as "the last defiant gesture of the Dark Ages, the final stand of masculine stupidity against the triumphant advance of the hosts of our wives and mothers."[70]

On 30 March 1922, when the Committee of Privileges recommended that the petition be granted, the opposing peers were ready to challenge it. Lord Birkenhead opposed the motion and proposed an amendment which would require the case to be referred to an enlarged Committee of Privileges on which he wished to serve. While such an action was not without precedent, it was unusual.[71] But the force of the lord chancellor's support and the realization that an important constitutional issue and a significant precedent were at stake allowed the amendment to carry easily. The reconstituted Committee of Privileges consisted of twenty-six peers, an addition of eighteen members. Before the case could be heard again, Attorney General Sir Gordon Hewart had become lord chief justice and was replaced by Sir Ernest Pollock, a man known to be considerably less enthusiastic about the admission of women.

At the second hearing, the previously simple arguments devolved into a controversial discussion of both semantics and the intentions of the statute. Lady Rhondda's lawyers argued that the intent of the Sex Disqualification (Removal) Act was to place men and women on an equal footing in public affairs by removing all barriers based on gender. If the House of Lords were not meant to be included in this political restructuring, the law would have specifically made that exception. Further, they contended, the summons to Parliament (the official invitation to take one's seat) was attached to the peerage. Therefore, it did not rest with the king or the lords to refuse the petitioner's request.[72]

The attorney general countered by arguing that the holding of a peerage was not a public function but a personal grant and dignity. He further suggested that in defining the terms of the act upon which the petition was based, it would be necessary to look beyond the mere words to consider extraneous circumstances, legislative intent, and precedents which might lead their lordships to reach an interpretation contrary to the exact letter of the law. Commenting that the claim was based on "a doubtful interpretation of an ambiguous word," he further argued that had the legislature planned to make such a vital alteration in the composition of the upper house, it would have specifically stated its intention to do so.[73] That opening statement set the stage for a long technical argument led by Pollock and Birkenhead, which resulted in a twenty to four decision to rescind the first committee's decision. Only Lords Haldane, Selbourne, Wrenbury, and Ullswater voted to uphold Lady Rhondda's claim.

The justification for this unusual reversal was explained to the full House of Lords at length by Lady Rhondda's chief opponent, Lord Birkenhead. He stated that Lady Rhondda's lawyers had failed to provide adequate proof of either of the two vital questions: first, whether she was entitled to receive a writ but was disqualified by her sex; and

second, whether such a disqualification was indeed removed by the statute in question. Regarding the first issue, the lord chancellor claimed
that the terms of the original patent conferred on Lady Rhondda the
name and privileges of the viscountcy but did not expressly grant her
a seat in Parliament. Rather, he argued, by its silence on that issue—
while specifically granting D. A. Thomas and his male heirs a seat, place,
and voice in Parliament—the patent expressly differentiated between
the rights of a female peer and a peer of Parliament. Furthermore, he
stated, "A person who is a female must remain a female till she dies.
Apart from a change in the law, she could not before 1919 both be a
woman and participate in the legislative proceedings of the House of
Lords." Thus, she was never entitled to receive a writ of summons and
was therefore not disqualified by her sex except in a "wholly loose and
colloquial sense."[74]

Aside from that, there was the broader question of whether the Sex
Disqualification (Removal) Act had intended to grant such a privilege.
Using a mixture of common law, precedent, and past legislation, Lord
Birkenhead claimed that although no law prevented a writ of summons
to a woman, the fact that no woman had received one must be taken
to establish a precedent which could be superseded only by specific legislation. Quoting §9 of the Representation of the People Act (1918), which
read, "Any incapacity of a peer to vote at any election arising from the
status of a peer shall not extend to peeresses in their own right,"[75] the
lord chancellor argued that previous laws did not assume the right of
peeresses to hold the voting privileges of their male counterparts. Further, he quoted a statement made by Lord Haldane in the debate over
the passage of the Sex Disqualification (Removal) Act in which Haldane
specifically said:

> If this Amendent is accepted it does not enable women who are Peeresses
> in their own right to take their seat in this House; they can only do that
> if the terms of the Letters Patent or of the other documents creating the
> Peerage prescribe it, and also if a Writ of Summons is issued. It may or
> may not be necessary, if we admit the principle, that some Amendment
> may be required for the issue of the Writ of Summons.[76]

This, of course, indicated that the issue had arisen and been dismissed,
greatly strengthening Lord Birkenhead's claim that the law did not in-
tend to permit women into the House of Lords. Had Parliament meant
to make such a revolutionary change, it would, he suggested, have specifically so stated. In technical terms the lord chancellor's contentions

were accurate. Following the letter rather than the spirit of the law, the enlarged Committee of Privileges had reached a conclusion that may have run counter to the prevailing sentiments of the day but could nonetheless be legally justified. Until new legislation was passed, the House of Lords was safe from the potentially disruptive influence of women.

The decision evoked considerable comment from those who regarded the defeat as a serious miscarriage of justice and a breach of faith on the part of the government. Lady Rhondda's original response, shared with a select audience of women supporters, was that the word *Removal* in the act's title had never succeeded in getting outside its brackets. The case had proven, she continued, that injustice and prejudice would continue unabated unless the women forced their unwilling representatives to make the law into a reality.[77] Other feminists likewise responded indignantly. Millicent Garrett Fawcett, the grande dame of the suffrage fight, called the decision "simply scandalous" and asked if the few peers on the Committee of Privileges were to be allowed to disregard an act of Parliament because it ran counter to their prejudices.[78] The Consultative Committee of Women's Organizations, chaired by Lady Astor and representing over thirty societies, sent a resolution to Leslie Scott, solicitor general for the House of Commons, charging the government with acting in bad faith and demanding the passage of an amendment which would allow peeresses to take their rightful place in the House of Lords. Scott replied that objections should have been raised three years earlier when the original act was being debated and that women would have never been allowed to hold peerages had voting privileges accompanied them.[79] Other officials proved no more receptive. In the House of Commons, Margaret Wintringham pressed Neville Chamberlain (lord privy seal) on the government's intentions and was told that the type of amendment being suggested had no chance of passing and that the government would not pledge inclusion of the question of women's eligibility in the anticipated House of Lords reform bill.[80]

Such statements fed general dissatisfaction with the ruling. The *Times* categorically stated that there was no logical reason to continue to exclude women from the upper chamber,[81] and the women's organizations prepared to continue the fight to achieve the political equality that would remove this remaining stigma of female inferiority. The Sex Disqualification (Removal) Act, heralded as a charter of women's rights, had proven to be a failure. It was, in Lady Rhondda's words, "a leaky saucepan,"[82] and the leaks had to be plugged. Margaret Wintringham's question in the House of Commons had been the first shot in a campaign that would finally succeed between 1958 and 1963.

The disappointment and frustration of the 1922 defeat did not prevent Lady Rhondda from continuing to press her battle for admission. Since, however, the Lords had spoken on the issue of the existing law, future attempts concentrated on legislative changes that would allow peeresses entry into the forbidden chamber. In 1927, 1930, 1946, and 1949 they were rebuffed, and the issue again became tied up with the broader question of reform of the House of Lords, particularly the Labour Party's opposition to any extension of the hereditary chamber. In each attempt Lady Rhondda played a major role, using her talents, her contacts, and her weekly review to break down the barrier, and gaining for herself a new nickname, "the Persistent Peeress." The Life Peerages Act, which opened the doors of the House of Lords to a select group of females, passed just months after her death in 1958. In November 1963 hereditary peeresses finally took their seats.[83]

Throughout Lady Rhondda's life, however, the ban stood despite the indignation of women's groups, the disapproval of the general public, and reasonable suggestions that laws or the terms of patents should be changed to conform to the realities of women's position in the modern world. Women did not yet have the political power to pressure government officials into treating them fairly. The 1918 suffrage act had granted the vote only to those women over thirty who met specific property holding or residential qualifications, leaving large numbers of women wage-earners disfranchised and without any effective means of either protecting their interests or helping remedy the injustice of feminine exclusion. The fight for an equal franchise became the primary focus of women's political agitation after the defeat of the 1922 peerage claim.

Until 1925 the campaign languished under the illusion that the government would surely act soon to eliminate the disparity in the franchise. But continued inaction by the government made those feminists who had grown tired of empty promises turn once more to activism. Perhaps because of her recent experience, Lady Rhondda was less inclined to wait patiently than many. Writing to Lady Astor about the possibility of bringing Emmeline Pankhurst back from Europe to take part in the new campaign, she indicated that Mrs. Pankhurst's presence and the memories it would evoke could prove of inestimable value.[84] Lady Astor, probably fearful that the great militant's presence might prove provocative, responded optimistically that it was unnecessary to enlist Pankhurst, as the government was certain to grant equal suffrage anyway.[85] Not content to wait passively for legitimate grievances to be addressed, Lady Rhondda became the driving force behind the formation of the Equal Political Rights Campaign Committee, whose sole aim was to unite the various feminist societies in a massive push for votes for twenty-one-year-old women.

The new committee received tremendous support; some fifty-four women's groups eventually affiliated with it. The joint effort kicked off with a giant demonstration in Hyde Park on 3 July 1926. Representatives from equalitarian and social feminist societies were joined by thirty-five members of the U.S. National Woman's Party in a show of solidarity and determination. The demonstration was greeted by *Time and Tide,* rapidly establishing itself as a leading feminist organ, as marking the end "of a period of lassitude, the beginning of a fresh period of enthusiasm and courage."[86] In deputations to Prime Minister Baldwin and letters to the press over the following two years, the committee made it clear that only a franchise based on the same terms as those for men would be satisfactory. Any suggestions of a conference or an inquiry would be seen as just one more attempt to evade the issue of equality. Considering the Conservative Party the greatest obstacle, the committee planned to exert particular pressure in traditionally Conservative districts. Their pressure apparently worked: the prime minister announced in April 1927 that women would be granted the same voting privileges as men.[87]

The announcement heralding the enfranchisement of approximately 5.3 million women received mixed reviews.[88] While it was welcomed by the feminist, Liberal, and Labour presses, the Conservative organs were predictably less enthusiastic. The *Daily Telegraph* and the *Daily Express* accepted Baldwin's statement as inevitable and likely to help the Conservatives, but others expressed serious doubts.[89] The *Daily Mail* feared that the granting of votes to "impulsive and politically ignorant girls" might prove hazardous, leading to the possible exclusion of the Conservative Party for thirty years. The *Daily Mirror* titled its correspondence column "Flapper Vote Folly" and suggested that it would be more reasonable to raise the voting age than to "shower more votes upon muddle-headed amateurs."[90]

Despite the press accounts, women remained optimistic, but their patience began to wear thin as Baldwin's pledge remained just that. Mass demonstrations again dramatized the issue in July and November 1927. Even Lady Rhondda's spirits began to fail. While it was perhaps neces-

sary for her to express certainty of victory at home, she was at least free
to share her doubts in private correspondence with American friends
and supporters. To Doris Stevens, a prominent American militant and
equalitarian feminist, she confided in late December 1927 that final victory was beginning to look "a little shaky."[91] Her optimism returned
in mid-January, shortly before the Franchise Act of 1928 removed the
political disability which she had long regarded as a symbol of female
inferiority. She wrote to Helen Archdale that the victory had brightened
feminist prospects and left men extremely conscious of the fact that majority power now lay in women's hands.[92] She attributed the victory to
a change in public opinion brought about by the agitation done by an
active minority, acceptance of reality, and a recognition of the fine
achievements of individual women in all areas of public life.[93] Writing
about the incident in her autobiography, Lady Rhondda admitted that
she was relieved at the conclusion of the struggle. She had never really
been interested, she confessed, in legal details, and she now felt free to
concentrate on more important projects, presumably *Time and Tide*.[94]

   While Lady Rhondda devoted herself increasingly to the journal, she
did not abandon the feminist cause. During her struggle for admission
to the House of Lords, extension of the female franchise, and removal
of economic barriers, she had frequently come in contact with supporters from other countries and had developed close ties with women of
similar sentiments. The resulting sense of sisterhood led her to turn
her attention to international feminism. The first signs of Lady Rhondda's
interest in international cooperation had appeared in April 1925 with
the formation of a British advisory group to cooperate with the U.S.
National Woman's Party in an informal alliance designed to press for
full equality. As the vanguard of a worldwide equal rights movement,
this alliance was formed to ensure that women's interests received adequate attention in all international agreements, treaties, and conventions, and to provide a nucleus for a concerted movement for equal rights
for men and women throughout the civilized world.[95] Over the next
five years, both of Lady Rhondda's pet organizations, the Six Point
Group and the Open Door Council, became prime instruments in
educating British feminists in the need for international cooperation.
Her personal notoriety (a result of both her business contacts and the
publicity surrounding the House of Lords proceedings) made Lady
Rhondda a natural asset to the campaign. The American feminist Doris
Stevens wrote that she and Alice Paul were very excited to have her "mar-
shal the European sentiment" in favor of their goals.[96] Inter-American

Commission of Women releases refer to her as "a great international leader," while giving only a national affiliation for other international advisory board members.[97]

The International Women Suffrage Alliance (IWSA) Congress held in Paris in June 1926 provided Margaret with an opportunity to capitalize on her reputation and help set in motion the machinery for broader collective action of interest to women. Meeting with delegates from Belgium, Czechoslovakia, Denmark, Egypt, France, and Germany, she explained the need for joint action, especially in light of the refusal of the 1926 congress to take a firm stand against protective legislation for women only. This action, she implied, made the formation of a new international organization dedicated to industrial equality and worldwide action to achieve it an absolute necessity.[98]

Much of the international feminist community was not yet prepared to accept either the responsibility or the philosophy Lady Rhondda wanted. The international movement, like the British movement, was in the throes of the debate between social and equalitarian feminism. The major controversy of the IWSA Congress arose over the admission of the National Woman's Party, the American equalitarian society. The moderate American League of Women Voters campaigned strongly against its equalitarian rival on the grounds that it was too extremist and was manipulating the press for its own ends. In deference to the League of Women Voters, the IWSA voted to exclude the National Woman's Party. The arbitrary nature of the decision, best indicated by the simultaneous admission of its British counterpart, the Six Point Group, provoked a backlash which widened the developing ideological split. Lady Rhondda asked to address the congress and soberly announced that she felt honorbound to withdraw the Six Point Group's application for membership unless the rejection was overturned. Ending her solemn rebuke, she offered this challenge: "If you vote to keep the Woman's Party out you will be voting for the past. If you vote to take them in it will be a vote for the future."[99]

Her challenge caused a stir of excitement, and it appeared that the decision might be overturned. IWSA officers, however, turned the challenge into a credibility issue, arguing that a reversal would be seen as a vote of no confidence in the leadership which would signal that the women's movement lacked direction and consensus. This argument brought all but the most independent in line—the rejection stood.[100] Lady Rhondda responded by officially withdrawing the already accepted application of the Six Point Group, claiming that the tactics used in the campaign—innuendos, exaggerated charges, and petty intranational jealousies—made it impossible for her to affiliate with an organization capable of such underhanded dealings.[101] This dramatic gesture, while not affecting the outcome, marked Lady Rhondda as a woman of principle and as a major force in the international women's movement.

Lady Rhondda took advantage of her new international prestige to meet with feminist leaders, to develop a more consistent understanding of the status and needs of women in other parts of the world, and to seek possible solutions to issues of mutual concern. She had emerged from the Paris congress with a vague feeling that the protective policies and actions of the League of Nations' International Labour Office (ILO) should be attacked. After conversation and correspondence with prominent feminists, including Doris Stevens and Alice Paul, she came to see this as a negative and counterproductive policy, since the ILO meetings would always be overshadowed by press attention to the League of Nations assemblies. A much more plausible and more widely publicized campaign, she believed, could be waged against the League of Nations itself. If the league could be encouraged to adopt an international agreement prohibiting the placing of legal disabilities on women's work, it would create a valuable propaganda effect and set a strong precedent for equal treatment.[102]

Lady Rhondda and the Six Point Group took the lead in gathering the forces for international agitation. In the early stages, partly because the British were involved in their own fights at home, primary attention focused on making women's presence felt at League of Nations meetings and ensuring adequate press coverage of the league's unacceptable stand on protective legislation and other antifeminist positions.[103] From the beginning, however, this line of attack had a fatal flaw. Without an official international society to add legitimacy to the Six Point Group activities, the group could hardly expect to be taken seriously or to be accepted as the voice of worldwide feminism.

But once the full franchise was gained at home, British feminism could turn its attention to organization on the international level, first concentrating on economic issues and then on broader political concerns. The Open Door Council took the lead in forming an international organization to work for women's labor equality and to attack what they considered the antifeminist policies of the Labour Bureau of the League of Nations. In June 1929, the Open Door International was formed to unite men and women concerned about the growing tendency toward gender-biased protective measures which encouraged continued economic inequality. The new organization's manifesto stressed the outdated character of present economic legislation, which by "protecting" women from the evils of the workplace prevented them from being recognized as a legitimate force in the marketplace. Only through complete economic emancipation, it continued, could the international economy function at its maximum potential and the prosperity of all citizens be guaranteed. Turning to specific methods of achieving this end, the members signed the *Women Workers' Charter of Economic Rights*, which placed primary emphasis on ensuring that protective legislation was job-related rather than sex-related, that married women's right to work be recognized, and that pay be based on performance.[104]

But economic agitation alone was not sufficient to create international unity or to achieve significant gains, and attention turned to the broader issue of worldwide political equality. As early as 1926, Lady Rhondda worked with Doris Stevens and Alice Paul to develop a comprehensive equal rights treaty which they hoped would be signed by representatives of all major nations.[105] In the autumn she chaired an international committee of the Six Point Group charged with directing all international activity and launching the equal rights treaty idea in Europe.[106] For Lady Rhondda, still committed to equalitarianism, the passage of such a treaty immediately assumed primary importance, but other leaders feared that such an all-embracing plan would not be acceptable to the majority of feminists. They continued instead to work as independent units fighting for specific issues. International consultation and cooperation continued, but international organization and commitment to true equality was stalled until 1930.

The Six Point Group continued to press the need for true internationalism, but the initiative passed to American hands. The one issue which crossed national boundaries and might create a precedent for future cooperation was the question of a female's loss of nationality rights on marriage to a foreigner. Since women of all nations were affected, the issue was perfect for a temporary alliance to achieve a specific goal. If successful, it was hoped, women would learn that power lay in numbers and organization. The American feminists, led by Doris Stevens and Alice Paul, were the guiding forces behind the early developments, but because of continuing hostility between the IWSA and the NWP, American leaders proposed that Lady Rhondda chair a World Committee on Nationality to last only until the convening of the Hague Conference on Codification of International Law at which the issue was to be discussed. Lady Rhondda's leadership, they asserted, would ensure numbers and prestige. While flattered by the request, Lady Rhondda was unhappy at the decision to concentrate on such niggling details at the Hague conference while true feminism demanded a broader attack on inequality at the League of Nations Assembly in Geneva. She also refused to lead the new movement on the grounds that the chairmanship should be held by one of the true leaders, Doris Stevens or Alice Paul, since they were better informed on the issues and had the total commitment necessary to sustain the fight, while she regarded *Time and Tide* as her primary concern. Also, she admitted to being a very poor internationalist, commenting that: "The laws against women in some small South American Republic don't make me see *properly* red like they do you. I just have a general feeling a tidal wave would probably do that part of the world good, which is the wrong attitude of mind for a World Chairman!"[107] To allow anyone not totally committed, no matter how supportive, to direct the campaign would cripple the fight from the beginning.

Lady Rhondda did agree, however, to chair the British support group, in part because she saw no acceptable alternative. No one but she among British feminists possessed the two vital qualifications: complete trust in the American leaders and complete acceptance by the British equalitarian societies.[108] Even so, she was still not certain that she would be able to persuade the British societies to support so limited a program or to accept American leadership. The Hague conference, she suggested, would draw little press attention and evoke limited enthusiasm. If attention were focused instead on the League assembly at Geneva the following year (1929), greater support would probably be forthcoming.[109]

Lady Rhondda's objections carried some weight, and the plan of action in Europe was revised to focus on the broader issue of an equal rights treaty. The new plan called for Doris Stevens to approach the French foreign minister Aristide Briand on behalf of the International Committee of the NWP. She would ask him to arrange a conference between delegates of all countries slated to sign the Kellogg-Briand Pact and representative women from each of these nations to discuss the status of the world's female population. If he agreed, the women planned to surprise the delegation with a full-blown equal rights treaty (much as the Americans had done at the Pan-American Congress in Havana in 1928). While the treaty was fairly certain to be defeated, the publicity would focus attention on it. The Americans were optimistic that Briand would agree, but Lady Rhondda expressed serious reservations that such tactics would work with European leaders.[110]

Lady Rhondda cooperated with the effort, but she was never particularly enthusiastic about it. Doris Stevens recorded in her diary that Lady Rhondda accompanied her to a meeting at the American embassy in Paris on 25 August 1928 to make preliminary arrangements for the women's delegation to meet with the plenipotentiaries.[111] The attempts to persuade Frank Kellogg and Aristide Briand to receive the women fell short, and the American contingent decided to force the issue after Margaret had returned to London. On 28 August, Doris Stevens led a group of about a dozen women, including the Six Point Group representative Vera Brittain, to Rambouillet (the summer chateau of the president of France). When Stevens tried to present her petition, the women were arrested for not having French identification cards (required only for extended visits of a month or more) and were detained until the plenipotentiaries concluded their business.[112] Stevens regarded Rambouillet as "the last militant act . . . to have been staged for women's rights."[113] But Lady Rhondda considered it a serious tactical mistake. She wrote that the movement should have stopped with Briand's refusal. To go public and be refused was a rather inauspicious beginning for the equal rights treaty, and the militant spirit seemed particularly unsuitable to her in this case. In a letter to Vera Brittain, who as representative of the Six Point Group had found herself in the uncomfortable position of having to support the NWP stand despite her own reservations, Lady Rhondda wrote: "Militancy is right after one has tried other methods. But to open with militancy is like a naughty child which howls before it has any cause—I'm all for howling in due season, but I object to doing it when I feel a fool myself to do it. But you were *absolutely* right not to dissociate the S.P.G. or me from Rambouillet at the cost of giving the lie to the Woman's Party—whatever we do we can't do that!"[114] Challenging the acknowledged leaders publicly would cast doubt not only on them but on the cause as well.

The abortive Paris campaign did nonetheless discredit the NWP and shifted responsibility back to Lady Rhondda's Six Point Group. The group lobbied strongly but unsuccessfully for acceptance of the Inter-American Commission of Women's (Alice Paul's) equal rights treaty at the 1929 League of Nations Assembly. The lack of success again emphasized the need for international coordination to fight not for narrow economic rights, already the territory of the Open Door International, but for the adoption, ratification, and practical application of an equal rights treaty designed to combat economic, social, and political discrimination against women.[115] The Six Point Group took the initiative in planning for an international equality organization, contacting various feminist societies, sounding out key political figures, publicizing the common needs of advanced and underdeveloped nations, and consistently urging an equal rights treaty as the best means of ending discrimination and improving the status of women.[116] Lady Rhondda does not appear to have taken a significant role in this preparatory stage, choosing to leave the task in the hands of the Six Point Group's international secretary, Helen Archdale, and her daughter Betty.

By September 1930, the groundwork had been laid for the formation of a worldwide equality group, the Equal Rights International. The new organization brought together women of various nations who pledged that they would try to obtain support for the passage of the equal rights treaty in their countries. Taking the chair at the organizational meeting for the new group, Lady Rhondda claimed that an equal rights treaty was necessary both to secure for women an equal say in future international decisions and to ensure that reactionary countries could not act to hinder advances in more progressive nations. Prominent feminists, including Alice Paul of the United States, Lily van der Schalk Schuster of Holland, Jessie Street of Australia, María Boscoff Zoty of Romania, and Blanche Z. de Baralt of Cuba, pledged their support and elected Helen Archdale chairman.[117] Having gotten this latest venture off to a promising start, Lady Rhondda felt free to leave the conclusion of the international campaign to others. By November 1930, she had separated herself from the organization and was expressing some doubts about its future. Writing to Doris Stevens of her future plans, Margaret confessed: "I am clearing out of feminist things altogether so far as I can except in so far as they come in to T. & T. If I can make the paper go in a big way (as is beginning to seem possible) I shall have done as big a thing for feminism as I am capable of."[118]

By 1931, Lady Rhondda had indeed dissociated herself from active participation in feminist organizations, but not from the feminist cause. Instead, she channeled her efforts in a different direction. In her career as an active feminist organizer she had served the movement well. Aside from the primary commitments previously noted, she had participated in a number of other more specialized groups and activities. Between 1921 and 1924, she served as president of the National Women's Citizens' Association, an organization dedicated to promoting active, responsible citizenship and securing equal representation for men and women in public life at the local, regional, national, and international levels. She was also a member of the executive committee of the National Union of Societies for Equal Citizenship, a founding member of the Women's Election Committee (an organization established to help finance women candidates for Parliament),[119] and a representative to the Women's Consultative Committee, which coordinated political work. She was active in the British Commonwealth League, a feminist society concerned with the position of women throughout the empire, the British Federation of Business and Professional Women, and various specialized groups and committees concerned with professional opportunities and recognition of outstanding female achievement.

Lady Rhondda was particularly interested in issues pertaining to education and public health, two vital components of satisfying personal lives and national progress. Always believing that the hope of the future lay in the education of a nation's populace, she was a tireless defender of the rights of all Britons, whether male or female, rich or poor, to an adequate education. She advocated training individuals according to talents, abilities, and personal interests rather than by artificial gender or financial distinctions. Any country which attempted to educate only a small part of its population and did so according to outdated principles, she held, could not hope to maximize its national potential or promote the fullest possible well-being of its citizenry.

This commitment to the best possible education for the greatest number prompted the childless Lady Rhondda to become a spokesperson for curriculum improvement, raising of the national school-leaving age, and more adequate funding of education.[120] Her own commitment to adequate financing was most notable in her fund-raising activities and private bequests for the impoverished Oxford women's colleges. At various times in her career she was the treasurer of the Oxford Women's Club Fund (designed to provide money for salaries, pensions, advanced research, and structural improvements), a patron of the Crosby Hall Appeal Fund (to build an international residence hall for women postgraduates studying in London), and a supporter of Somerville College. As a gesture of thanks for her continuing support, the one-year Somerville student was awarded an honorary membership in the British Federation of University Women.

Concurrent with her commitment to education ran a humanitarian concern for improved public health which led Lady Rhondda into numerous campaigns for better public housing, sanitation, infant welfare, and improved unemployment allowances. She was also appointed president of the Women Sanitary Inspectors and Health Visitors' Association and a member of the Advisory Committee of the Ministry of Health. She served as honorary treasurer for the Food Education Society, an agency which undertook educational campaigns to promote hygienic and dietary awareness. Her concern for public health also led her to become a patron of the New Sussex Hospital for Women and Children and the Josephine Butler Memorial Foundation.[121]

Such broad-based commitments necessarily kept Lady Rhondda in the public eye and earned her a reputation as a responsible, useful citizen. That reputation allowed her the opportunity to plunge into the debate on one of her favorite subjects, the menace of the "leisured woman." Having attended a private boarding school, participated in the London Season, and moved in the circles of the wealthy for much of her life, she had closely observed the women of her class and was not particularly impressed by what she saw. In the fall of 1927, she began to contribute articles on the leisured woman to *Time and Tide* under the pseudonym "Candida" and to participate in public debates on the subject, of which the most notable was with G. K. Chesterton. Lady Rhondda used these forums to criticize upper-class women for being content to lead pleasant but useless lives of luxury which benefited neither themselves nor their community. She argued that despite the liberalizing tendencies of contemporary society, wealthy British women were still leading empty, idle lives.[122]

These ideas were further developed in an extended essay entitled *Leisured Women*. In Lady Rhondda's opinion, the average upper-class woman, freed from the burdens of child rearing and domestic work, and having little to do except pamper herself, served no useful purpose. Instead, she constituted a serious danger to British society because she perpetuated poisonous qualities in her offspring. Idleness, materialism, and hypocrisy, according to Lady Rhondda, were the trademarks of these leisured women, and their prominent status gave them a visibility and an influence which affected all women and society negatively.[123] Through her own actions, she had tried to point the way to an active, more fulfilling life style which would benefit both the individual and the broader community.

In fighting for her vision of women's equality, Lady Rhondda had helped keep feminism alive during the interwar years, when many grew complacent. By alerting women to the political and economic disabilities they faced and keeping up consistent pressure for change, she had helped remove a few of the most blatant disabilities and had perhaps helped prevent discrimination from becoming worse. Her commitment to securing women's rights earned her a reputation as a "feminist, heart and soul, consistent to the last degree."[124] Hazel Hunkins Hallinan, a longtime friend and Six Point Group associate, perhaps said it best: "Margaret Haig was one of the best. Her commitment to women, the women's movement, and a better society was total."[125]

6 · THE PRIVATE MARGARET

By the 1920s, Lady Rhondda had become a public person in many respects. Her championship of women's rights, her war work, and her success in commercial affairs had brought her to the attention of the press and the general public. The public persona, created largely by journalists and feminist commentators, depicted a formidable and slightly remote woman, totally secure in herself and her status. She emerges from contemporary accounts as a passionate defender of the oppressed, a staunch social critic, and an exemplary career woman able to move freely and comfortably between the worlds of business and high society.

To an extent this public image is accurate. Lady Rhondda was indeed an active and concerned citizen. She had a passionate sense of duty and responsibility and a deep sympathy for the less fortunate. Her privileged upbringing and slightly elitist inclinations sometimes added a patronizing note to her humanitarian gestures. George Bernard Shaw once asked her if she was certain she did not have a family bias toward classifying "poor devils with only £1,000 a year" as the poor,[1] but her commitment to public justice and her strong humanitarian principles cannot be questioned. She often provided moral and financial support for international relief schemes, historical preservation, the arts, and various charitable organizations. Frequently her support was offered anonymously, a clear indication that she was not simply seeking publicity or acclaim for her contributions.[2]

Concomitant with this image as a philanthropist and social crusader was her reputation as a popular, attractive, and slightly unconventional hostess. Standing about five feet six inches tall, the adult Lady Rhondda was a large-boned, stocky woman, with fair skin and light brown hair with a hint of natural curl. Clear blue eyes softened the wide jaw, broad forehead, and determined mouth, creating a pleasant but by no means beautiful countenance. Contemporary accounts report that she often wore a harried expression and frequently frowned when preoccupied. Concerned more with comfort and practicality than fashion, she generally preferred utilitarian suits or trousers, long sleeves, and low-heeled shoes. She possessed high spirits, a sharp wit, and a genuine appreciation of good companionship which transformed her into an appealing hostess.

Lady Rhondda considered good company and good conversation essential to her personal well-being and her professional success. She entertained frequently, despite chronic anxiety that her parties would fail, and drew a mixture of praise and ridicule for the odd assortment of individuals she gathered around her. Neither a true intellectual nor a social snob, she chose her friends because they shared her tastes and interests or because she found them intriguing and amusing. Parties at her London flat or her country house (first in Kent, later in Surrey) drew guests from industry, the arts, politics, and journalism. Since Lady Rhondda's own life spanned so many areas, her home often provided a meeting ground where men and women from different worlds could engage in friendly discussion and animated argument. The caricaturist of businessmen, George Bernard Shaw, could be invited to meet some average representatives of the species in hopes of broadening his mind and toning down his criticism.[3] Young, relatively unknown writers could come into contact with living legends, and politicians could confront their press critics in a neutral environment filled with stimulating talk and excellent food and drink.

The mixture of diverse personalities and stimulating conversation to be found at her gatherings earned Lady Rhondda high marks from many contemporaries. In trying to explain her effectiveness as a hostess, Vera Brittain, herself a frequent guest, cited as Lady Rhondda's foremost asset the fact that she was a perfect listener, always attentive, informed, and genuinely interested. Another frequent visitor, Winifred Holtby, emphasized Lady Rhondda's ability to draw people out and persuade them to share confidences. People opened up to her because she seemed truly concerned and was always well informed about her guests and their special interests.[4] Veronica Wedgwood, on the other hand, attributed Margaret's success to her insecurities. Because she was shy herself (Wedgwood believed), Lady Rhondda understood and sympathized with the socially awkward or insecure and worked doubly hard to ensure that no one was left out and that all went away feeling better about themselves.[5]

Others were less impressed by Lady Rhondda's social skills. Virginia Woolf, an occasional guest at Margaret's social engagements, often expressed amusement at the "oddities" her hostess gathered around her and disdain for what she considered the shallow conversation. She regarded Lady Rhondda as "a good able superficial woman" but was critical of her ostentation and her indecisive, tentative nature. It is not surprising that the worldly sophisticates of the Bloomsbury circle should not have found Lady Rhondda totally to their liking, given her slightly puritanical streak and her highly developed critical faculties. The Bloomsbury crowd appealed to Lady Rhondda because of their provocative literary works, their self-assurance, and their "liberated" life styles, but the more contact she had with them, the less enthusiastic she became. She could never accept their more blatant affectations or their narcissistic tendencies.[6] She was welcome on the fringes of Bloomsbury, but she was never really inducted into the inner sanctums.

Despite her widespread reputation as businesswoman and social hostess, little is known about the private Lady Rhondda. Although she was frequently interviewed by prominent commentators and journalists, she remained unquantifiable. She graciously consented to talk with journalists—but revealed little. Carefully weighing her words and deftly parrying personal queries, she left many a frustrated reporter feeling he "only partially got her to talk."[7] While reticence was fairly typical of one of her class and upbringing, Lady Rhondda appears to have been even more reluctant to discuss her life than most people. She valued her privacy highly and jealously guarded her innermost thoughts and emotions even from her closest friends. This self-imposed isolation provided a protective buffer which separated the insecure, vulnerable Margaret from the confident, assertive viscountess.

Those who turned to her autobiographical writings for an insight into Lady Rhondda's character found themselves perplexed and a little disappointed. Hoping to find intimate confidences or scandalous gossip,[8] they discovered instead a coming-of-age tale of a slightly atypical young woman facing the challenges, uncertainties, and complexities of growing up in a transitional period. In choosing the title *This Was My World*, Lady Rhondda made it quite clear that she intended to confine her comments to the past, to formative years and influences. Writing in 1933, she chose to end her story with her entry into business in the early 1920s, depriving curious readers of the personal detail they craved. Explaining this decision, she wrote: "The me of twenty years ago is so little of me that I can talk of that creature with freedom. The me of even ten years ago is so much me that I find it difficult to say a word about her."[9] Always willing to speak out on the social, economic, political, or ethical issues of her day, Lady Rhondda was not inclined to share her private emotions on anything other than abstract principles or past occurrences. The present and the recent past were not suitable topics for public scrutiny in her view.

This selectivity results in a curiously impersonal, but still enlightening, autobiography. She began writing it as a project to fill time on long train trips, but it became an attempt to come to grips with past emotions and resentments and to understand the woman she had become better. She clearly had no intention of letting readers into the inner recesses of her mind or her soul, but only of throwing some light on the collective experience of "ordinary" Edwardian young women. Brought up with one foot in the Victorian epoch and the other in the modern age, these women faced a constant challenge to make a place for themselves in a rapidly changing world.[10]

Upper-class young women grew up in a world of limited opportunities to use their wealth or their talents at a time when the public was beginning to challenge idle lifestyles and the misuse of personal resources in general. They grew up in a world obsessed with efficiency and the meaning of life, yet they had few outlets to prove their efficiency and few opportunities to find purpose in their own lives. The urban, industrial England of their experience often seemed at odds with the pastoral island of the prescribed literature and the school curriculum. Many young women sought liberation through one or more of the moving forces of the early twentieth century—suffragism, psychology, socialism.[11] Margaret, being too firmly committed to private property and individualism to be attracted to socialism and too reluctant to open her private life to scrutiny and self-analysis to be drawn to psychology, chose suffragism as the path to her liberation. She believed in the universality of her message enough to share the publishing costs of *This Was My World*, confident that she would see some, if not all, of her money back.[12]

The autobiography succeeded in portraying the internal conflicts of Lady Rhondda's generation and received rave reviews from prominent literary and political figures. Winifred Holtby, a prolific journalist, minor novelist, and close friend of Lady Rhondda, considered the book vigorous, courageous, vital, and "splendidly free from bunk." E. M. Delafield, author of the charming *Diary of a Provincial Lady*, characterized it as a signal contribution to a better understanding of the unsettling times. Virginia Woolf wrote that she liked the honesty of the book but found it lacking in subtlety. Norman Angell, prominent economist and editor of *Foreign Affairs*, counted his copy among his personal treasures, and he particularly praised her penetrating description of the wartime state of mind. Vera Brittain, whose *Testament of Youth* was recognized as a brilliant portrait of the same period, wrote that Margaret's portrayal had a special charm reminiscent of the simple, direct man-of-action poetry of the Elizabethan lyricists.[13] But the portrait left her slightly unnerved and even more uncertain about the real Lady Rhondda. Writing to Winifred Holtby, Brittain admitted that she could not help thinking "what a really charming and honest and honourable person emerged from it, and puzzling over *why* I'd never liked her and she never liked me when we have almost everything in common except, perhaps, my faculty as an artist and her business experience."[14] It often seemed that Lady Rhondda's business career made her just a bit too "common" for many of the aristocratic and artistic types. Despite her wealth and their respect for her breaking down the barriers to females, women like Vera Brittain and Virginia Woolf were sometimes bothered by her association with the actual world of big business. It is likely, too, that part of the reason that Brittain and Lady Rhondda did not always get along well was that each resented the other's influence on their mutual friend Winifred Holtby.

Today's reader would probably come away with much the same impression as Brittain did. It is indeed an illuminating portrait of the times and the formative influences on young ladies of the day. But in this as well as the later *Notes on the Way* (1937) – a series of reflections on human nature, social institutions, political values, people, and books – there is an amazing lack of personal candor. Lady Rhondda writes with passionate intensity about the abstract values of justice, truth, equality, democracy, and peace. Female education, barriers to advancement, individual or national complacency, and social or political repression draw her fire. Public issues are generally treated with clarity and keen analysis, but only in her occasional digressions does one glimpse the true depths of her emotions and her intellect. There she lets the reader inside her mind briefly, and readers then and now are left with the impression that they have been allowed just to skim the surface. Lady Rhondda had a broad-ranging mind, comfortable in generalizing about a wide variety of issues, able to synthesize masses of information quickly and clearly, but uncomfortable with specifics and occasionally blind to inconsistencies. She often tended to blur arguments, to oversimplify difficult issues, to look for easy answers. Many of her pronouncements on economic and political issues seem almost trite, but her analysis of women's issues is clear and penetrating – an indication that Lady Rhondda applied her analytical power only selectively, to those issues which deeply touched her. Through all her writings the private Lady Rhondda remains safely hidden behind the formidable public image.

Yet the glimpses she does provide throw a good deal of light on the nature of her experiences, and it is possible at least partially to strip away the veil of privacy through use of supporting archival materials, particularly surviving letters to some of her closest friends. On first consideration it appears that there were actually two Margarets — one public, one private — constantly at war with each other. On the one hand is the shy, timid, reserved woman, happiest on her country estate with a few intimate friends and clearly bound by the conventions of her past and by her own romantic and idealistic tendencies. On the other is the confident, assertive career woman, restless away from the city's center of power for any length of time and influenced by the practical, utilitarian values of the business world. Closer examination reveals one Margaret, a woman struggling with the complex strands of her character and of the times in which she lived.

From reading her letters one can see that Margaret was often uncomfortable with her public image and had to work hard to maintain a balance between the public perceptions and the private realities of her life. She regarded herself as ordinary and had trouble reconciling her desire for privacy with her ambitions and her pride in her increasing notoriety. The private Margaret found it difficult to assert herself for her own ends, but the public Margaret could demand for women, the underprivileged, and the oppressed the respect and consideration that she was uncomfortable demanding for herself. The public Margaret was known as a passionate crusader, while the private woman could scarcely express her emotions.

The strong public persona actually camouflaged a deep shyness and an emotional reserve that served as a protective barrier that few breached. Her reserve was not debilitating, but it was sometimes limiting. It frequently caused her to avoid intimate contact and to adopt a cavalier attitude that was easily misconstrued as arrogance, coldness, or impatience. Widely read, widely traveled, and genuinely sympathetic, she could carry on an effective conversation with the match lady outside her office or with heads of state, but she often worried later if she had said the right thing or, more important, whether she had unwittingly offended anyone. She longed desperately for the approval of those close to her.

The pressure of a busy professional life, an active social calendar, and her personal insecurities manifested itself in both emotional and physical forms. While normally a very controlled person, Lady Rhondda was prey to bouts of moodiness and sullenness that were intense but generally short-lived. She usually kept her anger and frustration turned inward, but suffered from occasional outbursts of temper followed by intense guilt and shame.[15] Periodically the pressures contributed to bouts of depression, illness, and enforced rest cures that belie the public reputation of a hardened, self-assured woman in total control of her life. The nature of Margaret's illnesses ranged from specific cases of influenza and pneumonia to more generalized diagnoses of exhaustion, a delicate nervous system, and unspecified back and gynecological problems. Some of these illnesses were undoubtedly caused by viral infections or other medical phenomena, but it is obvious that others were simply the result of overextension and the internal tensions typical of high achievers among Edwardian women.[16] Margaret's physicians frequently ordered rest cures in the form of extended vacations or short-term stays in convalescent homes.

This is not to suggest that she was in any sense a hysterical hypochondriac or a depressed invalid. For the most part she was a vital, active woman who engaged in six-mile walks across the Kentish moors, enjoyed swimming and skiing, and occasionally climbed mountains. But she worked and worried herself into exhaustion on occasion and needed time and peace to let down the public mask and seek physical and emotional renewal.

Those few who were allowed to see behind the public facade and enter into the tight inner circle of friends discovered a sensitive soul, a loyal but not uncritical supporter, and a sympathetic confidante. Lady Rhondda kept in close contact with school chums and family members throughout her life, and she had a fairly wide circle of acquaintances and a significant number of close friends, both male and female. Because she was an only child and a divorcee, these relationships were a critical source of emotional support and acceptance of her chosen life style. And because she was at the center of a network of richly rewarding relationships, she could never be mistaken for the lonely, embittered spinster or the hardened, emasculating professional female of Victorian folklore.

In choosing male friends, Lady Rhondda seems to have been drawn primarily to men of intellect, creativity, and influence. Her male acquaintances were most often representatives of the worlds of politics, literature, and journalism. Among her frequent houseguests were rising political figures like Sir Charles Peake, Richard Law (later Lord Coleraine), and Herbert Morrison. The diaries of her companion, Theodora Bosanquet, are filled with references to visits by these three. They shared a strong camaraderie with Lady Rhondda and engaged in lively political discussions lasting into the early morning hours. Lady Rhondda relished the idea of pitting her mind and her political knowledge against these insiders and gleaning information from them. Her circle of friends also included established men of letters, most notably G. K. Chesterton and George Bernard Shaw, who once wrote that she was one of his "most valued friends."[17] The few letters in the Shaw collection indicate a healthy respect and a willingness to criticize on both sides. Lady Rhondda clearly admired these strong, creative, and influential men and enjoyed their company, but existing records cast little light on the personal dimension of these male friendships.

What is apparent from the records is that most of Margaret's closest friends were women and that she found in them a level of commitment and support that she had been unable to find in her marriage or her other relationships with males. Strong, influential women like Winifred Cullis, eminent educator and physiologist, and Ellen Wilkinson, prominent socialist member of Parliament and cabinet minister, were frequent guests and sources of intellectual stimulation and emotional support for more than thirty years, while a younger generation of feminists like Winifred Holtby looked to Lady Rhondda for guidance and encouragement.

This close association with females, combined with her failed marriage to Humphrey Mackworth and her intense privacy about personal affairs, led to frequent hints of lesbianism,[18] but the scarcity of private papers makes it difficult to determine the nature of Lady Rhondda's private relationships. She certainly shared a very close and special relationship with at least three women: Winifred Holtby, promising journalist, feminist, and minor novelist; Helen Archdale, female activist and first editor of *Time and Tide;* and Theodora Bosanquet, a prominent spokeswoman for the British Federation of University Women, former secretary to Henry James, and one-time literary editor of *Time and Tide*. All three of these relationships originated as political alliances based on mutual commitments to the feminist struggle; they developed into long-term, supportive, affectionate relationships. Lady Rhondda deliberately chose to seek personal fulfillment within the community of women, and she found in her companions a level of intimacy and satisfaction lacking in the relationships with the men in her life.

While these special friendships were undoubtedly very intimate emotionally, it is unclear whether or not there was a corresponding sexual intimacy. The difficulty in determining the limits of relationships between these women lies in part in the lack of sources and in part in the public perception of friendships between women during the interwar years. As late as the 1890s, very close emotional bonds between women were generally regarded as perfectly "normal," innocent (asexual), and acceptable. But as twentieth-century physicians, psychologists, and sexologists began to reinterpret women's sexuality – particularly when they acknowledged the female sex drive – such relationships came under close scrutiny. New definitions of normality and abnormality were developed, and same-sex relationships were tainted and labeled deviant.[19] Lesbianism was acknowledged but seldom discussed in polite society. Many feminists deliberately shied away from any overt association with lesbianism in order not to discredit their cause.[20] Undoubtedly Lady Rhondda's experiences would at least qualify as what Lillian Faderman has classified as "romantic friendships" – loving, nurturing relationships between women who deliberately remain sexually and emotionally independent of men, but which do not necessarily involve physical sexuality.[21] A number of modern feminists would classify such a relationship as lesbian. For instance, Blanche Wiesen Cook argues, "Even if they did renounce all physical contact . . . women who love women, who choose women to nurture and support and to create a living environment in which to work creatively and independently are lesbians."[22] By that definition, Lady Rhondda's relations with these women would be classified as lesbian. Evidence indicates that she was concerned about being labeled a lesbian, but that she nonetheless chose to spend most of her adult life in the company of women. While her intense privacy and deliberate silence on sexual matters prevent a verifiable judgment, her relationships might well have been viewed as lesbian by her contemporaries. Women were central to her life both at work and at home.

Of all Lady Rhondda's relationships, the one with Winifred Holtby was probably the deepest and most intense of her life. Their eleven-year friendship began in 1924 as a professional relationship between the older, established journal owner and the promising young author. Holtby submitted an article on education for *Time and Tide* which so impressed Lady Rhondda that she hired her as a regular leader writer. Within two years, Holtby had become an indispensable member of the journal's staff and a director in Lady Rhondda's publishing company. Given the overriding importance Lady Rhondda attached to *Time and Tide*, perhaps the strongest evidence of her confidence in her young protégée is the fact that she trusted Holtby to run the journal during her frequent bouts of illness.[23]

Professional partnership quickly developed into close personal friendship as well. At their first conference the two found they had so much in common that a simple business luncheon turned into a three-hour discussion ranging over such diverse topics as marriage and family, education and religion, loyalty and fidelity, and war and peace.[24] In Winifred Holtby Lady Rhondda found a woman combining the passionate commitments and personal vitality that she found so intellectually and emotionally stimulating. Holtby's roots in rural Yorkshire reminded Lady Rhondda of her own ties to rural Wales. She thoroughly enjoyed her young companion's north country raciness and Yorkshire simplicity, qualities of a class far removed from the professional and social circles in which Lady Rhondda normally traveled.[25] More important, she valued the strength and depth of her young friend's commitments. Holtby was devoted to the causes of women's rights, peace, racial justice in South Africa, and social reform at home. While Lady Rhondda was generally less reformist and less pacifist than Holtby, their mutual commitment to feminism and their collaboration on *Time and Tide* paved the way for a deep and intense friendship.

The few extant letters between the two reveal a warmth and an openness lacking in much of Lady Rhondda's other surviving correspondence. She acknowledged that Holtby was one of the few people with whom she could share her hopes and fears and really be herself. Holtby was one of those special people who could be trusted to "do the kind of thing that makes a difference . . . and that one never forgets."[26] While much of the correspondence concerns strategies for *Time and Tide* or various feminist ventures, the writing is colored by their intimacy and by Lady Rhondda's sense of vulnerability. Letters are sprinkled with admonitions that Winifred watch her health, commiseration over failed relationships, and Lady Rhondda's hopes and fears for the journal that had assumed central importance in her life. Many of the letters carry affectionate salutations like "My dearest Winifred" and close with endearments like "Much Love." Lady Rhondda often signed her letters simply "Margaret" rather than her usual "Rhondda" or "Margaret Rhondda."

The two women vacationed together in France, and Holtby was a frequent visitor in Lady Rhondda's country home. There were rumors of a lesbian relationship between the two, but Vera Brittain, Holtby's dearest friend and frequent flatmate, vehemently denied them in her *Testament of Friendship*.[27] Still, the warmth of the correspondence, the promises of discretion in the use of Holtby's letters in Lady Rhondda's own writings,[28] and a reference to "my last love-letter"[29] in correspondence marked PRIVATE indicate a relationship built on common interests and an affection that went beyond friendship. When Holtby's health began to fail, contemporary accounts show that Lady Rhondda was genuinely concerned and committed to making her last days more pleasant. She had planned to take Holtby to Tunis to recuperate in the sunshine, but the rapid acceleration of the illness prevented that journey. Instead, Lady Rhondda could only join Holtby's parents and her other close friends in a final vigil as her dear friend lost the battle against Bright's disease.[30] Margaret was devastated by the untimely death; she had lost not only a loyal employee, but her closest confidante as well.

But the relationship was not entirely one-sided. For Holtby Lady Rhondda became a combination of friend, patron, critic, and role model, as is evident in the dedication to her collection of short stories, *Truth Is Not Sober,* published shortly before her death. The inscription reads:

For VISCOUNTESS RHONDDA
To the leader, with homage
To the editor, with gratitude
To the friend, with love.

Their relationship could also be less than idyllic. Lady Rhondda's wealth, position, and fifteen years' seniority created strains and made it difficult for someone of Holtby's humble origins and sensitivity to feel completely at ease. And while Lady Rhondda could be a compassionate and supportive friend, she could also be judgmental, critical, demanding, and remote. She frequently criticized Holtby's writing, informing her that her novels were immature and her critical study of Virginia Woolf dull and confused.[31] She often intimated that her friend should give up these frivolous pursuits and concentrate on her true calling—political journalism for *Time and Tide.*[32] Lady Rhondda's one major shortcoming was that she could never understand that the journal which had become her life did not necessarily inspire the same all-consuming passion in others.

Lady Rhondda was also a jealous friend. She expected total devotion and often felt slighted over trivial incidents. She was piqued because Holtby sent St. John Ervine a copy of *Poor Caroline* before she received one, although Holtby's action was understandable considering the comments Lady Rhondda had made about her novels.[33] Yet while demanding complete devotion and primary consideration for herself, Lady

Rhondda kept her distance even in her most intimate relationships. Holtby, who was at the time probably closer to her than any other living person, found it strange "to know someone so well and so little." She reported never quite being able to overcome the awe that made her feel she should stand up when Lady Rhondda entered a room.[34]

The tensions in Lady Rhondda's relationships may have been representative of the problems facing the new class of professional women. Martha Vicinus argues that professional women were forced to imitate male values, including emotional distancing, to prove themselves in a man's world. The pressures created inflexibility and severe strains in close relationships. According to Vicinus, professional women demanded too much from themselves and from their friends. They often expected total loyalty, leaned very heavily on trusted friends—but maintained their own distance.[35] Rebecca West made a similar judgment when she wrote that Lady Rhondda "had deep affections of a number and of a degree which were the more remarkable because she often had difficulty in understanding other people's points of view. Only her capacity for love enabled her to bridge the gulfs of misapprehension that sometimes opened between her and her friends."[36]

Nowhere was this tension in her personal relationships more evident than in her often troubled friendship with the prominent British feminist and peace activist Helen Archdale. Since no direct correspondence between the two has survived, and since Lady Rhondda's autobiography closes before the beginning of the relationship, very little is known of their life together. They became acquainted through committee work during World War I and then became allies in the postwar feminist struggle, first through the WIL and later through *Time and Tide*. Archdale was an original director of the company and the journal's first editor between 1920 and 1926. Unlike the Holtby-Rhondda friendship, which bound the slightly awed junior feminist to the established suffrage leader, the Archdale-Rhondda relationship originally seems to have been more a meeting of equals drawn together by the intimacy and camaraderie of the struggle for women's rights and bound by the sense of sisterhood so vital to that fight. By the early 1920s, the two women were sharing a London flat and a country home, Stonepitts, in Kent. They admired each other's work for the cause and enjoyed each other's company, taking frequent trips and hosting "feminist weekends" at Stonepitts. The circumstances and letters to third parties indicate that these women must have been fond of each other. In letters to the American feminist Doris Stevens, Lady Rhondda admitted that she cared deeply for Archdale[37] and frequently expressed admiration for her contributions to the cause. Likewise, Archdale's letters to Stevens talk of a desire for a reconciliation with Lady Rhondda, but only if Margaret would commit herself to spending at least a fortnight with her in the United States or Canada.[38] As late as 1931, Lady Rhondda indicated that the two had reached an understanding and were no longer thinking of separating.[39]

Isolated references indicate that this friendship had romantic overtones, but it is likewise apparent that it was very troubled, fraught with tensions over personal and philosophical disagreements. Until about 1926, the relationship seems to have been very close and mutually supportive. Lady Rhondda's preoccupation with her business career perhaps kept the partnership on an even keel during those years. After 1926, however, Lady Rhondda's ascendancy within the women's movement and her increasing intervention in *Time and Tide* affairs created resentment and backbiting that spilled over from the working partnership into the private sphere. As editor of the journal, Archdale naturally resented being bypassed by contributors and advertisers who preferred to take their business or complaints directly to the proprietor. Lady Rhondda's intervention undermined Archdale's authority and hindered her work. Tensions in the workplace climaxed in 1926 when Lady Rhondda assumed the editorship of the journal herself, forcing Archdale out and reshaping the editorial policies in line with her own thinking.

The rift widened as it became increasingly apparent that serious philosophical disagreements over feminist priorities separated the two women. By 1928 Archdale was moving ever more fully into the mainstream of the international feminist and pacifist movements—at a time when Lady Rhondda was drawing back and refocusing her energies on *Time and Tide*. As Archdale became increasingly committed to her work for international feminism, she resented Lady Rhondda's unwillingness to make it her primary commitment. Archdale hinted that such an overwhelming commitment to *Time and Tide* amounted to a betrayal of the feminist cause. There may also have been an element of jealousy involved. Archdale apparently resented the time Lady Rhondda was spending on the journal, claiming that "at present *Time and Tide* is all and everything for her and I am excluded from that entirely." To her, Lady Rhondda's approach seemed too conservative and too slow.[40] She longed for a revival of the dramatic gestures reminiscent of the earlier suffrage struggle, while Lady Rhondda was leaning more toward parliamentary lobbying and educating women voters.

These philosophical disagreements drove a wedge between Lady Rhondda and Archdale professionally and personally, but it appears that the two women attempted to keep the fight private. While Lady Rhondda acknowledged that they had indeed drifted far apart, she gave no details and hastened to assure Doris Stevens that their relations were cordial and that their personal troubles would not prevent them from collaborating in feminist ventures.[41] While the two did come together again temporarily in 1929, their intimacy had been destroyed by professional and philosophical tension. They were two strong-willed women, each committed to her own vision. Their relationship continued into the early 1930s but ended with them barely on speaking terms.

The breakup of this romantic friendship after more than a decade caused Lady Rhondda a significant amount of emotional distress, which contributed to serious health problems in 1933. Recurring back and gynecological problems caused her to embark on a Mediterranean cruise to recuperate both emotionally and physically. Among her traveling companions was Theodora Bosanquet, permanent secretary for the International Federation of University Women (IFUW). Lady Rhondda characterized her as a sad but fine person, worried in herself and seeking peace and loneliness.[42] Bosanquet soon became a live-in companion for Lady Rhondda and remained her confidante until Lady Rhondda died. While probably less intense than either of her other primary relationships, the friendship with Bosanquet appears to have been the fullest and richest of the three. It was the longest lasting (twenty-five years) and was comfortably intimate instead of being intense and volatile.

Lady Rhondda and Bosanquet had become acquainted as early as 1922 through their mutual acquaintance with Winifred Cullis and their interest in the international women's rights movement. There is, however, no evidence of anything more than a passing acquaintance and no indication of any attraction. Their early contacts were limited and tense. Lady Rhondda considered Bosanquet's political position too narrow. As representative of the IFUW, Bosanquet was, not surprisingly, reluctant to endorse programs she viewed as falling outside the interests of university women.[43] For several years Lady Rhondda worked to persuade Bosanquet to support and lobby her membership for a broader commitment to an equal rights treaty as opposed to narrower programs serving just the interests of an elite group of university women.

In view of their slight—and slightly strained—acquaintance, it is clear that something happened on that trip to change the nature of their relationship drastically. Before the return voyage from Greece, the two women had already decided to live together. But no record explains this change of heart. Since the two set up housekeeping together within months and lived together without a break for the next quarter century, there is no enlightening correspondence. And though Bosanquet was a prolific diarist, a significant gap spans the years between 1930 and 1943. Since Bosanquet was so conscientiously committed to recording private emotions and activities before and after those dates, it is unlikely that she stopped writing for thirteen full years. What happened to the diaries is a mystery, and until it is solved most details of her life with Lady Rhondda will remain hidden.

Nonetheless, letters in the Winifred Holtby Papers make it clear that Lady Rhondda took great pains to have the original arrangement appear to be primarily a practical one. She expected gossip and enlisted Holtby's aid in deflecting the anticipated queries about her new living arrangements. Writing to Holtby in October 1933 from Greece (where she was vacationing with Bosanquet), Lady Rhondda confided that they had decided to live together, but they had no intention of broadcasting their decision. Holtby was, however, instructed about the proper line to take when word spread. She was to say that Lady Rhondda had been looking for a home for some time and had recently located the ideal place. Since the new home was too large for her needs, and since she and Bosanquet were now collaborating on a book about different means of influencing public opinion (a book never intended to be completed), she had persuaded Bosanquet to rent several rooms for her own use.[44] She asked Holtby to seek out suitable houses for their consideration.

Once the new home had been found, Lady Rhondda confided that while she would miss the lovely flat she had shared with Archdale, a clean break with the past was necessary if the new relationship were to work. The only explanation she offers is contained in one sentence: "I suppose the truth is," she admitted, "I do hate being alone."[45] In Theodora Bosanquet she had found a companion who would remain with her to the very end.

Over the next twenty-five years, the two shared a house in Hampstead, a country home in Surrey, and in the last years a flat overlooking Green Park. Bosanquet joined the staff of *Time and Tide* as literary editor. For a quarter of a century, she and Lady Rhondda were inseparable. Unlike the relationship with Archdale, this one appears to have been companionable, stable, and relatively free from strife. By the early 1930s, Lady Rhondda was an acknowledged leader in both the feminist and journalistic realms. Bosanquet, it appears, was content to remain in the background. While she was undoubtedly a capable and creative woman, she chose not to challenge Lady Rhondda but to maintain her independence through involvement in areas outside her companion's sphere of interest, most notably psychical research.

While the Bosanquet diaries are silent on the physical nature of this relationship, they are very informative about the two women's daily life during the last fifteen years of their cohabitation. Unfortunately, we have only Bosanquet's side of the story. The diaries paint Lady Rhondda as a generous provider, a warm companion, and a supportive friend. There are frequent expressions of appreciation for thoughtful and often unexpected gifts—a warm winter coat, a special book, or money for "something frivolous." In return, Bosanquet offered emotional support, loyalty, and companionship of mind and body. She acted as secretarial assistant, trusted confidante, and later as spiritual adviser and nurse. Her reflections portray a life of genuine affection. They shared simple pleasures—taking long walks in the Welsh countryside, cutting flowers from the garden they lovingly tended, and playing chess before the blazing fireplace. Both women loved good literature and stimulating conversation. They led an active social life filled with theater engagements, luncheons at their clubs, and frequent entertaining. Their relations seem to have been characterized by a special sensitivity and a certain peacefulness. Each respected the other's privacy and allowed her freedom and space to work through her problems—alone if she wished, but always within reach if needed. With Bosanquet Lady Rhondda could share all her hopes and dreams and unburden herself of many worries. With her she could show the vulnerability, the anger, and the frustration she tried to hide from professional colleagues. Over the years Bosanquet became increasingly protective of Lady Rhondda, conspiring with doctors behind her back to arrange much-needed rest cures, keeping minor office problems from her, and supporting her through financial and health crises. Bosanquet once wrote: "The difference between this flat without her [Margaret] and with her is the difference between a pool of 'static' water and a lake with a stream running through it."[46] Lady Rhondda very likely would have said the same of her companion.

All the closest and most important of Lady Rhondda's adult relationships were woman-centered, but it is also apparent that her commitment to women was less a rejection of men than a positive affirmation of women's strength and character. Her relationships with other women grew out of a common commitment to the feminist struggle and the natural camaraderie of women acting together in that movement. These affectionate romantic friendships sustained her through many difficult times and enabled her to continue her personal growth and her broader fight for personhood for the female sex. Through the women in her life Lady Rhondda found not only a great deal of personal satisfaction but a reaffirmation of her central belief in the community of women and the possibilities it offered for personal growth and for the improvement of society.

7 · PUBLISHER AND EDITOR

Despite her role as a militant suffragette, her success in the masculine realm of business, and her active participation in various British and international feminist societies, it is fitting that Lady Rhondda is best known today as founder and editor of the weekly *Time and Tide*. She saw the review as her unique contribution to the feminist movement, considering it her own instrument for breaking down barriers to female equality and for shaping the world into a better, more humane society. Over the years *Time and Tide* became increasingly important to Lady Rhondda. It drained away her fortune and her strength but infused her with a sense of dignity, purpose, and satisfaction which no amount of wealth, recognition, or social prominence had been able to provide. The journal became her life. As Anthony Lejeune, the last deputy editor, wrote: *"Time and Tide* was the twelve children . . . she would have liked, the seat in the House of Lords she tried to claim."[1] It was and remains the childless woman's legacy to a new generation of feminists.

The establishment of *Time and Tide* as a feminist forum in 1920 was for Lady Rhondda the fulfillment of a childhood fantasy. As a youngster, she had dreamed of editing her own magazine and had produced a "slightly irregular" one called *The Shooting Star* before she left for boarding school.[2] The experience fed her desire to publish a periodical which would reach a wider audience. Lady Rhondda reports that she knew she wanted to edit a weekly review by the time she was in her early twenties, but she did not actually begin the project until she was thirty-seven. Through her rise in the commercial world and her fight for a parliamentary platform, the desire to edit had always remained. At the first opportunity, she seized the chance.

Her decision to concentrate on a weekly review grew from her dissatisfaction with the daily press's coverage of the militant suffragette campaign and her desire to be at the center of controversy, molding and shaping the opinions of more prominent members of the public. Though they had a relatively small circulation, the weeklies were read by a select audience, which Lady Rhondda called the "keystone public"–the ministers, journalists, lawyers, teachers, politicians, and businessmen who exerted influence over the masses.[3] Further, she believed that a weekly review, whose contributors had "time to pause and think, to sum up, to eliminate the unessential, to achieve a proportioned whole, to give something of a considered opinion,"[4] would necessarily have a better perspective and more influence. The review of her dreams would be a platform for reaching thinking individuals, publicizing the issues she regarded as most important, and changing attitudes. Lady Rhondda wrote that she wanted passionately, urgently to alter customs, to influence ideas, and to have "the chance of reaching out to the people likeminded with oneself, who would understand what one was trying to say. That way I could find the people who were worth hearing, and see that they were heard, if not by the big multitude at least by the inner group–the keystone public who ultimately directed the multitude. I could put before the public that mattered the things I wanted them to hear."[5] A first-class weekly would allow her to mold opinions and promote social and legal changes and a world more in tune with her philosophy.

The first step toward achieving this goal was taken in 1920 when Lady Rhondda conferred with Lord Camrose about the feasibility of such an enterprise. The publishing magnate strongly advised against the risky venture, warning her that the appeal of a weekly review, particularly one with a feminist orientation, was limited and that it would be a slow and expensive struggle to gain advertisers, subscribers, and credibility.[6] But Lady Rhondda was always one for a challenge, and the negative response served only to stiffen her resolve. Since she was a wealthy woman, money was no issue. Time was. As she was already heavily involved in various business, feminist, and social commitments, and was preparing to contest her exclusion from the House of Lords, she was extended to the limits. For her to edit a weekly review herself was out of the question.

Yet the need for a review which would give primacy to the female viewpoint and educate women in the rights and responsibilities of citizenship was so pressing that a longer delay appeared unjustified. She founded and financed *Time and Tide* but was forced to allow others of like mind–friends from the suffragette struggle–the editorial responsibility during the first six years of its existence. Nominally owned by a limited liability company (Time and Tide Publishing Company) incorporated in May 1920 with £20,000 capital, the journal was from the beginning heavily subsidized by Lady Rhondda. She controlled 90 percent of the company's shares and served as vice chairman of the board

of directors (later as chairman and editor as well) and was in effect sole
controller of the review for most of its existence.[7] It was she who decided that it would be a journal modeled after the prestigious *New
Statesman* but directed and staffed by women only and owing no alle-
giance to any particular party. As long as it was independent of party
squabbles, it would be free to attack injustice in any form, to demand
government accountability, and to present the widest possible array of
arguments.[8]

The all-female board of directors fully concurred in Lady Rhondda's
decision. The board, composed of Alexandra Chalmers-Watson (chairman and former director of the WRAF), Lady Rhondda, Helen Archdale
(the first editor), Dame Helen Gwynne-Vaughan (a prominent botanist),
Mrs. H. B. Irving, Christine Maguire (organizer of the Women's Clerks
and Secretaries Association), and Elizabeth Robins (a distinguished
author), shared a strong conviction that the female perspective on major
issues of the day was too valuable to go unheard and unheeded. Its
members also believed that, if the public were better informed, the validity of the woman's view would be quickly recognized. With the support
of such prominent women as Jean Lyon of *Punch* and the novelists Rebecca West, E. M. Delafield, and Cicely Hamilton, these women embarked on a unique venture—a woman's magazine of a very different
type. Instead of the typical emphasis on fashion and household affairs
designed to appeal to woman as consumer, *Time and Tide* would stress
general political, social, and literary interests appealing to woman as
citizen.[9] The odds were heavily against success, but the commitment
and dedication of these women carried the periodical through its first
trying years.

The first issue of the journal appeared on 14 May 1920 with the motto
"Time and Tide . . . wait for no man." The cover featured Big Ben with
the tide flowing under Westminster Bridge, clear indication that the
new review would have a political orientation. The editorial statement
made it apparent that the journal would be distinctly feminist in flavor
as well. Convinced that the world was on the verge of a new era and
that existing press enterprises were too tied to their Victorian and Edwardian past to realize or fully interpret the changed conditions, *Time
and Tide*'s promoters saw a need for a more independent press which
would recognize the new role of women in society and would treat
women and the issues dear to them as worthy of a fair hearing.[10] In the
pages of *Time and Tide*, women could take part in the political, social,
and ethical debates of the day, evaluate present policies, and suggest

new ones more in line with their needs and perceptions.[11] The journal
would be a feminist forum and would range over the whole spectrum
of human interests in the arts, politics, and industry. Here newly en-
franchised women could use their minds and their new-found influence in an attempt to raise society's consciousness.

From the beginning Lady Rhondda kept her finger on the pulse of
the weekly review she had founded, though other professional commitments prevented her from assuming the editorship. For the first six
years she played many different roles in the journal's production. She
assumed responsibility for the political side of the review, ensuring the
strict adherence to the nonparty principle that would leave the weekly
free to judge tested policies by their results and projected ones on principle. She pitched in to fill any vacancies, serving at various times as
financial consultant, book reviewer, drama critic, and leader writer.[12]
She also spent considerable time searching out new talent and appears
to have had final responsibility for approving contributors.[13] But as long
as she had other commitments, and as long as the journal followed her
interests, she was generally content not to interfere in day-to-day editorial
details.

During Helen Archdale's six-year tenure as editor, the tone of *Time
and Tide* was strongly feminist and slightly left-wing. The review was
conceived when women appeared to be on the threshold of achieving
some political power after years of exclusion, and political organization
and pressure had the highest priority in its first years. Editorial statements and leading articles seldom missed the opportunity to set forth
a feminist position on any issue that arose. The first volume carried perceptive comments on the plight of women workers, a none-too-generous
assessment of male parliamentarians' recent performances, and a critical
exegesis of the pending Bastardry Bill. Also included were brief profiles
of the prominent novelist Elizabeth Robins and the American women's
movement, and notices of upcoming events and meetings of interest to
women. While articles on the arts and nonfeminist political issues were
included, the primary concern was clearly feminist. Broad-ranging,
trenchant, and critical, this first issue set the pattern that *Time and Tide*
followed until the mid-1930s.

Hoping to ensure that the journal and the causes it espoused were
taken seriously, Archdale and Lady Rhondda gathered around them
some of the finest women writers and thinkers of the day. Politicians
like the conservative Lady Astor and the radical Ellen Wilkinson, novelists like Elizabeth Robins, Rebecca West, and Cicely Hamilton, the

well-known pacifist and journalist Helena Swanwick, and promising authors like Winifred Holtby and Vera Brittain all gravitated to the newly created feminist forum. Even established women of letters offered their support and contributed articles, short stories, or reviews. Among the more prominent of these were Virginia Woolf, Rose Macaulay, E. M. Delafield, and Naomi Mitchison. Influential men, too, lent their encouragement. George Bernard Shaw, G. K. Chesterton, and Gilbert Murray were perhaps the most supportive men in the early days. The inclusion of such famous people of both sexes and the tolerance of divergent opinions lent credibility to the review and prevented it from being regarded as a purely feminist propaganda organ. The review appears to have reached between twelve and fifteen thousand readers in the early 1920s.[14]

With talented writers, adequate financing, and Lady Rhondda at its helm, *Time and Tide* seemed destined to emerge as the preeminent voice of radical feminism. Among its highest priorities was the need to convince women of their own worth. Only when women took themselves seriously could others be expected to take notice of their demands. But centuries of conditioning had undermined the feminine ego and led women to acquiesce in their second-class citizenship. The habits of deferring to males and making light of women's needs and accomplishments had become so ingrained in the female population that the recently won vote seemed unlikely to achieve the type of change committed feminists hoped for. Before women could be welded into an effective political pressure group, they had to come to terms with the validity of the woman's viewpoint and the importance of the so-called women's issues. They had to wipe away the Victorian mores that prevented them from taking full advantage of the freer atmosphere and advantages of the postwar period.[15] Many of the journal's early articles were aimed at increasing women's pride in their gender by providing information about prominent women of the past and present, destroying the myths of feminine inferiority, and encouraging awareness of women's history. Through this process of consciousness-raising, the *Time and Tide* staff hoped to create a collective belief in womanhood that would translate into effective pressure against psychological, physical, and material exploitation.

Concurrent with this effort to raise women's consciousness the journal conducted an educational campaign designed to publicize continued legal, political, economic, and social discrimination and to inform women of the options available to them. Discrepancies in voting rights, pay,

employment opportunities, and educational training were ruthlessly exposed. Supposedly benevolent gender-based protective measures were
unmasked and revealed as working to women's detriment. Problems of
psychological and financial dependence, combining marriage and work,
and child rearing responsibilities were perceptively and sympathetically
discussed. The journal boldly confronted such controversial issues as
double standards for ethical behavior, birth control, marital rape, and
child assault, always with a view to stressing women's rights and responsibilities. By placing the controversies and inequalities before the public—both male and female—week after week, *Time and Tide* hoped to
sensitize people, make it more difficult to practice and accept blatant
discrimination, and encourage women to seek nontraditional options in
their professional and personal lives.

At the same time, the journal fought a campaign for parliamentary
reform and responsibility designed to remove existing legal disabilities
and to force politicians to be more cognizant of the needs and voting
power of women. *Time and Tide* spoke out unequivocally against restrictions on female voting, the exclusion of peeresses from the House of
Lords, and failure to enforce the heralded Sex Disqualification (Removal) Act. Unequal guardianship laws, marriage bars, and gender-biased
protective legislation were consistently condemned. Equality, with the
freedom of choice and the opportunity to succeed or fail it implied, became the keystone of the journal's feminist policy.

Realizing that criticism alone served little purpose, *Time and Tide*
sought to influence parliamentary decisions through exerting direct pressure and cooperating with feminist organizations like the Six Point
Group. Bills of special interest to women were carefully monitored and
critiqued, along with the voting records of members of Parliament. The
Six Point Group's Black and White Lists were printed, individual parliamentarians were praised or vilified, and inconsistencies between words
and actions were highlighted. The journal acted as a watchdog for women's
interests, always vigilant, alert to possible danger. Private members' bills,
the impending reform of the House of Lords, and the appointment of
boards and committees to investigate allegations of sexual inequality were
denounced as worthless ploys to divert attention from the pressing issues.
Women were encouraged to hold individual members of Parliament and
the party in power responsible for the continuing plight of womankind
and to vote for and support female candidates and parliamentarians.
They were advised to demand an end to talk and to insist on action.
The optimistic belief that it spoke for the majority of women and that

the potential of women would be shortly recognized pervaded the pages of *Time and Tide* during its first six years. While such confidence may appear unfounded and even naive today, one must remember that the suffrage victory was still recent and that old barriers were rapidly falling. Publicity, common sense, and political pressure were expected to erode the vestiges of gender inequality.

Women's issues dominated the early volumes, but other concerns received adequate coverage as well. Questions ranging from education, housing, and employment to public health, poverty, and physical fitness were discussed from the feminist perspective, as were issues of disarmament and peace. Contemporary trends in literature, the theater, and the arts received considerable attention, and correspondence columns were open to debate on almost any issue. Economic trends were followed, and financial advice was given. But as long as women were denied equal voting privileges, feminist concerns remained at the core of *Time and Tide*'s editorial philosophy and dominated its pages. By the mid-1920s, the journal had been recognized as a "highly rational and intelligent feminist periodical"[16] and had become one of the major organs of feminist thought. The feminist platform it espoused in the 1920s would fit surprisingly well in today's debates.[17]

Yet Lady Rhondda was not content for her journal to be seen primarily as a platform for feminism. She had always envisioned a respectable, influential weekly review which would deserve the unstinting confidence of all its readers, male and female. As a businesswoman she was also concerned about the journal's financial difficulties in its early years. As long as *Time and Tide* needed a sizable subsidy (between £5,000 and £10,000 per year in the early days; approximately £250,000 in her lifetime)[18] to exist, it could not be considered a complete success. As Helen Archdale became increasingly committed to her international feminist responsibilities and leaned more toward pacifist and socialist principles, editor and proprietor began to differ. Lady Rhondda decided to take the reins into her hands and put her stamp on the journal that she already considered her most important contribution to a more humane and just world.

By the mid-1920s Lady Rhondda had matured into a strong woman who knew what she wanted and longed only for the time to accomplish her goals. In the autumn of 1926, with her business reputation secured by her election as president of the Institute of Directors and the struggle for equal franchise well under way, Lady Rhondda finally felt free to devote herself to *Time and Tide*. She took over the editorship, a position she retained until her death, and began the long struggle to put the journal on a sound financial footing and establish it as one of Britain's leading weekly reviews.

In assuming the editorship Lady Rhondda had embarked on the most difficult and most rewarding task of her life. James Drawbell, editor of the *Sunday Chronicle,* summed up the editorial challenge effectively, stating: "There is no mumbo-jumbo about editing. It is not done by mirrors. It is a solid grind, inspired by flair and an egoistic belief in yourself, a standing up for what you believe to be right, a constant and unremitting infliction of your personality and your beliefs on your public."[19] Judging by that standard, Lady Rhondda was an effective editor. Her personality, commitment, and principles gave *Time and Tide* a distinctive character. Owning the paper gave her total freedom to champion the ideals in which she believed. She worked tirelessly to build a reputable journal when others in her position might have rested on their laurels and left the hard work to others. If dedication, money, and diligence could ensure success, the future of *Time and Tide* was secure.

From the outset Lady Rhondda took her editorial responsibility very seriously and made the journal her primary commitment. To her friend Doris Stevens she wrote that all the money, thought, and energy she had was going into *Time and Tide.* "If T & T is to succeed," she confided, "I've got to give it all I have & am for the next two or three years & — rightly or wrongly — that's what I mean to do."[20] She poured money into the enterprise, often at the risk of injuring her other financial holdings, determined to make the journal pay. As with her commercial career, money was never that important to Lady Rhondda; influence was. She wanted the review to prosper not because of the profits it would bring but because of the wide readership and credibility financial success would imply.

Lady Rhondda had always been heavily involved in the political side of the review, and she now took a more active part in shaping policy. In weekly meetings with key staff members, issues were discussed and possible responses were debated, but Lady Rhondda's position generally prevailed.[21] Veronica Wedgwood, a prominent historian and a director of *Time and Tide* in the final years, noted that to the very end, Lady Rhondda "shaped the editorial comment of the paper with meticulous care and insight."[22] She rejected or accepted all articles submitted (or delegated someone to do it in her absence) and carefully perused every issue to be sure that each volume maintained a high quality, a thoughtful and stimulating perspective, and a liberal and humane vision.[23]

In addition to forming policy and passing judgment on the finished product, Lady Rhondda continued to contribute articles and reviews and zealously worked to advance the journal's interests at every turn. She frequently traveled to Paris and New York to promote the journal and seek foreign correspondents. Contacts in all walks of life and in various countries, most notably France and the United States, were exploited for contributions, consultation and discussion, verification of information, and introductions to potential contributors, subscribers, and prominent individuals. For instance, Doris Stevens was asked to sound out the American author Willa Cather, and Marie Meloney, an American journalist and the editor of the *New York Herald Tribune Sunday Magazine,* was quizzed about American perceptions of British policies.[24] Ellen Wilkinson kept Lady Rhondda informed about parliamentary proceedings, and Pierre Camert (head of the Quay d'Orsay Press Bureau) arranged an interview with the former French premier Pierre Laval in April 1938.[25] The viscountess's broad contacts in politics, industry, journalism, and the arts ensured that *Time and Tide* would remain up-to-date, perceptive, and provocative.

Lady Rhondda increasingly wooed both new and established talent for the journal. Perhaps the greatest strength of *Time and Tide* was its variety of contributors. In filling staff positions, Lady Rhondda sought individuals of like mind (women only until the mid-1930s), but her journal was intended to be a forum for open discussion. Contributors were courted for the selling value of their names, for their ideas, and sometimes for their opposing viewpoints. To attract a wide audience for her views, Lady Rhondda originally attempted to lure major authors without regard to their philosophies. Her chief confidante and editorial assistant, Winifred Holtby, recorded just weeks after Lady Rhondda assumed control that the new editor intended to "aim high, and try to put salt on the tails of all the best men and women writers—from Shaw downwards."[26]

Appealing to Bernard Shaw was no particular problem. He was already an ardent supporter who had contributed occasional articles since 1923, seldom accepting payment. When he was too busy to write he sent "hasty scribbles" that someone on the staff could "fake an interview out of." His articles and letters attracted a wide readership, and Lady Rhondda was not above exploiting her friendship with Shaw for the benefit of her journal, always mindful that even the mention of his name had a significant effect on sales. Phyllis Bentley was wooed because it was "useful to be on good terms with these best-sellers." Even though

Wyndham Lewis bored her, his contributions were welcomed because he had a significant following, and one nameless major author could be as irritating and exasperating as he chose as long as he continued to be worth hundreds of readers a week.[27]

As the journal grew in prominence, literary giants like Bernard Shaw and H. G. Wells shared space with Rebecca West and Virginia Woolf, the economist Norman Angell, and the dramatist Sean O'Casey. Prominent literary figures occasionally contacted the review first, the most notable example being Ezra Pound, who wrote petulantly: "T and T appears to have printed nearly everyone ELSE."[28] Having an article published in *Time and Tide* was apparently becoming a badge of distinction by the early 1930s.

The costs of relying exclusively on such major figures would have been considerably more than a struggling young weekly review could possibly bear. George Bernard Shaw once advised James Drawbell, then striving to turn *John Bull* into a respectable periodical, that: "Instead of falling back on the established celebrities, your magazine should be discovering and exploiting the young talent of the country."[29] This sentiment was one that Lady Rhondda wholeheartedly shared from the beginning of her editorship. *Time and Tide* offered a place for promising young writers to exhibit their skills and test their public appeal. The articles they submitted would be given fair treatment according to their merits. Winifred Holtby and Vera Brittain received encouragement and support from the journal early in their careers. E. M. Delafield's *Diary of a Provincial Lady* was originally printed as a weekly feature, and Stella Benson's delightful short stories were also welcomed. Stephen Spender, W. H. Auden, and Christopher Isherwood displayed their early efforts as well. Many of these young or unknown authors, grateful for *Time and Tide*'s support, remained loyal contributors even after becoming established.

Lady Rhondda also attempted to broaden the scope of her journal by printing the opinions of foreign correspondents. Always an opponent of insulation and complacency, she wrote: "It is never wise to neglect opportunities of seeing ourselves as others see us and it is as well that we should know how the English mind strikes foreign observers."[30] A monthly supplement entitled "A View from America," written by the noted journalist Walter Lippmann, began in 1932, and from time to time articles from the foreign press which were deemed particularly perceptive or relevant were reprinted.

By gathering varied personalities around her, Lady Rhondda necessarily developed a fairly open policy. She claimed that a weekly review should function as a salon where writers and thinkers were free to ponder and reflect on the issues which most concerned them, and she believed the best strategy was to choose honest, vital, readable authors, give them free rein, and trust readers to draw their own conclusions.[31] The "Notes on the Way" section, inaugurated in the 7 June 1929 issue, especially allowed "brilliant misfits" to be heard, ensured a high quality of thought, and provoked spirited controversy.[32] The journal was, however, always careful to point out that the views in "Notes" did not necessarily coincide with editorial policy, and particularly exasperating authors were often singled out for editorial censure.[33] Writers were free to say anything they wished; but the editor was also free to express her opinions of their contributions.

Despite this free pen policy, Lady Rhondda sometimes rejected contributors because of their political sympathies, writing confidentially to her assistant Winifred Holtby that Konni Zilliakus, a League of Nations official (and later a Labour member of Parliament), should be used only sparingly because he was "a shade naive . . . and too frankly Labour."[34] She refused her deputy editor Anthony Lejeune permission to commission articles from Peregrine Worsthorne because she felt he was dangerously left-wing. Worsthorne had criticized Franklin D. Roosevelt, one of Lady Rhondda's personal favorites.[35] To Gordon Catlin, who had contacted her about an article on "Insulation and Internationalism," Margaret replied, "We are not in sufficiently close agreement for that to be possible."[36] This reluctance to commission articles from authors with socialist tendencies became increasingly apparent as Lady Rhondda's political sympathies shifted toward the conservative side after the Second World War. To those who were commissioned, however, the promise of unedited liberty was a welcome, if slightly frightening, prospect — welcome because they could freely express themselves without fear, frightening because responsibility was placed squarely on the contributor.

Freedom of written expression did not extend to staff members. Totally committed to the journal herself, Lady Rhondda expected the same devotion from others. "Those of us who are the *Time and Tide* type," she wrote, "should care for the paper more than we do for ourselves and should work for the creation and maintenance of something we know to be more important than we are."[37] She was, for example, accustomed to spending at least fourteen hours a day at her job, and she had difficulty understanding that her staff members had other interests and re-

sponsibilities. When Winifred Holtby took time off to write novels, or
Veronica Wedgwood placed the study of history first, or Patrick Thompson started his Securities Investment Service, Lady Rhondda's major
concern was that the paper would suffer.[38] She also demanded complete
devotion to the journal's policies. Staff members were, of course, not
expected to endorse every detail, but they were expected to support the
general principles. Employees not in harmony with the review's essential premises were encouraged to resign. In 1936, after a disagreement
over the extension of sanctions against Italy, Phoebe Gaye, assistant editor for four years, tendered her resignation. Even then Gaye was given
space to express her views and explain why she thought *Time and Tide*'s
policy too fainthearted.[39] Other disgruntled former employees sought
different forums in which to air their grievances. Sir John Betjeman,
the journal's literary editor in the mid-1950s (who was guilty of trying
to turn *Time and Tide* into a strictly literary review), described his termination in a caustic poem entitled "Caprice."[40]

Staff members and contributors generally, however, found Lady Rhondda
something of a benevolent tyrant to work for. Norman Angell found her
a kindly, if demanding, editor, while Malcolm Muggeridge thought
her generous but slightly menacing. Relating her story of the *Lusitania*
incident, in which she stared down a man who tried to grab the end
of a board she was clinging to, he wrote that he understood why the
man turned away. "Working for *Time and Tide*," he confessed, "was
rather like holding onto a spar with Lady Rhondda at the other end."
Yet he also admitted that *Time and Tide* was "a Salvation Army shelter . . . for destitute ideologues" where down-and-out authors found sanc-
tuary and succor. Holtby recorded that she loved the feeling of doing
worthwhile work and believed that Lady Rhondda's intensity and expectations brought out the best in her, while Shaw believed that she
had remarkable qualities as an editor but sometimes suffered from too
tender a conscience.[41] Staff and contributors who wished to satisfy
Lady Rhondda had to perform at a consistently high level.

Under Lady Rhondda's editorship, *Time and Tide* increased its readership and reputation so much that, according to Kingsley Martin, editor
of the *New Statesman and Nation,* it made a strong run at becoming
the leading weekly review in Great Britain in the 1930s.[42] But trying
to estimate the journal's influence poses problems. Any attempt to measure public opinion involves much guesswork, and in the case of *Time
and Tide*, the problems are compounded by the absence of subscription
lists and records. It is possible, however, to get some idea of the jour-

nal's readership and the esteem in which it was held by looking at the letters to the editor and various comments in the correspondence, diaries, and autobiographies of prominent individuals. The type of person who writes letters to the editor or is prominent enough to have writings published is not the average reader. But it is generally accepted that weekly reviews appeal to a more discriminating and better educated reader looking for a thoughtful and provocative commentary on political, social, and cultural developments. This audience differs from the average reader of a daily paper, and those who had letters or articles published in *Time and Tide* were probably closer to the journal's average reader than to the man or woman in the street.

Time and Tide frequently advertised for the right type of audience— "people who enjoy intelligent, detached comment on current political events, good literary articles, and critical and discriminating reading."[43] A survey of the letters to the editor in the 1920s and 1930s indicates that those discriminating readers came primarily from the realms of politics, the arts, and the professions. Politicians of all parties read the journal and often expressed their appreciation of its candor and comprehensiveness. Among the prominent political figures carrying on periodic correspondence with the editor were Lord Cecil, Robert Vansittart, Hugh Dalton, Richard Law, and Lord Balfour of Burleigh. The journal was read at the palace, in the prominent clubs, and in the halls of the Commons. It is said that at the height of the Suez Crisis in 1956, when the speaker of the House of Commons, Herbert Morrison, had to suspend the session until the uproar died down, he retired to his quarters with *Time and Tide* for company. Sir James Grigg, Churchill's secretary of war, reportedly told Ellen Wilkinson that *Time and Tide* was "the only weekly," and Prime Minister Clement Attlee expressed his appreciation of the journal in a private conversation with her.[44]

The arts were represented by correspondents including George Bernard Shaw, H. G. Wells, George Orwell, Dorothy Sayers, and Leonard Woolf. The composer Ethel Smyth, the dramatist Sean O'Casey, and the actor Noël Coward also contributed frequently. Coward privately described the journal as the "only really non-partisan weekly that is intelligent . . . and right-minded."[45] Prominent scholars and educators including Harold Laski, Gilbert Murray, J. H. Huizinga, and G. D. H. Cole were joined by unnamed senior history lecturers and public school teachers. The publishers Kingsley Martin (*New Statesman and Nation*) and Ivor Thomas (*The Athenaeum*) contributed letters, as did Catholic priests, Anglican bishops, civil servants, and doctors and nurses. Dur-

ing the war years, pleas from soldiers seeking relief from the intellectual
wasteland of foxhole or barracks bunk frequently appeared in the *Time
and Tide* correspondence columns.

Correspondents appear to have shared a common commitment to knowledge, an earnest desire to comprehend varying viewpoints, and a pro-
pensity to make up their own minds after carefully sifting and weighing
the evidence. Their concerns and interests encompassed the political,
diplomatic, social, and cultural currents of the day. Educated, intelligent, and opinionated, they respected the journal's broad scope, un-
flinching honesty, and liberal commitments even though they might
sometimes violently disagree with its judgments. Moreover, they trusted
the review explicitly to provide a reasoned and accurate commentary.
G. D. H. Cole said that the tendency of the millionaire-controlled press
to tell lies should be discouraged during any peaceful transfer to socialism but stated that he would leave *Time and Tide,* along with *Saturday
Review* and the *Independent,* free to say exactly what it liked, and would
even allow it a certain degree of latitude beyond the existing limits of
the law.[46]

That *Time and Tide* was read and respected by the moving forces of
British society is undeniable. Whether the journal changed people's
thinking or reinforced previously held ideas is impossible to ascertain.
Yet the fact that prominent members of Parliament, civil servants, and
respected literary figures perused the journal's pages indicates that it
must have had some influence in helping them to clarify their own viewpoints. Since many of these readers were widely read or widely heard
commentators on British society, politics, and culture, one can assume
that the journal had an indirect influence on the shaping of British opinion. Individual readers of lesser stature often wrote about the impact
of *Time and Tide* in shaping their own perceptions. The most eloquent
expression appears in a letter by a Susan Ertz:

> In my opinion, reading a weekly review ought to be like going for a
> country walk with an inspired geologist. His knowledge should open
> up fresh worlds for us; from a pebble on a beach or a rock on a hill-
> side he should be able to make deductions far beyond our powers. He
> doesn't go out to look for scorpions, but sometimes in turning over a
> stone he will find one. Snakes, too, he will meet in his rambles. They're
> not what he's after, primarily, but if they're dangerous to life he'll know
> how to deal with them. He'll always keep a cool head and a logical
> mind, and through his eyes we can read the footprints in the sand.

As *Time and Tide* takes me for just such excursions I, among many, await each issue with eager impatience.[47]

Of course not everyone responded in this vein. Kingsley Martin noted that the journal suffered from a "too feminist" flavor to have great influence among the British populace. H. G. Wells and Sir John Betjeman poked fun at the journal and its continued association in the minds of some with the radical feminism of its early days. Wells referred to it as "Wear and Tear, the ladies' paper," and Betjeman, in his years as literary editor, changed the logo on the paper's letterhead to read "Tame and Tade . . . Wait for Women" in correspondence with his friend Clive Bell. Edith Sitwell wrote to a friend that Wyndham Lewis had taken refuge with "the old ladies of *Time and Tide*, and from the shelter of their skirts and amidst the atmosphere of lavender and old lace is yelling defiance."[48] Despite such criticism, the journal did offer perceptive commentary on matters of domestic and international policy during the interwar years and undoubtedly reached a wide and potentially influential audience.

In seeking to explain *Time and Tide*'s success Lady Rhondda credited her absolute dedication, the careful selection of staff, the high quality of the contributors, and the journal's commitment to truth rather than popularity. Once she became editor she put the paper first — before her business interests, her health, and her financial security. She had gathered around her a loyal and devoted staff, prepared to do what she asked and to fill any position necessary. In screening potential contributions, she accepted only what she deemed worthy of consideration, regardless of authorship, and tried not to be too much influenced by labels or reputations.[49] More than anything else, however, it was *Time and Tide*'s sincere and steadfast advocacy of justice, equality, and individualism that brought the journal recognition and increased its circulation.

Throughout Lady Rhondda's tenure as editor, the philosophy of *Time and Tide* remained consistent in its general principles, promoting justice, women's rights, and individualism, and steadfastly opposing all forms of tyranny at home or abroad. She insisted in a 1936 interview that she had no definite agenda as editor. If, however, she were to draw one up, it would embrace democracy, individual liberty, and peace, rejecting racism, sexism, and class prejudice.[50] She elaborated on these basic considerations in an article entitled "The World As I Want It." The ideal world, as she saw it, was one free from war and the fear of war. She did not envision a wholly idealistic, utopian world but one which had made a conscious and practical decision "that it would rather keep itself in order than commit suicide." She wanted a world with sufficient food, adequate housing, and equal political and economic opportunity so that all individuals would be set free to develop their own talents and find their own happiness. Her ultimate hope was that every individual, regardless of sex, race, or class, would be accorded the respect and dignity that a human being deserved.[51] Throughout the journal's life the basic pledge to democratic and responsible government, assertive leadership, and opposition to tyranny remained constant. Lady Rhondda shaped *Time and Tide* to her wishes and controlled it absolutely, turning it into a liberal and reformist, rather than a strictly feminist periodical.

But *Time and Tide* did not by any means abandon the feminist cause when Lady Rhondda became editor. Until equal franchise was won in 1928, women's issues remained foremost in the editor's concerns, and she saw her total commitment to the journal as the best thing she could possibly do for the cause of women's equality. Since there had never been a serious weekly run by females, success in this venture, she contended, would be analogous to women's entry into medicine and education and would force open yet another closed door. At the same time, the journal was sending out weekly signals of "implicit and explicit feminism"[52] to an audience of intelligent activists who could be expected to sympathize and to help in the ongoing struggle. Under Lady Rhondda's guidance the paper continued to press for equal franchise, international cooperation, admission of peeresses to the House of Lords, and the removal of all sex-based barriers to advancement. With the franchise victory in 1928, however, Margaret felt free to shift the journal's emphasis to "the real task of feminism." The task now, she believed, was to "wipe out the overemphasis on sex that is the fruit of the age-long subjection of women. The individual must stand out without trappings as a human being."[53] This decision was a reflection of the general postfranchise optimism that invaded the broader feminist movement. Many activists believed that since equal franchise had been granted, future efforts should be concentrated on emphasizing the common humanity of men and women and their joint role as responsible citizens.[54]

For *Time and Tide* to play an effective role in the broader fight for human equality, its feminist label had to be removed. Lady Rhondda began deliberately to distance the journal from specifically feminist causes and to turn it into a broader review of politics, arts, and society.

Over the years she worked to balance male and female staff and contributors, writing to Vera Brittain that an excellent article she had submitted could not be used in the requested issue. Since a woman was writing the "Notes" that week, she explained, a man's name was needed to balance the issue.[55] She later confided to Virginia Woolf that each week she went through the entire journal, deleting references to women's names and special interests. While this practice was regrettable and even maddening, failure to do so, she believed, "would soon kill the paper."[56]

Such policies brought Margaret into conflict with old friends from the suffragette days. Ardent feminists, then and now, regarded the removal of their platform as a betrayal. Monica Whateley, secretary of the Six Point Group in the late 1930s, wrote a very critical letter charging that *Time and Tide*'s failure to give full coverage to the League of Nations' "Status of Women" report was a rejection of the original commitments that had made the journal a success. Lady Rhondda replied that *Time and Tide* had no desire to perpetuate the idea of women as a separate class but chose instead to present men and women working together on equal terms for the general good, hoping that someday such a picture would be regarded as natural and arouse no comment.[57]

Today's feminists, too, have expressed disappointment over the journal's changing tone. Dale Spender, a leading Australian feminist and author, wrote that the almost imperceptible drift of *Time and Tide* toward a "'safer,' more sober, and in establishment terms 'more suitable' weekly review for women is for me a matter of regret."[58] For Lady Rhondda, however, it was the best means of establishing the legitimacy her journal must have if her platform were ever to reach a wide audience and escape the female/marginal category.

While Lady Rhondda did begin to dilute the pure feminism of the review, she did not abandon the causes that feminists of different persuasions held dear. If anything, the journal's political commentary became more focused and its criticism of the existing power structure more trenchant in the 1930s. And while the explicit feminist tag was removed, the implicit understanding that educated female (and male) voters should pursue justice, social reform, and international peace remained. *Time and Tide* strove to be the conscience of concerned liberal people regardless of gender or party affiliation.

Throughout the 1930s the journal continued to fight for social justice for all groups and to demand a comprehensive response to the serious economic and social problems plaguing the nation. *Time and Tide* attempted to awaken the public conscience to the need for better health care, higher school-leaving ages, improved nutrition, and prenatal and infant care programs. It continued to oppose gender discrimination in social welfare programs and argued for a more humane prison system designed to rehabilitate offenders and to create productive, responsible citizens.

Yet, as was typical of Edwardian reformers, Lady Rhondda seldom offered concrete proposals for achieving such social improvements. That she felt strongly about social injustice is undeniable, but she was never able to translate her concerns into a program of action. Like other Edwardian-era reformers, she often treated social problems as quasi-moral and was content with pious denunciations of injustice and generalized prescriptions for a better society.[59] She wanted the government to provide equal opportunities, better education, and improved housing and health care, but she seldom considered the costs of such programs. She attacked inequities between rich and poor but fell short of supporting any redistribution of wealth. She resented the movement toward a planned economy and the growth of government power, regarding both as infringements on the rights of the individual and of free enterprise. Yet she still expected the government to act to ameliorate poverty and inequality and apparently never saw any contradictions in her demands for individual freedom and government protection in the social and economic realms.

Not surprisingly, the focus of Lady Rhondda's attention and of the journal's commentary shifted away from domestic issues during the 1930s as the international situation deteriorated. The rise of fascism focused world attention on the questions of isolationism, pacifism, disarmament, and internationalism. Lady Rhondda believed that involving women in the printed debate on international affairs through the pages of *Time and Tide* set another critical precedent for women's involvement in nontraditional spheres and clearly extended the feminist tradition. She had always believed that women voters could make a difference in foreign affairs and consistently pressed for a peace-making role for women. Unlike some feminists, Lady Rhondda did not claim that women were pacifists by nature or that their "innate" maternal and nurturant qualities made them particularly suited to the task. Instead, she believed that past exclusion from the councils of war might make women more objective and less inclined to justify past policies. She consistently stood behind measures to preserve peace and to include female delegates in national and international agencies dealing with questions of peace and war.

But Lady Rhondda made it very clear that she was not a pacifist.

> I do not hold—that force can never be justifiable. I am well aware that
> should we ever find ourselves embroiled in another big war I should
> be no more a pacifist than I was in the last one. I was not a pacifist,
> not because I passionately believed my country to be in the right,
> though on the whole I accepted the view of the big majority of my
> fellow countrymen that she was, but because when she was fighting
> for her life I knew that, right or wrong, the only thing I could do was
> back her with all my strength and cease from all criticism, which
> seemed to me merely defeatist.[60]

Still, she believed that peace was a necessary precondition for a better
and more humane world, and she was hopeful that informed women
voters would throw the balance in favor of global harmony. She decided
to use *Time and Tide* to educate men and women readers about the evils
of war and militarism and the practical methods of pursuing peace.

The journal's commentary on foreign affairs was heavily influenced
by the liberal internationalism of Norman Angell. Angell's diplomatic
philosophy centered on an appeal to reason and enlightened self-interest.
He argued for prevention of war not only because it was inhumane and
irrational but because it was economically counterproductive and self-
defeating as well. Angell was committed to peace through international
(not unilateral) disarmament and League of Nations arbitration. Unlike
many of his contemporaries, he was uneasily cognizant that collective
security might require a military show of force to ground principles in
fact.[61] Angell's thinking heavily influenced Lady Rhondda, leading her
to place her faith primarily in the League of Nations, arms limitations,
and close cooperation with the major democracies—the United States,
France, and the Scandinavian countries. Her hopes that the memories
of World War I and the moral censure of the League would prevent war
dominated the pages of *Time and Tide* until the mid-1930s. The journal
condemned aggression, excessive nationalism, and the rising tide of
fascism, and supported the Peace Ballot, League of Nations sanctions,
and "legitimate" revisions of the Versailles settlement. As the European
situation worsened following a series of unilateral repudiations of international agreements and rising German, Italian, and Japanese expan-
sionism, Lady Rhondda and *Time and Tide* consistently argued for a
policy of justice and rational compromise. But when it became evident
that European dictators would not listen to reason and that peace could
be maintained only through armed conflict, she urged that the policy

of appeasement be abandoned. While abhorring war as much as anyone, she fully believed that the values of democracy, individual liberty,
and justice were worth fighting for.

When the Second World War broke out, Lady Rhondda was fifty-six
years old and plagued by ill health; therefore, her options for active service were limited. She had to be content with sitting on civil defense
committees and using the pages of *Time and Tide* to support the war
effort. The significant technological advances of the past twenty years,
particularly those in aerial warfare, placed the British home front in
possible peril from the beginning of the hostilities, and it was apparent
that the war on the home front would be more important than in any
previous conflict. Journals of opinion like *Time and Tide* would play
an important role in keeping the educated public informed and in monitoring governmental action or inaction on the home front as well as on
the battlefield.

Lady Rhondda's primary concern when war broke out (aside from national survival) was for the future of her journal. She was determined
that *Time and Tide*'s voice—the voice of the liberal, concerned populace—must survive to help pave the way for a better world in the postwar era, but she realized that maintaining the journal's high standards
in the midst of the disruption accompanying the hostilities would be
difficult. The press faced frequent, but fortunately short-term, delays
because of military censorship, paper shortages, printers' strikes, and
heavy bombing damage.[62] For *Time and Tide* the conditions of the war
years were a mixed blessing. In a time of such turmoil and rapid change,
readers turned to the political reviews for a weekly digest and thoughtful commentary on the sometimes overwhelming mass of information
confronting them. All journals did well during the war years, and *Time
and Tide* reportedly increased its circulation to over 30,000 copies per
week and generally covered its costs.[63] Unfortunately, however, the increased circulation was offset by a decline in advertising revenues and
the loss of staff members to war service. Almost overnight advertisers
withdrew their notices, uncertain as to what the future might bring.
Younger staff members were called up for intensive training courses or
active service. Contributors took up positions in the armed forces or
the various ministries or sought refuge in the country or the United
States. Paper shortages, blackouts, disrupted mail services, and air raid
warnings created tremendous dislocation, sometimes making it seem
almost impossible to get the paper out.[64] Occasionally the staff had to
leave the presses running and go to the shelters, continuing their discus-

sions about layouts and design while waiting for the all-clear signal to sound. Often the printer's van drove through the dark during air raids to pick up the final pages.[65] Working with a skeleton staff, limited supplies, and totally unpredictable circumstances, *Time and Tide* prided itself on never having missed an issue during the war.

The journal actively supported the war effort, expanded its coverage of foreign affairs, and included brief reports of troop movements and morale. It even went so far as to print advertisements for the Ministry of Information and Ministry of Supply, some of which would have been deemed offensive a decade earlier. For example, the Ministry of Supply ran an advertisement in September 1940 appealing to Britain's Mrs. Smiths to render "a very valuable service" by carefully putting out every scrap of metal, bone, and paper for recycling. It seems unlikely that the editor voluntarily printed such a patronizing advertisement, and one assumes that there must have been governmental pressure brought to bear on her to do so.[66] The decision is definitely inconsistent with the journal's general policy regarding women during the war years.

Not surprisingly, the patronizing attitude of such government advertisements was indicative of a broader government reluctance to integrate women into the war effort, despite their proven success in World War I. As early as 1934 female veterans of the first war took the initiative and began organizing as the Voluntary Emergency Service. They received some unofficial encouragement and even instructors for summer training camps from the War Office and the Air Ministry. By spring 1939 the government had revived the women's branches of the services and had created the Auxiliary Territorial Service (ATS) for female volunteers.[67] But these were largely cosmetic actions; the government made no real attempt to utilize the large and proven reserve of womanpower, choosing instead to allow only minor participation in nonessential areas. Patronizing pamphlets advised women to fulfill their duties as housewives (their providentially ordained role) to the best of their abilities. They were counseled to shop wisely, avoid waste, and keep their men's spirits up.[68] For women who were allowed to participate in the war effort, unequal pay rates were justified as a reflection of practices in the private sector.[69]

The government's blatantly discriminatory policies triggered a temporary revival of feminism during the war years. Primary attention focused on involving women in decisions regarding use of existing womanpower, compulsion (the forced movement of people into critical jobs), equal compensation for war injuries, and equal pay. The movement lacked the unity and direction of the 1920s campaigns and again fell prey to class divisions, but it did succeed in publicizing discrepancies and achieving minor improvements.

Time and Tide played a very active role in disseminating information and drawing attention to official gender discrimination. The journal condemned patronization as archaic and potentially dangerous and called on the government to make use of the existing women's branches which had proven themselves during the First World War. The policy of denying trained women pilots nonbattlefield positions for which they were qualified and forcing them into poorly paid jobs like ferrying planes from the factories was ridiculed as a waste of valuable talent and resources. Prophetically, the journal warned that women who were now prepared to make the sacrifice might not be so willing in the future if they were rebuffed.[70] *Time and Tide* consistently called for more effective mobilization and the extension of compulsion to women, arguing that it would be fairer and more efficient and would provide a tremendous morale boost for all British women. It also warned that government propaganda posters appealing to women to stay at home or take subordinate jobs to free men for more important work indicated an "abysmal ignorance of the modern young woman's outlook" and could hardly be expected to engender enthusiasm.[71]

Time and Tide's belief that British women would welcome compulsion appears unfounded in light of recent research. By the summer of 1941, acute labor shortages forced the government to begin "direction" of workers into essential industries and to extend conscription to women. Many women were reluctant to take up war work because of the burden of domestic responsibilities, the unpleasant nature of much of the work, and the low pay. While about 200,000 women were actually directed into essential industries, 2,067 were prosecuted for failure to accept direction. It seems likely that many of the others joined the work force more to escape prosecution than out of any real commitment.[72] Once on the job, female workers and servicewomen again faced hostility from their male counterparts, segregation into unskilled or semiskilled jobs, low pay, and allegations of immorality and promiscuity. Married women faced the dual burden of poor pay and heavy housekeeping, which was made even more difficult by rationing.[73]

Time and Tide recognized many of these problems and frequently warned that only a true integration into the war effort would satisfy women. Confined to nonessential tasks and subjected to unequal pay and compensation rates, women could fail to fulfill their true potential.

The journal deemed government speeches declaring their high regard for women workers worthless unless their admirable sentiments were translated into action. Inadequate training centers, unequal rates and compensation, and too few child care centers were condemned for limiting effectiveness and increasing burdens on female volunteers – further weakening the morale of Britain's women.[74] The key to maintaining morale in the dark days that were sure to come lay in convincing each individual that he or she had an important part to play, "not the part patronizingly handed out . . . by broadcasting uplifters or imposed by dyed-in-the-wool soldiers, but our own real share in a people's war."[75] The food minister was encouraged to be more responsive to the needs of women workers who found it impossible to stand in long queues for coupon booklets. He was urged to keep regional centers open late enough for these working women to receive their fair share.

As the sacrifices became greater and the government was increasingly involved in all aspects of the civilian population's life, *Time and Tide* kept up pressure to ensure that the basic needs of the people behind the war effort were met. The journal urged that, within the limits imposed by wartime conditions, every possible measure be taken to provide adequate protection, ensure good health, and alleviate social problems. Such measures would not only reinforce the war effort but would also show good faith for the future.[76] The journal called for more thorough air raid preparations, deeper and better provisioned bomb shelters, and better arrangements for evacuees. It supported campaigns for equal pay, increased family allowances, public nurseries, state-financed boarding schools for the less privileged, and improved fire services and comprehensive rebuilding programs in bombed-out districts. Government ministries were constantly challenged to provide better information and services to the public and to maintain fairness in their policies. For instance, the Ministry of Food was constantly urged to use its power more fully to solve problems of skyrocketing prices and malnutrition among the lower classes.[77]

Time and Tide's support for greater governmental intervention in social affairs was neither new nor unique. Throughout the 1930s the journal had pressed many of these same issues and had joined with liberal improvers, progressive conservatives, and even some socialists in arguing that it was the state's duty to provide a better life for its citizens, particularly to ameliorate conditions for those most in need. Lady Rhondda joined a group of progressive capitalists, academics, professionals, and centrist politicians holding to a new "middle opinion" group which recognized the need for planning, but within the framework of a capitalist system.[78] The pressures of World War II intensified the move toward a more collectivist system. In reflecting on postwar domestic needs, *Time and Tide* supported the consolidation and extension of wartime advances in social and economic reform, calling specifically for broader health care, unemployment, and education programs. It favored a continued merger between socialism and capitalism in postwar Britain, claiming that a system which combined the organizing power of the state with the driving force of the individual would be of the greatest benefit to all Britons.[79] The journal and its proprietor had come to believe, with many others, that the extension of the state's role was not necessarily an abrogation of personal freedom but a necessary tool to free many from an unsatisfying life.[80]

No one doubted as the war drew to its conclusion that six years of conflict had taken their toll on British resources and had brought some significant changes in domestic policy. High taxation was assumed to have equalized incomes; rationing and civil defense programs were thought to have submerged class distinctions; broader female participation in the work force was expected to undermine traditional gender roles. Recent research casts doubts on many of these assumptions. Penny Summerfield has suggested that while incomes may have risen for many workers, there was no consistent "leveling up" because of widespread pay differentials, the inability of the working classes to acquire property, and postwar reversals of fiscal policies favoring the working classes.[81] Likewise, Harold Smith has shown that government policies maintained strict sex differentiation for the female work force and that campaigns for equal pay met stiff resistance. More important, the unpleasant nature of much of the work and the dual burdens placed on married women actually strengthened traditional gender roles and led to a revival of domesticity in the postwar years.[82] The anticipated social revolution never occurred.

Women made a number of superficial gains during the war, but many were temporary or symbolic. The fact of conscription stood as a tacit acknowledgment of "more than rhetorical equality" in the eyes of some observers. Likewise, Princess Elizabeth's joining an ATS Transport Corps provided a symbolic legitimizing of women's military service. Wartime dilution agreements supposedly guaranteed women on "men's work" the full men's rate after a specified time on the job, but employers exploited loopholes in the agreements to justify unequal pay. Women's average earnings increased, but the increase was partially offset by longer hours and a higher cost of living.[83]

For Lady Rhondda the war had little immediate impact. Increased taxation was offset by the success of her journal. *Time and Tide* came through the war with an elevated reputation among British intellectuals in part because of its unwavering commitment to democratic values and in part because of its judicious commentary on both foreign and domestic affairs. Its reputation was further enhanced when publication of the "Nazi Black List" in September 1945 showed the journal to be one of the papers the Germans would have banned when they invaded England. Its editor and numerous contributors were marked for immediate arrest.[84]

In the postwar years, the struggle for equal rights for women once again consumed much of Lady Rhondda's time. Many of the gains of the war years quickly eroded after the conflict ended. Although employment opportunities for married women increased, women continued to face gender-based discrimination in the workplace. They remained concentrated in "female" jobs at the lowest end of the pay scale and were offered limited avenues for advancement. Despite supposedly liberating wartime experiences, large numbers of men and women continued to idealize the role of happy homemaker and to stigmatize women expressing dissatisfaction with that role as "unfeminine," "deviant," or sexually repressed "man-haters."

The postwar climate was not hospitable to female activism. As middle-class women lost their domestic help and entered the work force in increasing numbers, fewer were able to undertake the voluntary work which had traditionally formed the backbone of feminist activism.[85] Direct benefits from the extension of the welfare state, most notable in medical care, access to education, and family allowances, obscured the fact that the system was built on the traditional notion of a "natural" family structure and further reinforced the economic dependency of married women. Married women's access to the welfare system came through their husband's payments; thus, it was the husband's rights that were recognized. And married women who did pay into the system received lower benefits when sick or disabled than did men or single women.[86] The feminist movement entered a quiescent phase during the postwar years, leading what Elizabeth Wilson has trenchantly characterized as a "Sleeping Beauty existence" in a society which claimed to have wiped out gender-based oppression.[87] Only a small but committed minority was left to keep the fight for true equality alive in the face of widespread apathy, and Lady Rhondda again played an active role.

In the last ten years of her life, Lady Rhondda continued to work through a number of existing organizations to press for recognition of women and for a broader role for women in policy making. She worked with the Association of Women Journalists and the Women's Press Clubs to establish a fellowship for outstanding female journalists. She frequently presided over fundraisers for women's colleges and spoke to various organizations on topics relating to women's rights. She continued to work with the British Federation of University Women and the British Business and Professional Women's Association to open doors to advancement. In 1955 Lady Rhondda was named President of Honour of the Six Point Group.[88] For the woman who had founded the organization and guided it through its early years, this was a fitting tribute. In her final days, Lady Rhondda formally reentered the community of women activists.

Yet, as in the earlier years, Lady Rhondda's primary interest focused on the use of *Time and Tide* to bring remaining barriers to full equality to public notice and on the lonely fight to secure a seat in the House of Lords. The exclusion of females from the upper chamber of Parliament remained a highly visible symbol of women's inequality which Lady Rhondda hoped to see removed during her lifetime. Renewed efforts in 1946 saw only limited success, in the form of an admission from the Lords that the exclusion was a type of unjust discrimination.

When the usual appeals through newspapers, journals, and political channels failed to bring success, feminists turned to other media to broadcast their demands. Here too Lady Rhondda's public notoriety and longstanding battle for the cause made her a prime candidate to be featured in the media campaign. In October 1948 she participated in a film entitled *Women of Today* for a series entitled *This Modern World*. The film contained a segment with Lady Rhondda explaining to her interviewer, Anne Purvis, the status of women in the modern world and outlining measures to bring them full equality.[89]

Time and Tide consistently censured the continued exclusion of women from the Lords, ridiculing the 1946 and 1949 rebuffs.[90] In 1953 the journal lent its support to proposed modifications of the upper chamber, including the nomination of life peers whose public service and careers had marked them as individuals of ability and sound judgment. From then until passage of the Life Peerage Act in 1958, the journal urged that women be considered on the same terms as men in appointing life peers. Lady Rhondda's last public appearance, just three months before her death, was on a television program discussing the latest efforts to secure voting privileges for peeresses.[91]

While the fight for broader female representation consumed much of her time during her last years, Lady Rhondda also continued her crusade for justice in the nation's domestic policy, again using *Time and Tide* as her primary tool. By the 1950s, however, her commitment to individualism, justice, and equality had forced her and the journal into the Conservative camp. Her shift to a conservative stance was not unique but reflected a general shift to the right by many thirties radicals in response to past advances and disillusionment with the socialist state created after the war.[92] But, just as important, it paralleled significant changes in the Conservative Party's philosophy. With the promulgation of the *Industrial Charter* in May 1947, the party committed itself to "greater individualism within the central planning framework."[93] It reconciled itself to the welfare state and made a commitment to extend social services and reduce taxation through a return to competitive free enterprise.[94] That policy shift made it feasible for Lady Rhondda to abandon her traditional nonparty stance.

As the Labour government forged ahead with its plans to reorder British social and economic life along socialist lines, Lady Rhondda became increasingly convinced that the expanding bureaucracy and the dangers of nationalization outweighed the benefits of the social welfare measures. She regarded the bureaucratic aspect of the programs as dehumanizing and believed that individuals were treated as mere cogs in the great machinery of an increasingly impersonal state. The clearest assertion of this view appeared in the 24 May 1952 issue of *Time and Tide:* "We believe that the concentration of industrial power in the hands of the State leads directly to totalitarianism. Socialism may be theoretically and even practically possible, but it *is* possible only at the price of making the citizen the slave of the State from the cradle to the grave. It is possible only at the price of subordinating all life (and all human liberties) to its economic aspect."[95] Nationalization programs in particular drew censure for destroying political liberty, undermining individual initiative, and subsidizing inefficient industries.[96] The socialist experiment had failed, in Lady Rhondda's view, because it diminished the individual's role and responsibility in government and infringed on personal freedom.[97]

Lady Rhondda's shift to the political right was completed by *Time and Tide*'s formal affiliation with the Conservative Party. The 6 October 1951 issue of *Time and Tide* saw the words "Independent Non-Party" on the title page replaced with "The Independent Weekly." An editorial statement hastened to explain that the decision to campaign actively for a Conservative victory in the approaching general election symbolized no change in principle but an ongoing commitment to individual liberty and democratic government.[98] The *Times* parliamentary correspondent's column reprinted the explanation for *Time and Tide*'s change in policy that same day, a clear indication that the journal was still presumed to have some political influence. In the columns of *Time and Tide* Lady Rhondda continued to defend justice and individualism against the twin enemies of socialism at home and communism abroad for the rest of her life.

By the 1950s, however, the age of the weekly journals of opinion had passed. During the war, *Time and Tide*'s circulation had grown to about 40,000, but by the 1950s, increased production costs, competition for advertising, and the expansion of Sunday newspapers and television made publishing a weekly an extremely risky venture.[99] By 1955, circulation dropped to about 16,000, and *Time and Tide* was losing £400 to £500 per week.[100] Yet Lady Rhondda refused to let the journal which had been her life's work die, and she spent her last years trying to stop its decline.

But by this time her personal fortune was almost exhausted, and Lady Rhondda was forced to appeal to her readers. Their response was overwhelming. Expressions of sympathy, encouragement, suggestions for price increases, and monetary gifts ranging from two shillings to an anonymous £500 donation poured in. Many readers expressed guilt at having allowed Lady Rhondda to subsidize alone something which had given them such pleasure for so long. Letters and gifts came from all over Great Britain and from as far away as North America, India, Spain, France, and Malaya. Prominent readers rallied to the journal's support. T. S. Eliot wrote succinctly: "I should consider the termination of *Time and Tide* a national disaster."[101] T. H. Cubbitt added: "Life minus *Time and Tide* would indeed be bleak. I fear that it is a reflection of the barbarity of the present age that the revenue of a journal of the calibre of *Time and Tide* is not booming."[102] Rebecca West sent regrets that "the unkind age should have been so unkind to the work of your hands—and considering what you had made 'Time and Tide' the age has proved itself ungrateful as well as unkind."[103] The overwhelming response and generosity of the readers made the journal's immediate future secure and inspired Lady Rhondda with renewed hope. Peers, clergymen, students, housewives, literary giants, and royalty had rallied to the journal to the tune of £25,000, justifying its continued existence in her eyes as nothing else could have done. Claiming that it was impossible to think that a paper with such readers could fail, Lady Rhondda expressed confidence that a new era in the history of *Time and Tide* was beginning.[104]

The physical, financial, and emotional burdens of the struggle to keep the journal alive had taken their toll on Lady Rhondda's health as she grew older. Plagued with physical ailments throughout her adult life, she had experienced difficulties after fracturing a hip in an accident on board a cruise ship bound for South Africa in January 1957. The fracture had not healed properly and had left her partially immobilized. Over the next year, heart problems and a slowly spreading stomach cancer left her progressively weaker. In March 1958, an impending stomach operation which might have prolonged her life was canceled because of the *Time and Tide* crisis. Despite the pain of her illness, Lady Rhondda refused medication on the grounds that "*Time and Tide* demanded her mind."[105] Over the next few months, worries over the fate of the journal and her personal financial crisis combined with physical ailments to bring her to the brink of mental and physical exhaustion. On 5 July 1958 *Time and Tide* informed its readers that Lady Rhondda, now certain of the review's immediate future and exhausted by the four-month struggle, had entered the hospital for a period of rest and relaxation. In reality she had been rushed to the hospital bleeding profusely on 30 June and was given no chance for recovery. The cancer was too advanced.[106]

Death came quickly on 20 July 1958, and her ashes were buried at her beloved Llanwern five days later. It was announced shortly after her death that Lady Rhondda had spent over a quarter of a million pounds on *Time and Tide* and had so far dissipated her fortune that even the principal legacies of her will could not be met. In her will, as in her life, the reputation of *Time and Tide* had been placed first, with a provision that all the journal's overdrafts be taken care of before any personal bequests. After the journal's debts were discharged almost nothing was left. That would not have mattered to Lady Rhondda. She died content in the knowledge that the paper would live—the only thing that truly mattered to her. But her death deprived the journal of its spirit, and it did not long survive her absence.[107]

Lady Rhondda's passing drew comments from many of the leading journals and newspapers of the day. The *Times* devoted an entire column to her obituary, characterizing her as a "truly exceptional woman" and "champion of her sex" whose prominence in business and political journalism marked her as one of Britain's leading women. Claiming that her successful business style proved that she had above average capacity for commercial dealings, the *Times* emphasized her lifelong commitment to equality, her long record of achievement in business and civil affairs, and her generous sponsorship of young talent.[108]

Much the same sentiments were expressed in numerous remembrances printed in *Time and Tide* during the two weeks after her death. Letters poured in from prominent individuals in business, politics, and literature. Among the better known contributors were T. S. Eliot, C. V. Wedgwood, Norman Angell, Richard Law, Lord Salisbury, and Lord Birkenhead. These tributes were supplemented by letters from unknown readers who knew Lady Rhondda only through the pages of *Time and Tide* but nonetheless felt a special affinity for her because of shared viewpoints and intellectual bonds fostered by years of seeing glimpses of her soul and personality in signed contributions to the journal. Through all the notices runs a sincere appreciation for the values Lady Rhondda espoused and a recognition of the sacrifices she made. From those who knew her well came tributes to her generosity, her warmth, and her passionate commitment to the values and the causes she believed in. Recognition that she could have easily lived out her life in leisure and luxury made her friends even more willing to praise the qualities they admired in her. Of all the tributes published in *Time and Tide*'s pages, Rebecca West's seemed to sum up the essence of Lady Rhondda's life most accurately: "With her there died one of the last women whom Charlotte Brontë foresaw in *Shirley;* daughter of the men who had made great fortunes from modern industry, who were resolved to give more service to society than had been the habit of rich women."[109] Twenty-seven years after her death, a former colleague, Anthony Lejeune, could still write that, for him, touching the pages of *Time and Tide* evoked the richest memories of its remarkable editor. She was "one of those rare figures whose absence leaves an almost perceptible gap in the world."[110]

CONCLUSION

Lady Rhondda emerged from a privileged background to become one of the leading feminists of the interwar years. Originally swept up in the passions of a movement which promised some relief from the narrow boundaries of female existence, she became a committed feminist and spent her life as a crusader for women's rights and a more humane world. Her pilgrimage from proper young lady to rebellious suffragette to mature feminist and political activist provides an excellent vehicle for exploring the formative influences on women raised in the transitional years bridging the nineteenth and twentieth centuries, the partial transformation of their social and political milieu, and the changing course of modern British feminism.

Women born in the 1880s grew up with one foot in the Victorian era and the other in the modern world. During childhood they were imbued with the ideology of separate spheres for men and women and were conditioned in a way that fostered "feminine" virtues of service, compassion, and decorum and stamped out "masculine" traits of competitiveness, independence, and ambition. But changes in educational philosophy and gains from midnineteenth-century feminist agitation were beginning to undermine traditional gender expectations, opening new paths to these girls who would reach maturity in the freer Edwardian era. Lady Rhondda, born into a wealthy, liberal Victorian family, was raised in an atmosphere conducive to feminism. Her parents were less conventional than many and had the money to send her to St. Leonard's, one of the most enlightened of the new academically oriented girls' schools. As an only child, she was less bound by traditional gender expectations than was the norm. Nonetheless, she completed her schooling and returned home to await fulfillment through marriage and motherhood. Yet in doing so she was vaguely troubled by the dependent status such a role implied and the lack of other options.

Shortly after her marriage Lady Rhondda was introduced to the militant suffragette movement. Although she played only a peripheral role at this stage of the suffrage struggle, she found in it a sense of personal release and fulfillment that allowed her to shed her self-doubt and embark on a struggle for equality. It would have been easy for her to accept her privileged status as a birthright and to ignore the plight of less fortunate women. But she recognized that only chance (being the only child of a wealthy businessman and attending progressive schools) separated her from the average woman, and that given the same advantages and opportunities, others could match or exceed her achievements. Her recognition that all women were condemned to a subordinate position because of their gender led her to become a lifelong advocate of women's rights and responsibilities. She believed that every individual, regardless of gender, had unique talents and contributions to make. No barriers should stand in the way of fulfilling individual potential.

Lady Rhondda's support for women's (and men's) rights was more than a philosophical commitment. While her original commitment to militancy was purely emotional, her decision to risk her reputation and freedom by committing arson resulted from serious study and a feeling of solidarity with her oppressed sisters. Shortly after her militant career ended, she was given a unique opportunity to contribute to the women's movement when Lord Rhondda appointed her his business assistant. At the time, the female presence in the boardroom was nearly unknown and certainly unwanted. There she had an opportunity to prove by example that women could function in traditionally masculine realms. Shortly thereafter Lady Rhondda, like many other women, was given an even greater chance to prove herself as she was called on to contribute to the war effort. In war work, British women gained valuable administrative experience and a sense of dignity that translated into increased demands for a broader role in the postwar world.

After the war Lady Rhondda inherited her father's commercial concerns and for a time devoted herself to them with fair success. As a pioneer in the field she broke down barriers for women and became a visible symbol of women's ability to perform well in traditionally masculine fields. She became a model of the active, responsible woman citizen using her talents, her money, and her influence to help create a better world. Yet her commercial career reflects one of the essential problems of the postwar feminist movement, as women increasingly struggled over how to be a woman but not *only* a woman. Her father's patronage brought her into the boardroom; it was up to her to stay there and to earn her acceptance.

After World War I women not only entered the work force in increasing numbers but formally entered politics as well. Lady Rhondda's philosophical commitment to equality led her to become an ardent campaigner for the removal of all legal barriers to women's advancement and for full participation in all phases of British society. Her early involvement in the suffrage campaign led her to support a two-pronged rationale for women's participation. On the one hand, she invoked the Lockean natural rights argument; on the other, she emphasized the social benefits to the community that would supposedly accompany women's participation. While she always stressed women's right to enter the masculine spheres of business and politics, it is evident that she expected women to help redefine those spheres. She envisioned women as full and equal partners in building a better, more humane, more peaceful world.

Once the vote was granted (even on a restricted basis), Lady Rhondda and most feminists rejected militancy in favor of parliamentary pressure. When women had been wholly excluded from the system, they had had no choice but to make their presence felt outside it. Now that some had the vote, Lady Rhondda believed it was time to work within the system to exert political pressure and effect legal change. The altered circumstances required new strategies, and Lady Rhondda was again in a unique position to press for a broader political role for women. As a peeress in her own right, she claimed the right to take her place in the House of Lords. Although she never took her seat, despite repeated efforts, her actions helped publicize the incompleteness of postwar advances. In her personal battle against exclusion she demonstrated the defiant, persistent woman who would not be denied what she believed was hers by right and who would not settle for second best (in this case, a seat in the House of Commons). Here, too, her experiences illuminate an essential problem for postwar feminists: new laws like the Sex Disqualification (Removal) Act could bring about only limited political and social change as long as basic attitudes remained unaltered.

Although women were not allowed to sit in the Lords, the vote did give them some means to exert political pressure. But the removal of the unifying demand for the vote unfortunately threw the feminist movement into disarray. The 1920s saw the movement fragment into specialized pressure groups lobbying for the removal of particular legal, economic, or social disabilities rather than for the greater goal of equal status as human beings. Lady Rhondda detested this piecemeal approach, but she helped found a number of organizations with specific aims, most notably the Six Point Group, the Open Door Council, and the Equal Rights International. All of these groups insisted on absolute equality, coming into conflict with the rising tide of social feminism, which emphasized gender differences and sought recognition of women's special needs, particularly in the areas of industrial protection and maternity rights. This philosophical division did not prevent the two types of feminists from working together in the 1920s to secure specific reforms involving child and female labor, increased economic opportunities for women, and an equal franchise, but the schism still seriously weakened the women's movement. In the complacent years following the franchise victory, pressure groups helped to remove some of the most blatant disabilities and kept others before the politicians. Their vision may have been naive by today's standards and their victories incomplete, but the legal position of women gradually changed for the better. Unfortunately, as various groups worked toward specific ends, the underlying feminist identity was eroded away.

To help counter the erosion of the feminist identity and mold British women into a more knowledgeable and effective pressure group, Lady Rhondda undertook yet another challenge—the founding of a serious feminist periodical, *Time and Tide*, probably her greatest contribution to the interwar feminist movement. She was well aware that women's enfranchisement would have little impact until attitudes changed and women accepted the responsibilities of active citizenship. *Time and Tide* allowed Lady Rhondda to break down another barrier to women and to give the lie to the idea that women were not interested in politics. The journal gave feminists a voice—a public forum for expressing discontent and demanding change—and it was read in the most influential circles. In the pages of *Time and Tide* gender discrimination was ruthlessly exposed, and new visions of a more feminized society were given an airing. Readers were offered the type of intelligent analysis that would help them understand past injustices, and generalized prescriptions for the way to a better world as well. The journal continued to publicize women's issues throughout Lady Rhondda's lifetime. As women became better educated and more experienced *Time and Tide* tried to provide the broad coverage that would help them make intelligent choices. Through a tripartite approach of education, consciousness-raising, and political lobbying, Lady Rhondda worked to advance the cause of women and to increase their awareness and assertiveness.

With the franchise victory of 1928, many feminists believed their battle was won. The movement fragmented further. Prominent leaders turned their attention to other issues and joined mainstream political organizations emphasizing issues like socialism or pacifism. The socialist movement in particular undermined feminism by insisting that issues be considered along class rather than gender lines. Lady Rhondda, too, shifted her focus, not to any narrow issue but to the issue of human equality. Arguing that as long as political, economic, and psychological distinctions between men and women were emphasized, women would not be treated as full and equal human beings, she began to distance herself from specifically feminist causes. Far from abandoning the cause once equal suffrage was granted, as feminist critics then and now have charged, she pressed for a broader vision that would benefit both sexes and would advance the causes of justice and fairness. She was convinced that if women were treated fairly, they could and would succeed. Her goals remained much the same, but her methods differed with circumstances.

This process of distancing herself from strictly feminist causes seemed to Lady Rhondda the best way to ensure that *Time and Tide*'s arguments for a better world built on justice, equality, and individualism would be given a fair hearing. She continued to support women's rights through her example and in the journal, but within a broader reforming tradition. During the most active phase of her feminist commitment she had done everything in her power to advance the cause of women. As militant suffragette, prominent businesswoman, member of numerous national and international feminist societies, and editor and publisher of a feminist weekly, she was part of a determined minority which kept the issue of women's rights constantly before the public. Her career was a living demonstration of committed feminism in action.

But for all she gave the feminist movement, it gave her at least as much. It gave her the satisfaction of serving a worthwhile cause and a sense of belonging. For most of her adult life Lady Rhondda operated primarily within a community of women whom she met in connection with the feminist struggle. She drew her inspiration and support from these women friends and found a high degree of satisfaction in these relationships. These women were the sisters she had always wanted. The movement also gave her the self-respect and the courage to break out of restrictive bonds and face the challenges of the modern world. It made her feel that she was a human being, not just some invisible appendage of the men in her life. And it introduced her to the skills and qualities (organization, public speaking, persistence, lobbying) she needed to survive in the formerly masculine strongholds of commerce and political journalism.

By the mid-1930s the feminist movement had virtually broken down. Various pressure groups existed, but there was no real direction or organization. The sense of solidarity the suffrage campaign had brought had vanished along with the voting restrictions, and no single new issue had emerged to mobilize a concerted effort. Instead, the remaining issues tended to separate women. Questions of equal pay, marriage bars, and alternative life styles sparked bitter divisions. Past advances had improved women's status to the point that younger women were not interested in further agitation and often thought the older generation was out of step with the times. Many of the former leaders were nearing sixty or seventy and had tired of the fight or become disillusioned by the lack of more substantive progress.

The issue of equal rights for women lost its urgency in the troubled 1930s as serious economic and political problems threatened to undermine all liberty. Worldwide economic depression and the rise of fascism made specifically women's issues seem parochial and even dangerous at a time when national survival demanded unity and personal sacrifice. Antifeminist intellectual currents created a new and idealized version of the old domesticity. While obvious discrimination and official patronization temporarily revived the feminist movement during the Second World War, the postwar reaction and the surface gains of the welfare state combined to undermine both feminine solidarity and the feminist movement in the postwar years.

Through it all, Lady Rhondda continued to use her influence, her money, and her journal to demand a truer equality for women and to highlight the discrepancies betwen legal rights and women's reality. But in the postwar era her vision of feminism seemed passé to a younger generation which had grown up after suffrage was granted, after the professions were opened, and after the welfare state was incorporated. Women had made progress in political rights and to an extent in economic opportunities, and these gains helped obscure the fact that the majority of British women remained economically dependent, politically underrepresented, and socially stereotyped. The revival of British feminism would have to wait for the politicization of a new generation and the renewal of the type of female support networks and feminist identity that Lady Rhondda's generation had tried to distance themselves from.

NOTES

Chapter 1: Formative Influences: Family and School

1. Margaret Haig Mackworth, Viscountess Rhondda, *This Was My World* (London: Macmillan, 1933), 19–24.
2. *Times* (London), 15 April 1941; Rhondda, *This Was My World*, 19, 93.
3. Quoted in John Vyrnwy Morgan, *Life of Viscount Rhondda* (London: H.R. Allenson, 1919), 49.
4. Rhondda, *This Was My World*, 18.
5. Bentley Brinkerhoff Gilbert, *David Lloyd George: A Political Life – The Architect of Change, 1863–1912* (Columbus: Ohio State University Press, 1987), 96.
6. The biographical details of David Alfred Thomas' life are drawn from Morgan, *Viscount Rhondda*, and Margaret Haig Mackworth, Viscountess Rhondda, *D. A. Thomas, Viscount Rhondda: By His Daughter and Others* (London: Longmans, Green, 1921).
7. Gilbert, *David Lloyd George*, 19.
8. José Harris, "Bureaucrats and Businessmen in British Food Control, 1916–1919," in Kathleen Burk, ed., *War and the State: The Transformation of British Government, 1914–1919* (London: George Allen and Unwin, 1982), 142–43.
9. Deborah Gorham, *The Victorian Girl and the Feminine Ideal* (Bloomington: Indiana University Press, 1982), 10.
10. Ibid., 9–11.
11. Rhondda, *This Was My World*, 5–7; Sidney Walton, "The Man As I Knew Him," *Evening News*, 3 July 1918, D. A. Thomas Collection.
12. Lady Rhondda's childhood insecurities are a recurring theme of both her autobiography, *This Was My World*, and chapter 1 of her *D. A. Thomas*.
13. Gorham, *The Victorian Girl*, 3, 187; Walter E. Houghton, *The Victorian Frame of Mind, 1830–1870* (New Haven: Yale University Press, 1957), 187.
14. Winifred Holtby to Vera Brittain, 31 October 1925, in Vera Brittain and Geoffrey Handley-Taylor, eds., *Selected Letters of Winifred Holtby and Vera Brittain, 1920–1935* (London: A. Browne and Sons, 1960), 64; Rhondda, *This Was My World*, 5.
15. Rhondda, *D. A. Thomas*, 50; idem, *This Was My World*, 9.
16. This attitude was unwittingly reinforced by her mother's clannishness. In her autobiography Lady Rhondda relates how her mother trusted no one outside the family and did not really care to socialize with outsiders. She used family status rather than individual character as the yardstick of suitability and worth.
17. Rhondda, *This Was My World*, 9–10, 35–36.
18. Ibid., 14.
19. Gorham, *The Victorian Girl*, 3–12; Carol Dyhouse, *Girls Growing Up in Late Victorian and Edwardian England* (London: Routledge and Kegan Paul, 1981), 2–30.
20. Jane Mackay and Pat Thane, "The Englishwoman," in Robert Colls and Philip

Dodd, eds., *Englishness: Politics and Culture, 1880–1920* (London: Croom Helm, 1986), 192–93; Pat Thane, "Late Victorian Women," in T. R. Gourvish and Alan O'Day, eds., *Later Victorian Britain, 1867–1900* (New York: St. Martin's, 1988), 183.

21. Margaret Haig Mackworth, Viscountess Rhondda, *Leisured Women* (London: Hogarth, 1928), 22–24; Rhondda, *This Was My World*, 27.

22. Dyhouse, *Girls Growing Up*, 2.

23. Rhondda, *This Was My World*, 174.

24. Ibid., 11–12.

25. Gorham, *The Victorian Girl*, 105.

26. Rhondda, *This Was My World*, 11, 43.

27. Dyhouse, *Girls Growing Up*, 40.

28. Martha Vicinus, *Independent Women: Work and Community for Single Women, 1850–1920* (Chicago: University of Chicago Press, 1985), 166–70. See also Joyce Senders Pederson, "The Reform of Women's Secondary and Higher Education: Institutional Changes and Social Values in Mid and Late Victorian England," *History of Education Quarterly* 19 (Spring 1979): 61–91; and Sara Delamont, "The Domestic Ideology and Women's Education," in Sara Delamont and Lorna Duffin, eds., *The Nineteenth Century Woman: Her Cultural and Physical World* (London: Croom Helm, 1978), 164–87.

29. Julia Marie Grant, *St. Leonards School, 1877–1927* (Oxford: Oxford University Press, 1927), 35.

30. Rhondda, *This Was My World*, 79.

31. Grant, *St. Leonards*, 82; Rhondda, *This Was My World*, v, 58–59, 234. The fragmentary evidence about their relationship which appears in Lady Rhondda's autobiography makes it impossible to determine the exact nature of the friendship. It is not certain whether it was a case of simple admiration and respect for a much-loved teacher or more of a schoolgirl crush. On schoolgirl crushes in general, see Martha Vicinus, "Distance and Desire: English Boarding-School Friendships," *SIGNS* 9 (Summer 1984): 600–22.

32. Rhondda, *This Was My World*, 233.

33. Ibid., 96.

34. Ibid., 43.

35. Ibid., 52.

36. Vicinus, "Distance and Desire," 604.

37. Rhondda, *This Was My World*, 49–50.

38. Ibid., 82–83.

39. Ibid., 70–75. Despite her doubts, Margaret possessed something of a mystical temperament. She retained more belief than she could intellectually justify and continued to be troubled by her doubts. In later life, she became wholeheartedly Christian, but she continued to shy away from organized religion.

40. Leonore Davidoff, *The Best Circles: Society, Etiquette, and the Season* (London: Croom Helm, 1973), 17–18.

41. Ibid., 37–50.

42. Pat Jalland, *Women, Marriage, and Politics, 1860–1914* (Oxford: Clarendon, 1986), 22.

43. Rhondda, *This Was My World*, 82–85.

44. Ibid., 93.

45. Ibid., 97, 101–3.

46. Vicinus, *Independent Women*, 139–44.

47. Dyhouse, *Girls Growing Up*, 65.

48. Rhondda, *This Was My World*, 107.

49. Ibid., 104–8.

Chapter 2: Loosening the Bonds

1. Margaret Haig Mackworth, Viscountess Rhondda, "Notes on the Way," *Time and Tide*, 14 November 1936, 1582.

2. Rhondda, *This Was My World*, 108–17.

3. For a clear exposition of the antisuffrage mentality, see Brian Harrison's *Separate Spheres: The Opposition to Women's Suffrage in Great Britain* (London: Croom Helm, 1978). See also Martin Pugh, *Woman Suffrage in Britain, 1867–1928* (London: Historical Association, 1980).

4. Sandra Stanley Holton, *Feminism and Democracy: Women's Suffrage and Reform Politics in Britain, 1900–1918* (New York: Cambridge University Press, 1986), 14–18.

5. Ibid., 30.

6. Ibid., 32.

7. Ibid., 35–37.

8. Even at its height, the WSPU had only eighty-eight branches, located mainly in London and the southeast. Later its increasingly militant position diminished the organization's numbers significantly until in the end there remained only "a rump of family followers" more and more isolated from the real movement for women's suffrage. Pugh, *Woman Suffrage*, 25. A solid account of the rationale, organization, and activities of the WSPU is Andrew Rosen's *Rise Up Women! The Militant Campaign of the Women's Social and Political Union, 1903–1914* (London: Routledge and Kegan Paul, 1974).

9. Holton, *Feminism and Democracy*, 46.

10. Vicinus, *Independent Women*, 247–49.

11. Sandra Holton's study indicates that this is not unusual. The choice between a constitutional or a militant organization was frequently determined by the example of family or friends, by class, or by party ties. Holton, *Feminism and Democracy*, 39.

12. Rhondda, *This Was My World*, 121.

13. Lady Rhondda's autobiography totally neglects the content of the speeches, focusing instead on the sense of excitement and release. For a contemporary account that evokes both the spirit and the content, see Kitty Marion, typescript autobiography, 1938, Suffragette Fellowship Collection.

14. Rhondda, *This Was My World*, 119.

15. Rhondda, *D. A. Thomas*, 185–86.

16. Rhondda, *This Was My World*, 121.

17. There is some inconsistency in Margaret's recollections. In "My Introduction to the Press" (*Time and Tide*, 31 October 1924, 1051), she tells of an incident that she says took place when she was fifteen or sixteen. Her father introduced her to the editor of a daily paper in Wales and asked if she could submit articles on militant suffragism. Since the militant WSPU was not organized until 1903, when she was twenty, there is clearly a discrepancy.

18. Rhondda, *This Was My World*, 148–50.

19. Midge MacKenzie, *Shoulder to Shoulder: A Documentary* (New York: Allen Lane, 1975; Penguin, 1975), 54; Vicinus, *Independent Women*, 250–53.

20. Rhondda, *This Was My World*, 233.

21. Ibid., 103.

22. "Diary," *Time and Tide*, 6 February 1943, 103.

23. Marion, typescript autobiography, 173–74.

24. Rhondda, *This Was My World*, 121.

25. Ibid., 121–23.

26. Ibid., 125.

27. Ibid.

28. Ibid., 135–36.

29. Harrison, *Separate Spheres*, 193.

30. Rhondda, *This Was My World*, 144–45.

31. Pugh, *Woman Suffrage*, 22.

32. Sheila Rowbotham, *Hidden from History: 300 Years of Women's Oppression and the Fight against It* (London: Pluto, 1973), 80.

33. Rhondda, *This Was My World*, 150.

34. Ibid., 153–54.

35. *Times* (London), 28 June and 12 July 1913; Rhondda, *This Was My World*, 154–56.

36. Rhondda, *This Was My World*, 155–61.

37. For a full description of the process see Helen Gordon, "The Prisoner: A Sketch—An Experience of Forcible Feeding by a Suffragette," 1912, typescript, Suffragette Fellowship Collection.

38. For typical accounts from participants, see Christabel Pankhurst, *Unshackled: The Story of How We Won the Vote* (London: Hutchinson, 1959), and Emmeline Pankhurst, *My Own Story* (London: Evelyn Nash, 1914). Typical of later accounts is MacKenzie's *Shoulder to Shoulder*.

39. Balanced interpretations appear in Pugh, *Woman Suffrage*, and Holton, *Feminism and Democracy*.

40. Jill Liddington and Jill Norris, *One Hand Tied behind Us: The Rise of the Women's Suffrage Movement* (London: Virago, 1978), 219.

41. Holton, *Feminism and Democracy*, 3, 128.

42. Vicinus, *Independent Women*, 254.

43. See, for instance, her comments in "Diary," *Time and Tide*, 6 February 1943, 103, and Margaret Haig Mackworth, Viscountess Rhondda, "The Political Awakening of Women," in *These Eventful Years: The Twentieth Century in the Making As Told by Many of the Makers* (New York: Encyclopaedia Britannica, 1924), 2:558–60.

44. Rhondda, *This Was My World*, 120–21.

45. Dale Spender, *Women of Ideas and What Men Have Done to Them: From Aphra Behn to Adrienne Rich* (London: Routledge and Kegan Paul, 1982), 436–37; Rhondda, *This Was My World*, 125–27.

Chapter 3: Entry into a Man's World

1. Rhondda, *This Was My World*, 118.

2. Margaret Haig Mackworth, Viscountess Rhondda, *Notes on the Way* (London, 1937; reprint, Freeport, N.Y.: Books for Libraries, 1968), 69.

3. Rhondda, *This Was My World*, 118; Rose Feld, "Lady Rhondda on Two Democracies," *New York Times*, 10 September 1922, sec. 7, p. 2.

4. Rhondda, *This Was My World*, 225.

5. Ibid., 223–24.

6. Holton, *Feminism and Democracy*, 131–32.

7. This trip is often erroneously reported as a government mission, but Lady Rhondda's autobiography and the records of the trip in the D. A. Thomas Collection do not support this assertion. It was a personal business trip and has been confused with a later venture on behalf of Lloyd George to arrange for the purchase of munitions.

8. Rhondda, *This Was My World*, 239–40.

9. Ibid., 240.

10. Rhondda's own account of the incident can be found in *This Was My World*, 242–

60, in "May 7th, 1915," *The Spectator* 130 (5 May 1923): 747–50, and in "A Crowded Sea," *Western Mail* (Cardiff), 10 May 1915. The *Western Mail* article is in the Clipping Collection in the D. A. Thomas Collection.

11. Rhondda, *This Was My World*, 240–41.

12. Rhondda, "May 7th, 1915," 749.

13. Rhondda, *D. A. Thomas*, 200.

14. Arthur Marwick, *The Deluge: British Society and the First World War* (New York: W.W. Norton, 1970), 89–92; Ruth Adam, *A Woman's Place, 1910–1975* (New York: W.W. Norton, 1975), 45; John Williams, *The Other Battleground: The Home Fronts – Britain, France, and Germany, 1914–1918* (Chicago: Henry Regnery, 1972), 56–57; Trevor Wilson, *The Myriad Faces of War: Britain and the Great War, 1914–1918* (Cambridge: Polity, 1986), 710–18.

15. Evidence of women's willingness to work is widespread. In March 1915, the Board of Trade issued an appeal to all women willing to do paid work in trade, industry, and agriculture to register for service. It received 124,000 responses. Williams, *The Other Battleground*, 56–57.

16. Adam, *A Woman's Place*, 45.

17. Wilson, *Myriad Faces of War*, 718.

18. Rhondda, *This Was My World*, 223; *New York Times*, 1 July 1915.

19. Rhondda, *This Was My World*, 263.

20. Ibid., 265–67.

21. National Service Department, Women's Section, memorandum on the policy and organization of the section, May 1917, Women's War Work Collection, Emp. 49.1–48; and Margaret Haig Mackworth, "Suggestions for Recruiting Camp in Wales," 13 July 1917, NATS 1/1297, Public Record Office (henceforth PRO).

22. "Women and the War," *South Wales Daily News*, 17 July 1917, Emp. 49.2–23, Women's War Work Collection.

23. Margaret Mackworth to Miss Clapham, n.d., NATS 1/1268, PRO; Margaret Mackworth, *Monthly Report for June 1917*, 23 July 1917, NATS 1/1305, PRO.

24. Edith Lyttleton to Violet Markham, 22 May 1917, NATS 1/1307, PRO.

25. Violet Markham to Margaret Mackworth, 22 May 1917, NATS 1/1307, PRO.

26. This is attested to by voluminous correspondence in the file NATS 1/1307, PRO.

27. Interview with Miss Blackwell and Mrs. Chalmers Watson by Agnes Conway, December 1918, Emp. 49.1–51, Women's War Work Collection; memorandum by May Tennant and Violet Markham, 25 March 1917, NATS 1/1306, PRO.

28. *Brief Record of Service*, NATS 1/1297, PRO; "Woman Power: Lady Mackworth and Her Plans," *Pall Mall Gazette*, 8 February 1918, Emp. 49.2–32, Women's War Work Collection.

29. Memorandum, NATS 1/1272, PRO.

30. Margaret Mackworth, "Memorandum on Woman Power," 16 April 1918, NATS 1/1267, PRO.

31. Blackwell interview, Emp. 49.1–5, Women's War Work Collection; Rhondda, *This Was My World*, 268.

32. Rhondda, *This Was My World*, 268.

33. NATS 1/1280, PRO; extract from Rhondda, "Report on Conditions in Regard to Women Employed on War Work in Camps," in United Kingdom, Parliament, *Parliamentary Papers* (Commons), Cmd. 254 (May 1919). *Further Correspondence Related to the Termination of the Appointment of the Honourable Violet Douglas-Pennant as Commandant of the Women's Royal Air Force*, 845.

34. United Kingdom, Parliament, *Parliamentary Debates* (House of Lords), 5th ser., vol. 36 (1919), cols. 6–43.

35. Confidential memorandum no. 32, in United Kingdom, Parliament, *Parliamentary Papers* (Commons), Cmd. 182 (May 1919), *Air Ministry Correspondence Relating to the Termination of the Appointment of the Honourable Violet Douglas-Pennant as Commandant of the Women's Royal Air Force*, 813-32.

36. The full story can be gathered from Cmd. 182 and Cmd. 254. The case is rehashed in *Douglas-Pennant Case: In Defense of the Public Servant* (London: Publication Committee for Douglas-Pennant Case, 1931).

37. *Times* (London), 12 November 1918.

38. *Times* (London), 12 July 1918.

39. Evelyn Wrench to Lady Mackworth, 20 June 1918, NATS 1/1290, PRO.

40. For examples of the fulsome praise, see Sir Aukland Geddes, "Great Britain's Army of Workers," ix-xii, and Sir Leming Worthington-Evans, "The Miracle of Munitions," xv-xviii, in a special supplement to *Overseas* 3 (August 1918).

41. Margaret Haig Mackworth, Viscountess Rhondda, "The Women of Great Britain," *Overseas* 3 (August 1918): xx. The original draft was written by a Ministry of Information employee and corrected by Margaret (NATS 1/1290). These ideas do, however, recur in Margaret's later statements and articles. See particularly Rhondda, "The Political Awakening of Women," 557-70.

42. Minutes of meetings, Staff Investigating Committee, Ministry of Munitions, MUN 5/27/362/19; Final reports, Staff Investigating Committee, Ministry of Munitions, MUN 5/17/263/25, PRO.

43. She did not, however, appear before the committee, probably because of a serious illness during the period when the committee was meeting.

44. Wilson, *Myriad Faces of War*, 719.

45. Report of the Women's Advisory Committee, Ministry of Reconstruction, 18 December 1918, RECO 1/751, PRO.

46. United Kingdom, Parliament, *Parliamentary Papers* (Commons), Cmd. 67 (1 March 1919), *Report of the Women's Advisory Committee on the Domestic Service Problem*, 7.

47. Pugh, *Woman Suffrage*, 30; Elizabeth K. Nottingham, "Toward an Analysis of the Effects of Two World Wars on the Role and Status of Middle-Class Women in the English Speaking World," *American Sociological Review* 12 (1947): 667-69.

48. Dyhouse, *Girls Growing Up*, 6-7.

49. Wilson, *Myriad Faces of War*, 726.

50. J. M. Winter, *The Great War and the British People* (Cambridge: Harvard University Press, 1986), 153, 244.

51. Nottingham, "Toward an Analysis," 669.

52. See Martin Pugh, "Politicians and the Woman's Vote, 1914-1918," *History* 59 (October 1974): 358-74; David Close, "The Collapse of Resistance to Democracy: Conservatives, Adult Suffrage, and Second Chamber Reform, 1911-1928," *Historical Journal* 20 (1977): 893-918.

53. Holton, *Feminism and Democracy*, 130.

54. David Sweet, "The Domestic Scene: Parliament and People," in Peter H. Liddle, ed., *Home Fires and Foreign Fields: British Social and Military Experience in the First World War* (London: Brassey's Defense Publishers, 1985), 17.

55. Ibid.

56. Rhondda, *This Was My World*, 271.

57. David Lloyd George to Lord Rhondda, 18 June 1918; quoted in Rhondda, *D. A. Thomas*, 273.

58. Lord Rhondda left an estate of £883,645 (net personalty of £376,957). Margaret inherited his property and commercial interests.

59. Rhondda, *This Was My World*, 295.

60. Margaret Rhondda to Elizabeth Robins, 21 December 1921, Elizabeth Robins Collection.

61. Jeffrey Weeks, *Sex, Politics, and Society: The Regulation of Sexuality since 1800* (London: Longmans, 1981), 213.

62. Humphrey Mackworth to Margaret Mackworth, 24 November 1921; quoted in the *Western Mail* (Cardiff), 22 December 1922.

63. The account of these proceedings is taken from reports in the 22 December 1922 issues of the *Western Mail* and the *Times*.

64. Adam, *A Woman's Place*, 94.

65. Vera Brittain to Winifred Holtby, 23 December 1922; quoted in Brittain and Handley-Taylor, eds., *Selected Letters*, 21.

66. Theodora Bosanquet, diary, entry for 4 May 1948, Theodora Bosanquet Collection.

67. Margaret Rhondda to Winifred Holtby, 9 December 1933, Winifred Holtby Papers. Further comments on the value of marriage appear in Lady Rhondda's pamphlet *Marriage Is News* (n.d. [1938?]).

68. Rhondda, *This Was My World*, 294.

Chapter 4: Independent Businesswoman

1. While contemporaries regarded Lady Rhondda's business career as perhaps the most outstanding aspect of her early life, an attempt to understand her role in the commercial world is limited by the lack of comparative data available. Writing for Political and Economic Planning, Michael Fogarty stated in *Women in Top Jobs: Four Studies in Achievement* (London: George Allen and Unwin, 1971) that information on women in higher professional and management fields was extremely limited and that statistical analysis provided little or no help because of the small numbers involved and the scattered distribution of women in the occupations (13). He further reported that no record of the numbers or strategies of women in business existed, primarily because business itself is not classed as a profession and has no central body responsible for gathering data (181). Jane Lewis' study *Women in England, 1870–1950: Sexual Divisions and Social Change* (Bloomington: Indiana University Press, 1984) sounds the same theme but in even broader terms. Emphasizing the limited attention paid to the whole realm of women's work, she specifically laments that the interwar years are "virtually uncharted territory" (xiv).

2. Dorothy Thompson, "Women, Work, and Politics in Nineteenth-Century England: The Problem of Authority," in Jane Rendall, ed., *Equal or Different: Women's Politics, 1800–1914* (London: Basil Blackwell, 1987), 81.

3. Vicinus, *Independent Women*, 286.

4. Rhondda, *This Was My World*, 232. There is an absence of supporting material for businesswomen in general, but Lady Rhondda's personal recollections fit quite well with the data on pioneer professional women in Rosalie Silverstone and Audrey Ward, eds., *Careers of Professional Women* (London: Croom Helm, 1980).

5. *Liverpool Post*, 8 July 1918, Clipping Collection, D. A. Thomas Collection.

6. See Gorham, *The Victorian Girl*, 101–20; and Dyhouse, *Girls Growing Up*, 2–30.

7. Rhondda, *This Was My World*, 229–31.

8. For representative examples, see Lady Rhondda's comments in "Business and Commerce," in *Careers for Girls*, comp. J. A. R. Cairnes (London: Hutchinson, 1928), 58–59; "The Business Career for Women," *The Ladies' Field*, 28 April 1917, 353; *This Was My World*, 229–31.

9. Rhondda, *This Was My World*, 232.

10. Dyhouse, *Girls Growing Up*, 35.

11. Rhondda, *This Was My World*, 229.

12. Margaret Rhondda to Virginia Woolf, 6 February 1938, Virginia Woolf Collection.

13. Margaret Rhondda to Rebecca West, 1 June 1931, Rebecca West Collection.

14. Kathleen Woodward, "Lady Rhondda Besets the House of Lords," *New York Times*, 25 May 1924, sec. 9, p. 2; *Manchester Dispatch*, 14 June 1923, Clipping Collection, D. A. Thomas Collection.

15. Sandra Winston, *The Entrepreneurial Woman* (New York: Newsweek Books, 1979), 24.

16. Rhondda, *This Was My World*, 228.

17. W. D. Rubinstein, *Men of Property: The Very Wealthy in Britain since the Industrial Revolution* (New Brunswick, N.J.: Rutgers University Press, 1981), 178.

18. Rhondda, *This Was My World*, 265–66; interview in the *Los Angeles Times*, 31 March 1921, Clipping Collection, D. A. Thomas Collection.

19. For representative arguments, see Woodward, "Lady Rhondda," and the *Los Angeles Times*, 31 March 1921.

20. Winifred Holtby to Vera Brittain, 16 April 1924, in Brittain and Handley-Taylor, *Selected Letters*, 34.

21. This synthesis of Lady Rhondda's business philosophy is drawn from comments and interviews in the *Aberdeen Journal*, 4 July 1918; the *Monmouthshire Evening Post*, 5 July 1921 (both in the D. A. Thomas Collection); the *Times* (London), 23 November and 13 June 1931; Rhondda, "Business and Commerce," 58–64.

22. Martin J. Wiener, *English Culture and the Decline of the Industrial Spirit, 1850–1980* (Cambridge: Cambridge University Press, 1981), 127.

23. Milton Bronner, "Lady Rhondda, Industrialist and Editor to Visit U.S.," *New York World Telegram*, 14 December 1936, Schwimmer-Lloyd Collection.

24. Margaret Rhondda to Doris Stevens, 28 May 1927, 8 May 1931, Doris Stevens Collection.

25. For an overview of the problems of British industry between the wars, see Derek H. Aldcroft, *The Interwar Economy: Britain, 1919–1939* (New York: Columbia University Press, 1970), and John Stevenson, "Myth and Realities: Britain in the 1930s," in Alan Sked and Chris Cook, eds., *Crisis and Controversy: Essays in Honour of A. J. P. Taylor*, 90–110 (London: Macmillan, 1976). Problems in the coal industry are dealt with in Michael P. Jackson, *The Price of Coal* (London: Croom Helm, 1974), and W. H. B. Court, "Problems of the British Coal Industry between the Wars," *Economic History Review* 15 (1945): 1–24. The decline in iron and steel is treated in T. H. Burnham and G. D. Hoskins, *Iron and Steel in Great Britain, 1870–1939* (London: George Allen and Unwin, 1943).

26. Changes in Lady Rhondda's business holdings can be traced through the Institute of Directors' *Directory of Directors*.

27. *Times* (London), 18 January 1923; *Western Mail* (Cardiff), 2 December 1926, Clipping Collection, D. A. Thomas Collection.

28. Unfortunately, few documents exist to help explain Lady Rhondda's election to this prestigious position. The records of the Institute of Directors for this period are scant. The minutes of the 29 June 1926 meeting of council members indicated that Lady Rhondda had been interviewed by the chairman, W. Arthur Addinsell, but include no report on the subjects of that discussion. The Institute's *Report to the Annual General Meeting*, 28 July 1926, reports that a motion by Sir John A. Cockburn seconded by Addinsell to nominate her for the presidency was unanimously accepted by the council but again gives no comments on any debate. Institute of Directors, *Minute Book #2, 1911–1937*, 142, 145, Institute of Directors Library, London.

29. *Western Mail* (Cardiff), 29 July 1926.

30. *Paris Telegram and Continental Express*, 8 August 1926, Clipping Collection, D. A. Thomas Collection.

31. As no exact figures are available, this estimate is taken from P. G. Bailey Parker's *British Women in Business* (London, 1932; deposited in the Fawcett Library). Parker admits that this figure may be low because married women who were directors of companies often were not listed as such in the census.

32. *Public Ledger* (Philadelphia), 29 May 1921, Clipping Collection, D. A. Thomas Collection; *Time and Tide*, 4 November 1921, 1071.

33. *The Northern Whig*, 24 April 1926, Clipping Collection, D. A. Thomas Collection.

34. *Bristol Times and Mirror*, 27 June 1924, and *Westminster Gazette*, 3 December 1924, both in the Clipping Collection, D. A. Thomas Collection.

35. Since W. D. Rubinstein (*Men of Property*, 178) attributes similar qualities to successful businessmen, Lady Rhondda's candor seems uncalled for. Rubinstein states that most businessmen of the period had no special gifts but were carried along as successors to their fathers into their positions and forced to make the best of their situations—just as Lady Rhondda did.

36. Rhondda, *This Was My World*, 295.

37. Ibid., 296.

Chapter 5: Equalitarian Feminist

1. Margaret Rhondda, "Future of Women in Industry," 11 December 1918, Emp. 71.1, Women's War Work Collection.

2. Women's Industrial League, *Constitution*, Emp. 71.4, Women's War Work Collection.

3. Women's Industrial League, *Memorandum to the Prime Minister on the Future Employment of Women in Industry and Mr. Lloyd George's Reply Thereto*, December 1918, Emp. 71.6, Women's War Work Collection.

4. A. H. M. Fairbanks, "Women's Position in Industry," *The Englishwoman* 41 (January 1919): 3.

5–9. Women's Industrial League, *Memorandum to the Prime Minister*; *Times* (London), 7 December 1918, 17 February, 14 January, 13 February, 10 July, and 10 March 1919.

10. War Cabinet Committee on Women in Industry, minutes, 19 December 1918, Emp. 70, Women's War Work Collection.

11. Gail Braybon, *Women Workers in the First World War: The British Experience* (London: Croom Helm, 1981), 201–2.

12. Dale Spender, *Time and Tide Wait for No Man* (London: Pandora, 1984), 4.

13. For full details of the journal's history and Lady Rhondda's expanding role, see chapter 7, below.

14. Records for the Six Point Group are located in the Fawcett Library, but material for the early years is sketchy. Some early records can be found in the Nancy Astor Collection.

15. Elizabeth Wilson, *Only Halfway to Paradise: Women in Postwar Britain, 1945–1968* (London: Tavistock, 1980), 182; Dorothy M. Stetson, *A Woman's Issue: The Politics of Family Law Reform in England* (Westport, Conn.: Greenwood, 1982), 106, 112.

16. Elizabeth Robins, "Six Point Group Supplement, Introductory Number: The Six Points and Their Common Center," quoted in Spender, *Time and Tide*, 177–81.

17. *Time and Tide*, 2 March 1923, 243.

18. Margaret Rhondda to Vera Brittain, 15 August 1928, Vera Brittain Papers.

19. Vera Brittain, *Testament of Youth: An Autobiographical Study of the Years 1900–1925*

(London: Victor Gollancz, 1933), 583; David Mitchell, *Women on the Warpath: The Story of the Women of the First World War* (London: Jonathan Cape, 1965), 384.

20. *Time and Tide*, 19 January 1923, 52.

21. "The Power of the Vote," quoted in Spender, *Time and Tide*, 132–34.

22. Quoted in the *Manchester Guardian*, 15 March 1922, Clipping Collection, D. A. Thomas Collection.

23. *Daily Telegraph*, 1 March 1924, Clipping Collection, D. A. Thomas Collection.

24. Margaret Rhondda, "Labour and Women: Government's Broken Pledge," *Sunday Times* (London), 13 July 1924. Her statements proved true at least for herself, as she expressed no enthusiasm for Clement Attlee's Labour government after World War II.

25. *Daily Telegraph*, 17 December 1924, Clipping Collection, D. A. Thomas Collection.

26. The tests were apparently strict. The White List contained only 22 names in 1922, 20 in 1923, 18 in February 1924, and 12 in December 1924.

27. Brittain, *Testament of Youth*, 591–92.

28. George Viscount Curzon to Six Point Group, 5 July 1926, Nancy Astor Collection.

29. Quoted in Edith How-Martyn, *The Need for Women Members of Parliament* (London: Women's Election Committee, 1922), 4.

30. *Times* (London), 24 October 1924.

31. *The Nation* (London), 12 February 1921, Clipping Collection, D. A. Thomas Collection.

32. Six Point Group, *Forty-Fifth Anniversary Announcement*, 1966, Six Point Group Records.

33. Six Point Group, *The Six Point Group*, n.d. [1975?], Six Point Group Records.

34. Perhaps the fullest explanation of the old versus the new feminism appears in Mary D. Stocks's *Eleanor Rathbone: A Biography* (London: Victor Gollancz, 1949). More succinct but often more analytical treatments can be found in Rosalind Delmar, "Afterword" to Vera Brittain's *Testament of Friendship: The Story of Winifred Holtby* (London: Virago, 1981), 443–53, and Jane Lewis, "In Search of Real Equality: Women between the Wars," in Frank Gloversmith, ed., *Class, Culture, and Social Change: A New View of the 1930s* (Sussex: Harvester, 1980).

35. Jane Lewis, "Beyond Suffrage: English Feminism in the 1920s," *Maryland Historian* 6 (1975): 6, 13; Delmar, "Afterword," 451; Olive Banks, *Faces of Feminism: A Study of Feminism as a Social Movement* (Oxford: Martin Robertson, 1981), 171.

36. National Union of Societies for Equal Citizenship, *Equal Rights Milestones: Presidential Addresses at the Annual Council of Meetings of the* NUSEC (London, 1929), 8.

37. Delmar, "Afterword," 449–50; Lewis, "In Search of Real Equality," 230–31; and Lewis, "Beyond Suffrage," 14.

38. Margaret Rhondda, "The Political Awakening of Women," 558–69; Spender, *Time and Tide*, 42.

39. Quoted in the *Yorkshire Evening Post* (Leeds), 13 January 1923, Clipping Collection, D. A. Thomas Collection.

40. Quoted in "Speech Made by Lady Rhondda at NWP Luncheon in Paris, June 2," *Equal Rights*, 19 June 1926, 150.

41. Spender, *Time and Tide*, 42.

42. Margaret Rhondda, review of Elizabeth Robins, *Ancilla's Share*, *Time and Tide*, 27 June 1926, 616–17.

43. Herbert Marder, *Feminism and Art: A Study of Virginia Woolf* (Chicago: University of Chicago Press, 1968), 29.

44. Margaret Rhondda to Virginia Woolf, 6 February 1938, Virginia Woolf Collection.

45. An excellent discussion of women's interwar economic status appears in Neal

A. Ferguson, "Women's Work: Employment Opportunities and Economic Roles, 1918–1939," *Albion* 7 (Spring 1975): 55–68.

46. Open Door Council, *First Annual Report, 1926–1927*, Open Door Council Records.

47. Idem, *The Open Door Council*, n.d., [1929?], Open Door Council Records; Banks, *Faces of Feminism*, 170.

48. Open Door Council, *Third Annual Report, 1928–1929*, Open Door Council Records.

49. *Times* (London), 27 January 1927.

50. *Times* (London), 11 November 1926.

51. A good general statement of the argument appears in a pamphlet published jointly by the Open Door Council and the Equal Rights Committee entitled *The Factories Bill: Women Wage-Earners Need REAL Protection: Equal Status and Equal Safeguards* (London, 1929).

52. Lewis, "In Search of Real Equality," 212; Ferguson, "Women's Work," 65.

53. Kathleen Woodward, "Lady Rhondda Exalts Pin-Money Labor," *New York Times*, 19 January 1930, sec. 5, p. 7.

54. *Times* (London), 21 November 1935.

55. Not until 1970 did Parliament pass an Equal Pay Act.

56. United Kingdom, *Parliamentary Debates* (Lords), 5th ser., vol. 37 (1919).

57. Alice Fraser, "The Persistent Peeress," *Independent Woman* (December 1948): 346.

58. Milton Bronner, "Lady Rhondda, Industrialist and Editor"; Rhondda, *This Was My World*, 298.

59. For a brief account of the proceedings from the perspective of the major combatants, see Margaret Rhondda, "Women and the House of Lords," in G. Evelyn Gates, ed., *The Woman's Year Book, 1923–1924* (London: Woman Publishers, 1924), 82–83; and F. E. Smith, *Judgments Delivered by Lord Chancellor Birkenhead, 1919–1922*, ed. Roland Burrows (London: John Wiley and Sons, 1951), 467–91.

60. *Church Times* (London), 10 March 1922, Clipping Collection, D. A. Thomas Collection.

61. *New York Times*, 5 March 1922.

62. *Birmingham Post*, 8 March 1922, Clipping Collection, D. A. Thomas Collection.

63. *Western Mail* (Cardiff), 25 March 1922, Clipping Collection, D. A. Thomas Collection; Susan D. Becker, *The Origins of the Equal Rights Amendment: American Feminism between the Wars* (Westport, Conn.: Greenwood, 1981), 163.

64. *The Vote*, 10 March 1922; *Le Figaro*, 3 March 1922; and *Le Petit Parisien*, 8 March 1922; all in Clipping Collection, D. A. Thomas Collection.

65. *Sunday Times* (London), 5 March 1922, Clipping Collection, D. A. Thomas Collection.

66. *Evening News* (London), 7 March 1922, Clipping Collection, D. A. Thomas Collection.

67. Quoted in "Ladies' Day in the Lords," *Literary Digest* 73 (8 April 1922): 24.

68. *Western Mail* (Cardiff), 7 March 1922, Clipping Collection, D. A. Thomas Collection.

69. *Time and Tide*, 10 March 1922, 217.

70. *Sunday Chronicle* (London), 19 March 1922, Clipping Collection, D. A. Thomas Collection.

71. Lord Donoughmore, who had presented the motion, said there had been three or four cases where this had been done, but none had ever passed. Not surprisingly, this one did. United Kingdom, Parliament, *Parliamentary Debates* (Lords), 5th ser., vol. 49 (1922), col. 1027.

72. Rhondda, "Women and the House of Lords," 82–83.

73. Ibid., 83–84.

74. Smith, *Judgments*, 469, 477.

75. *Parliamentary Debates* (Lords), 5th ser., vol. 49, col. 1017.

76. United Kingdom, Parliament, *Parliamentary Debates* (Lords), 5th ser., vol. 37 (1919), col. 173, quoted in *Parliamentary Debates* (Lords), 5th ser., vol. 49, col. 1022.

77. Brittain, *Testament of Youth*, 582–84.

78. *Times* (London), 14 June 1922.

79. *Times* (London), 28 June 1922.

80. *Times* (London), 15 June 1922.

81. *Times* (London), 28 June 1922.

82. *Daily Sketch* (London), 16 October 1922, Clipping Collection, D. A. Thomas Collection.

83. Edward Iwi, "Women and the House of Lords," in Sydney D. Bailey, ed., *The Future of the House of Lords* (London: Hansard Society, 1954), 102–8; P. A. Bromhead, *The House of Lords and Contemporary Politics, 1911–1957* (London: Routledge and Kegan Paul, 1958), 255–56.

84. Margaret Rhondda to Nancy Astor, 5 November 1925, Nancy Astor Collection.

85. Nancy Astor to Secretary, attached to Margaret Rhondda to Nancy Astor, 5 November 1925, Nancy Astor Collection.

86. *Time and Tide*, 9 July 1926, 617.

87. *Times* (London), 4 February 1927; *New York Times*, 13 March 1927.

88. Noreen Branson, in *Britain in the Nineteen Twenties* ([London: Weidenfeld and Nicolson, 1975], 201), reports that 1.8 million women over thirty who had previously been excluded (domestic servants, women in furnished lodgings, widows living with married children, sisters keeping house for brothers) plus 3.5 million between twenty-one and thirty were affected. This would then make 14.5 million women eligible to vote, as opposed to 12.25 million men.

89. Ibid.

90. *Daily Mail* (London), 16 and 20 April 1927, and *Daily Mirror* (London), 14 April 1927; both quoted in Branson, *Britain in the Nineteen Twenties*, 201, 204.

91. Margaret Rhondda to Doris Stevens, 29 December 1927, Doris Stevens Papers.

92. Margaret Rhondda to Helen Archdale, 13 July 1928, extracted in Doris Stevens Papers.

93. Margaret Rhondda, "Women of the Leisured Classes," *Century* 115 (April 1928): 684.

94. Rhondda, *This Was My World*, 299. It is interesting to note that Lady Rhondda apparently later expressed to her close friends some doubts about the "flapper vote," intimating that it had been a mistake to grant the vote to such an immature group. Anthony Lejeune to Shirley Eoff, 28 November 1983.

95. Crystal Eastman, "International Cooperation," *Equal Rights*, 9 May 1925; quoted in *Crystal Eastman on Women and Revolution*, ed. Blanche Wiesen Cook (New York: Oxford University Press, 1978), 169.

96. Doris Stevens to Jane Norman Smith, 23 May 1928, Jane Norman Smith Collection.

97. Inter-American Commission of Women, press release, 1928–30, Doris Stevens Papers.

98. Open Door Council, *First Annual Report, 1926–1927*, Open Door Council Records.

99. In Crystal Eastman, "The Great Rejection: Part II," *Equal Rights*, 26 June 1926; quoted in Cook, *Crystal Eastman*, 206.

100. *New York Times*, 1 June 1926.

101. Margaret Rhondda to Margery Corbett Ashby in Eastman, "The Great Rejection: Part II"; quoted in Cook, *Crystal Eastman*, 200.

102. Margaret Rhondda to Alice Paul, 31 August 1926, Equal Rights Treaty File, Equal Rights International and Equal Rights Treaty, Records and Correspondence.

103. Winifred Holtby to Vera Brittain, 19 June 1926, in Brittain and Handley-Taylor, *Selected Letters*, 145.

104. Open Door Council, *Manifesto and Women Workers' Charter of Economic Rights* (1929), Nancy Astor Collection.

105. Vera Brittain, *Geneva: The Key to Equality* (London: Six Point Group, 1930), 6, Suffragette Fellowship Collection, 50.82/368.

106. Six Point Group, *Newsletter* (November–December 1928), Nancy Astor Collection.

107. Margaret Rhondda to Doris Stevens, 3 June 1928, 9 July 1928, Doris Stevens Collection.

108. Margaret Rhondda to Doris Stevens, 9 July 1928, Doris Stevens Collection. Apparently it took some persuasion. Helen Archdale wrote to Doris Stevens on 27 August 1928 that it was good that she had been able to persuade Margaret to participate.

109. Margaret Rhondda to Doris Stevens, 14 and 30 July 1928, Doris Stevens Collection.

110. Doris Stevens to Margaret Rhondda, 16 August 1928, and Margaret Rhondda to Doris Stevens, 20 August 1928, Doris Stevens Collection.

111. Doris Stevens, diary entry for 25 August 1928, Doris Stevens Collection. The reports here are contradictory. Press releases of the Inter-American Commission of Women credit Lady Rhondda and Alva Belmont with first demanding a hearing for the treaty from the World Peace Plenipotentiaries.

112. Full details of the Rambouillet incident are in the Doris Stevens Collection file on the subject.

113. Doris Stevens to Jonathan Mitchell, 29 April 1958, Doris Stevens Collection.

114. Margaret Rhondda to Vera Brittain, 4 September 1928, Vera Brittain Papers.

115. Betty Archdale for the Six Point Group to Mary Sheepshanks, 19 April 1930, Women's International League for Peace and Freedom, Series 5, 14, 13.

116. Betty Archdale to Lily van der Schalk Schuster, 8 July 1930, Equal Rights International File, Equal Rights International and Equal Rights Treaty, Records and Correspondence.

117. International Equal Rights Committee Inaugural Meeting minutes, 9 September 1930, Equal Rights International File.

118. Margaret Rhondda to Doris Stevens, 9 November 1930, Doris Stevens Collection. By the end of 1930 Lady Rhondda's withdrawal was officially confirmed by Helen Archdale, who informed Lily van der Schalk Schuster that Lady Rhondda had resigned from the council, saying she could no longer lend her name to organizations she had no time to support actively. Helen Archdale to Lily van der Schalk Schuster, undated, Equal Rights International File.

119. National Women's Citizens' Association, *National Women's Citizens' Association, 1918–1968* (London: National Women's Citizens' Association, 1969), 1; *Daily Sketch* (London), 3 February 1922, Clipping Collection, D. A. Thomas Collection.

120. See, for instance, the *Times* (London), 4 June 1924 and 16 July 1934.

121. Information about Lady Rhondda's commitments is available in contemporary press accounts located in the D. A. Thomas Collection.

122. Crystal Eastman, "Lady Rhondda Contends That Women of Leisure Are Menace," *Christian Science Monitor*, 8 March 1927; quoted in Cook, *Crystal Eastman*, 103.

123. Rhondda, *Leisured Women* (London: Hogarth, 1928), 33.

124. Eastman, "Lady Rhondda Contends," 103.
125. Quoted in Spender, *Time and Tide*, 41.

Chapter 6: The Private Margaret

1. George Bernard Shaw to Margaret Rhondda, 12 August 1932, George Bernard Shaw Collection.

2. The secretary of PEN wrote to Lady Rhondda on behalf of John Galsworthy (the current president) and the executive committee that her generous support was appreciated but agreed that it "should not be made a cause of heartburning to less fortunate members by any publication of name or other intimation." Secretary of PEN to Lady Rhondda, 30 September 1930, PEN Collection.

3. Margaret Rhondda to Charlotte Shaw, 29 November 1928, George Bernard Shaw Collection.

4. Vera Brittain, *Testament of Friendship*, 177.

5. *Time and Tide*, 26 July 1958, 904.

6. Virginia Woolf to Vanessa Bell, 21 June 1935, in Virginia Woolf, *The Letters of Virginia Woolf*, 6 vols., ed. Nigel Nicolson (New York: Harcourt Brace Jovanovich, 1975–82), 5:402–3; idem, *The Diary of Virginia Woolf*, vol. 2, *1920–1924*, ed. Anne Olivier (London: Hogarth, 1978), 167 (17 February 1922); vol. 4, *1931–1935*, ed. Anne Olivier (New York: Harcourt Brace Jovanovich, 1982), 123 (28 May 1933); Rhondda, *This Was My World*, 267.

7. *Daily Dispatch* (Manchester), 12 April 1924, Clipping Collection, D. A. Thomas Collection.

8. Lady Rhondda wrote shorty after the publication of her autobiography that she had received visits from individuals trying to sound her out about family scandals, her divorce, and her intimate relations, and criticizing her failure to include more personal information. Margaret Rhondda to Winifred Holtby, 4 March 1933, Winifred Holtby Papers.

9. Rhondda, *This Was My World*, xiii.

10. Ibid., vii.

11. See Samuel Hynes, *The Edwardian Turn of Mind* (Princeton: Princeton University Press, 1968), chaps. 5 and 6.

12. Margaret Rhondda to H. Macmillan, 5 April 1933, Macmillan Company Archives.

13. Quoted in Brittain, *Testament of Friendship*, 355; E. M. Delafield, review of *This Was My World*, *Manchester Guardian*, 24 February 1933, Biographical File; Virginia Woolf to Ethel Smyth, 12 March 1933, in Woolf, *Letters*, 5:167; Norman Angell to Margaret Rhondda, 11 March 1933, Norman Angell Collection; Vera Brittain to Winifred Holtby, 12 August 1933, in Brittain and Handley-Taylor, *Selected Letters*, 251.

14. Vera Brittain to Winifred Holtby, 5 April 1933, in Brittain and Handley-Taylor, *Selected Letters*, 251.

15. Frequent references to Margaret's moods and outbursts can be found in the diaries of her longtime companion, Theodora Bosanquet.

16. See Vicinus, *Independent Women*, 138.

17. George Bernard Shaw, "Authentic Shavian Democracy," *Time and Tide*, 10 February 1945, 114.

18. See, for instance, Vera Brittain's vehement denial of a lesbian relationship between Lady Rhondda and Winifred Holtby in *Testament of Friendship*, 328.

19. An excellent discussion of the changing attitudes toward sexuality during the early twentieth century can be found in Jeffrey Weeks, *Sex, Politics, and Society*, particularly

105–17. For the role of sexologists in developing an ideology hostile to women's relationships, see Sheila Jeffreys, *The Spinster and Her Enemies: Feminism and Sexuality, 1880–1930* (London: Pandora, 1985), 155–56.

20. Jeffrey Weeks, *Sexuality and Its Discontents: Meanings, Myths, and Modern Sexualities* (London: Routledge and Kegan Paul, 1985), 202.

21. Lillian Faderman, *Surpassing the Love of Men: Romantic Friendships and Love between Women from the Renaissance to the Present* (New York: William Morrow, 1981), 16–18.

22. Blanche Wiesen Cook, "'Women Alone Stir My Imagination': Lesbianism and Cultural Tradition," *SIGNS* 4 (Summer 1979): 738.

23. Margaret Rhondda, "Winifred Holtby," *Time and Tide*, 5 October 1935, 1392–93.

24. Winifred Holtby to Jean McWilliams, 21 February 1924, in Alice Holtby and Jean McWilliams, eds., *Letters to a Friend* (London: Collins, 1937), 240.

25. Brittain, *Testament of Friendship*, 266.

26. Margaret Rhondda to Winifred Holtby, 10 May 1930, Winifred Holtby Papers.

27. Brittain, *Testament of Friendship*, 317, 343.

28. Margaret Rhondda to Vera Brittain, 24 March 1936, Vera Brittain Papers.

29. The context of the phrase reads: "Did I in my last love-letter tell you I much like the poems and the sketch?" Margaret Rhondda to Winifred Holtby, 1 September 1932, Winifred Holtby Papers.

30. Brittain, *Testament of Friendship*, 328.

31. Margaret Rhondda to Winifred Holtby, 27 January 1931, Winifred Holtby Papers; Winifred Holtby to Vera Brittain, 5 August 1931, in Brittain and Handley-Taylor, *Selected Letters*, 186.

32. Margaret Rhondda to Winifred Holtby, 27 January 1931, Winifred Holtby Papers.

33. Ibid.

34. Winifred Holtby to Jean McWilliams, 28 May 1925, in Holtby and McWilliams, *Letters to a Friend*, 335–36; Brittain, *Testament of Friendship*, 328.

35. Vicinus, *Independent Women*, 161–62.

36. Rebecca West to editor, *Time and Tide*, 21 July 1958, 702.

37. Margaret Rhondda to Doris Stevens, undated [late 1928], Doris Stevens Collection.

38. Helen Archdale to Doris Stevens, 14 December 1928, Doris Stevens Collection.

39. Margaret Rhondda to Doris Stevens, 8 March 1931, Doris Stevens Collection.

40. Helen Archdale to Doris Stevens, 17 June 1928, 1 June 1929, Doris Stevens Collection.

41. Margaret Rhondda to Doris Stevens, undated [late 1928], Doris Stevens Collection.

42. Margaret Rhondda to Winifred Holtby, 11 and 23 April 1933, Winifred Holtby Papers.

43. Doris Stevens to Alice Paul, 13 September 1928, copy, Doris Stevens Collection.

44. Margaret Rhondda to Winifred Holtby, 17 October 1933, Winifred Holtby Papers.

45. Margaret Rhondda to Winifred Holtby, 16 November 1933, Winifred Holtby Papers.

46. Theodora Bosanquet, diary, entry for 18 July 1949, Theodora Bosanquet Papers.

Chapter 7: Publisher and Editor

1. Anthony Lejeune, "Lady Rhondda: Founder of *Time and Tide*," *Time and Tide* n.s. 1 (April 1985): 65–66.

2. Rhondda, *This Was My World*, 39–40.

3. *The Scotsman*, 8 March 1926, Clipping Collection, D. A. Thomas Collection; Anthony Lejeune, ed., *"Time and Tide" Anthology*, with an introduction by Margaret Rhondda (London: André Deutsch, 1956), 11.

4. Rhondda, *This Was My World*, 128.

5. Ibid., 304.

6. *Time and Tide*, 19 June 1954, 808–9; *Manchester Guardian*, 24 February 1933.

7. William Ewart Berry, Viscount Camrose, *British Newspapers and Their Controllers* (London: Cassell, 1948), 150.

8. Alice Fraser, "Persistent Peeress," 346.

9. *Time and Tide*, 14 May 1920, 24; Brittain, *Testament of Friendship*, 141.

10. *Time and Tide*, 14 May 1920, 4.

11. Spender, *Women of Ideas*, 438–39.

12. Many of Lady Rhondda's contributions in the early years were either unsigned or written under a pseudonym. She wrote theater reviews as "Anne Doubleday" (even after assuming the editorship), a series of articles on the leisured woman under the name "Candida," and diary notes as one of the "Four Winds."

13. *Time and Tide*, 5 October 1935, 1390.

14. This estimate is taken from *Time and Tide* financial reports for 1927 and 1928 in the Rebecca West Collection.

15. Perhaps the best exposition of this general argument in *Time and Tide* is "A Matter of Some Importance" (5 December 1924); reprinted in Spender, *Time and Tide*, 261–64.

16. *Morning Post*, 9 July 1923, Nancy Astor Collection.

17. Considering the relevance of *Time and Tide* comments to women and their affairs, one might be surprised that the journal is not better known or more frequently quoted by women writers. But the journal is not very widely available. Only two complete sets exist—one at the British Newspaper Library in Colindale, the other owned by Trust House Forte, which recently acquired the title and has revived the magazine. The prominent Australian feminist Dale Spender has written: "It can be argued that if there had been a conspiracy to keep this periodical out of the hands of young women then probably no more effective 'hiding place' than the present one [at Colindale] could have been found" (Spender, *Time and Tide*, 21).

18. *Times* (London), 21 July 1958; Lady Rhondda, in a letter to Rebecca West (1 June 1931, Rebecca West Collection), indicated that the cost was between £11,000 and £12,000 a year.

19. James Drawbell, *An Autobiography*, ed. Janet Morgan (New York: Pantheon, 1964), 275.

20. Margaret Rhondda to Doris Stevens, 28 May 1927, Doris Stevens Collection.

21. Lejeune, *"Time and Tide" Anthology*, 18. Frequent references to editorial conferences in the Bosanquet diaries, however, show the editor surrendering gracefully in the face of concerted opposition from staff members. When there was substantial disagreement she assumed responsibility for the final decision.

22. *Time and Tide*, 26 July 1958, 904.

23. Lejeune, *"Time and Tide" Anthology*, 18.

24. Margaret Rhondda to Doris Stevens, 21 August 1927, Doris Stevens Collection; Margaret Rhondda to Marie Meloney, 13 December 1938, Marie Mattingly Meloney Papers.

25. Margaret Rhondda to Marie Meloney, 15 April 1938, Marie Mattingly Meloney Papers.

26. Winifred Holtby to Jean McWilliams, 13 October 1926, in Holtby and McWilliams, *Letters to a Friend*, 429.

27. George Bernard Shaw to Winifred Holtby, 27 February 1931, Winifred Holtby Papers; Margaret Rhondda to George Bernard Shaw, 2 March 1930, George Bernard Shaw Collection; Margaret Rhondda to Winifred Holtby, 18 May 1932, 1 March 1935, Winifred Holtby Papers; Margaret Rhondda to Doris Stevens, 8 March 1931, Doris Stevens Collection.

28. Ezra Pound to Theodora Bosanquet, 23 September 1933(?), Winifred Holtby Papers.

29. Quoted in Drawbell, *Autobiography*, 220.

30. *Time and Tide*, 1 September 1934, 1073.

31. Margaret Rhondda, "Notes on the Way," *Time and Tide*, 9 February 1935, 184.

32. *Time and Tide*, 30 November 1935, 1735. "Notes on the Way" was originally conceived by St. John Ervine and was written by him until 1932, when it was turned into a clearinghouse for various intelligent, thoughtful viewpoints. Contributors ranged from George Bernard Shaw and T. S. Eliot to Richard Law (Lord Coleraine) and Herbert Morrison.

33. Representative examples can be found in Lady Rhondda's comment that nine-tenths of Malcolm Muggeridge's remarks were dangerous but provocative nonsense (*Time and Tide*, 30 November 1935, 1735) and her use of the editorial pages to criticize and "correct thinking" on A. L. Rowse's pro-Hitler comments (*Time and Tide*, 5 June 1937, 742–43).

34. Margaret Rhondda to Winifred Holtby, 6 October 1933, Winifred Holtby Papers.

35. Lejeune, "Lady Rhondda," 66.

36. Margaret Rhondda to Gordon Catlin, 16 December 1930, Gordon Catlin Papers.

37. Quoted in Lejeune, *"Time and Tide" Anthology*, 16.

38. Ibid., 13; Margaret Rhondda to Marie Meloney, 31 December 1937, Marie Mattingly Meloney Papers.

39. *Time and Tide*, 25 July 1936, 1067.

40. Anthony Lejeune reports ("Lady Rhondda," 66) that he omitted the particularly harsh final verse from the printed version. That verse read:

I fell on my feet. But what of those others,
    worse treated, Your memory's ghosts.
In gloomy bed-sitters in Fulham, ill-fed
    and unheated,
Applying for posts?
Do they haunt their successors and you as
    you sit there repleted?

41. Norman Angell, *After All: The Autobiography of Norman Angell* (London: Hamilton Hamish, 1951), 313; Malcolm Muggeridge, *Chronicle of Wasted Time*, vol. 2, *The Infernal Grove* (London: Collins, 1973), 63; vol. 1, *The Green Stick* (London: Collins, 1972), 191; Winifred Holtby to Margaret Rhondda, December 1931, Winifred Holtby Papers; George Bernard Shaw to Margaret Rhondda, 7 December 1931 and 3 November 1934, George Bernard Shaw Collection.

42. Kingsley Martin, *Editor: "New Statesman" Years, 1931–1945* (Chicago: Henry Regnery, 1968), 13.

43. *Time and Tide*, 12 October 1935, insert.

44. Lejeune, "Lady Rhondda," 65; Theodora Bosanquet, diary, entries for 2 October 1944 and 24 September 1945, Theodora Bosanquet Collection.

45. Noël Coward, *The Noël Coward Diaries*, ed. Graham Payn and Sheridan Morley (Boston: Little, Brown, 1982), 349.

46. Quoted in Rhondda, *Notes on the Way*, 46.

47. *Time and Tide*, 6 October 1934, 1224.

48. Martin, *Editor*, 13; Anthony West, *H. G. Wells: Aspects of Life* (New York: Random House, 1984), 141; John Betjeman to Clive Bell, 5 November 1952, Clive Bell Papers; Edith Sitwell to Christabel, Lady Aberconway, January 1935, in Edith Sitwell,

Selected Letters, 1919–1964, ed. John Lehmann and Derek Parker (New York: Vanguard, 1970), 47.

49. Lejeune, *"Time and Tide" Anthology*, 14–15.

50. Bronner, "Lady Rhondda, Industrialist and Editor."

51. Margaret Rhondda, "The World As I Want It," *Forum* 93 (April 1935): 243.

52. Margaret Rhondda to Doris Stevens, 28 May 1927, Doris Stevens Collection.

53. *Time and Tide*, 6 April 1928, 328.

54. Wilson, *Only Halfway to Paradise*, 162.

55. Margaret Rhondda to Vera Brittain, 4 October 1932, Vera Brittain Papers.

56. Margaret Rhondda to Virginia Woolf, 6 February 1938, Virginia Woolf Collection.

57. *Time and Tide*, 23 October 1937, 1402.

58. Spender, *Time and Tide*, 24.

59. Hynes, *Edwardian Turn of Mind*, 60.

60. Rhondda, *This Was My World*, 274.

61. For a useful synthesis of Norman Angell's philosophy and impact, see Albert Marrin's *Sir Norman Angell* (Boston: Twayne, 1979) and Louis Bisceglia's *Norman Angell and Liberal Internationalism in Britain, 1931–1935* (New York: Garland, 1982).

62. Kenneth E. Olson, *The History Makers: The Press of Europe from Its Beginnings through 1965* (Baton Rouge: Louisiana State University Press, 1966), 23–24.

63. No records exist. This information is taken from a letter from Anthony Lejeune, *Time and Tide*'s last deputy editor, dated 28 November 1983.

64. Margaret Rhondda, "Reminiscences of an Editor," 401.

65. *Time and Tide*, 21 September 1940, 941.

66. Ian McLaine's study, *Ministry of Morale: Homefront Morale and the Ministry of Information in World War II* (London: George Allen and Unwin, 1975) reported that the government issued confidential guidance letters to the editors suggesting the line their papers should take and frequently requested that certain nonsensitive material be voluntarily suppressed (92–93).

67. John Costello, *Virtue under Fire: How World War II Changed Our Social and Sexual Attitudes* (Boston: Little, Brown, 1985), 20.

68. Adam, *A Woman's Place*, 142.

69. Harold L. Smith, "The Problem of 'Equal Pay for Equal Work' in Great Britain during World War II," *Journal of Modern History* 53 (December 1981): 654.

70. *Time and Tide*, 3 December 1939, 1647; 9 March 1940, 236.

71. *Time and Tide*, 23 August 1941, 699.

72. Harold L. Smith, "The Effect of the War on the Status of Women," in Harold L. Smith, ed., *War and Social Change: British Society in the Second World War* (Manchester: Manchester University Press, 1986), 213. For an excellent discussion of the government's attempts to formulate and implement policy for women workers, primarily in the industrial trades, see Penny Summerfield, *Women Workers in the Second World War: Productivity and Patriarchy in Conflict* (London: Croom Helm, 1984).

73. Smith, "Effect of the War," 217–22.

74. *Time and Tide*, 22 November 1941, 1066; 23 November 1940, 1130.

75. *Time and Tide*, 16 May 1942, 397.

76. For a representative argument, see *Time and Tide*, 9 August 1941, 660.

77. *Time and Tide*, 10 May 1941, 375.

78. John Stevenson, "Planners' Moon? The Second World War and the Planning Movement," in Smith, *War and Social Change*, 65–66.

79. *Time and Tide*, 16 May 1941, 397.

80. José Harris, "Political Ideas and the Debate on State Welfare," in Smith, *War and Social Change*, 239.

81. Penny Summerfield, "The Levelling of Class," in Smith, *War and Social Change*, 200–7.

82. Smith, "Effect of the War," 221–25.

83. Mary Welch, "No Time For Tears," *Life*, 4 August 1941, 78; Costello, *Virtue under Fire*, 36; Summerfield, "The Levelling of Class," 186.

84. Germany, Geheime Staatspolizei, *Arrest List for England, 1940* (Stanford: Stanford University Photographic Department), 172, 270.

85. See Wilson, *Only Halfway to Paradise*, for a full discussion of the status of women during the postwar years.

86. Jane Jenson, "Both Friend and Foe: Women and State Welfare," in Renate Bridenthal, Claudia Koonz, and Susan Stuard, eds., *Becoming Visible: Women in European History*, 2d ed. (Boston: Houghton Mifflin, 1987), 540–42.

87. Wilson, *Only Halfway to Paradise*, 187.

88. Six Point Group, *Report of Annual General Meeting*, 8 November 1955, Six Point Group Records.

89. Theodora Bosanquet, diary, entries for 5 and 16 August and 15 October 1948, Theodora Bosanquet Collection.

90. Details of the 1946 and 1949 attempts, which were much the same as in 1922, can be found in Iwi, "Women and the House of Lords," 102–8, and in Bromhead, *The House of Lords*, 255–56.

91. Theodora Bosanquet, diary, entry for 30 April 1958, Theodora Bosanquet Collection.

92. Muriel Mellown, "Lady Rhondda and the Changing Face of British Feminism," *Frontiers* 9 (1987): 12.

93. T. F. Lindsay and Michael Harrington, *The Conservative Party, 1918–1970* (New York: St. Martin's, 1974), 151.

94. Alan Sked and Chris Cook, *Post-War Britain: A Political History* (Sussex: Harvester, 1979), 90.

95. *Time and Tide*, 24 May 1952, 539.

96. For representative criticisms, see *Time and Tide*, 5 July 1947, 709–10; 18 June 1949, 605; and 24 February 1951, 153.

97. Mellown, "Lady Rhondda," 11, 12.

98. *Time and Tide*, 6 October 1951, 933.

99. The circulation figure is reported in Camrose, *British Newspapers and Their Controllers*, 150.

100. Anthony Lejeune to Shirley Eoff, 28 November 1983.

101. *Time and Tide*, 12 July 1958, 862.

102. *Time and Tide*, 5 April 1958, 433.

103. Rebecca West to Margaret Rhondda, 13 February 1958, Rebecca West Collection.

104. *Time and Tide*, 15 March 1958, 315.

105. Theodora Bosanquet, diary, entry for 11 July 1958, Theodora Bosanquet Collection.

106. Theodora Bosanquet, diary, entry for 30 June 1958, Theodora Bosanquet Collection.

107. The journal continued under a board of directors appointed by Lady Rhondda for a few months before being sold to a private buyer. It was absorbed into *John O'London's Weekly* in 1962.

108. *Times* (London), 21 July 1958.

109. *Time and Tide*, 26 July 1958, 912.

110. Lejeune, "Lady Rhondda," 66.

BIBLIOGRAPHY

Primary Sources

A. Works by Lady Rhondda

Rhondda, Margaret Haig Mackworth, Viscountess. "Business and Commerce." In *Careers for Girls*, 58–64. Compiled by J. A. R. Cairnes. London: Hutchinson, 1928.

———. "The Business Career for Women." *The Ladies' Field*, 28 August 1917, 353.

———. *D. A. Thomas, Viscount Rhondda: By His Daughter and Others*. London: Longmans, Green, 1921.

———. Introduction to *"Time and Tide" Anthology*, ed. Anthony Lejeune. London: André Deutsch, 1956.

———. *Leisured Women*. London: Hogarth, 1928.

———. *Marriage Is News*, n.d. [1938?]. Pamphlet Collection. Fawcett Library, City of London Polytechnic, London.

———. "May 7th, 1915." *Spectator* 130, 15 May 1923, 747–50.

———. *Notes on the Way*. 1927. Reprint. Freeport, N.Y.: Books for Libraries Press, 1968.

———. "The Political Awakening of Women." In *These Eventful Years: The Twentieth Century in the Making As Told by Many of the Makers*, 2:557–70. New York: Encyclopaedia Britannica, 1924.

———. "Speech Made by Lady Rhondda at NWP Luncheon in Paris, June 2." *Equal Rights*, 19 June 1926, 150.

———. *This Was My World*. London: Macmillan, 1933.

———. "The Women of Great Britain." *Overseas* 3 (August 1918): xix–xx.

———. "Women and the House of Lords." In *The Woman's Year Book, 1923–1924*, 82–83. Edited by G. Evelyn Gates. London: Woman Publishers, 1924.

———. "Women of the Leisured Classes." *Century* 115 (April 1928): 684.

———. "The World As I Want It." *Forum* 93 (April 1935): 243.

B. Manuscript Collections

Norman Angell Collection. Bracken Library, Ball State University, Muncie, Indiana.

Nancy Astor Collection. University of Reading Library, Reading, England.

Clive Bell Papers. King's College Library, Cambridge, England.

Biographical File. Fawcett Library, City of London Polytechnic, London.

Theodora Bosanquet Collection. Houghton Library, Harvard University, Cambridge, Massachusetts.

Vera Brittain Papers. Mills Memorial Library, McMaster University, Hamilton, Ontario.

Gordon Catlin Papers. Mills Memorial Library, McMaster University, Hamilton, Ontario.

Equal Rights International and Equal Rights Treaty. Records and Correspondence. Fawcett Library, City of London Polytechnic, London.

Winifred Holtby Papers. Humberside Central Library, Hull, England.

Institute of Directors. Minutes and Evidence. Institute of Directors Library, London.

Macmillan Company Archives. University of Reading Library, Reading, England.

Marie Mattingly Meloney Papers. Columbia University Library, New York.

Open Door Council. Records and Correspondence. Fawcett Library, City of London Polytechnic, London.

PEN Collection. Humanities Research Center, University of Texas, Austin.

Elizabeth Robins Collection. Humanities Research Center, University of Texas, Austin.

Schwimmer-Lloyd Collection. New York Public Library, New York.

George Bernard Shaw Collection. Humanities Research Center, University of Texas, Austin.

Six Point Group. Records and Correspondence. Fawcett Library, City of London Polytechnic, London.

Jane Norman Smith Collection. Schlesinger Library, Radcliffe College, Cambridge, Massachusetts.

Doris Stevens Collection. Schlesinger Library, Radcliffe College, Cambridge, Massachusetts.

Suffragette Fellowship Collection. Museum of London, London.

D. A. Thomas Collection. National Library of Wales, Aberystwyth.

Rebecca West Collection. McFarlin Library, University of Tulsa, Tulsa, Oklahoma.

Women's International League for Peace and Freedom. Papers and Correspondence. University of Colorado Library, Boulder, Colorado.

Women's War Work Collection. Imperial War Museum, London.

Virginia Woolf Collection. University of Sussex Library, Brighton.

C. Government Records

Germany. Geheime Staatspolizei. *Arrest List for England, 1940*. Stanford: Stanford University Photographic Department.

United Kingdom. Parliament. *Parliamentary Debates* (Lords), 5th ser., vol. 36 (1919).

————. *Parliamentary Debates* (Lords), 5th ser., vol. 49 (1922).

————. *Report of the Women's Advisory Committee on the Domestic Service Problem*. Cmd. 67. 1 March 1919.

————. *Air Ministry Correspondence Relating to the Termination of the Appointment of the Honourable Violet Douglas-Pennant as Commandant of the Women's Royal Air Force*. Cmd. 182. May 1919.

————. *Further Correspondence Related to the Termination of the Appointment of the Honourable Violet Douglas-Pennant as Commandant of the Women's Royal Air Force*. Cmd. 254. May 1919.

United Kingdom. Public Record Office. Ministry of Munitions. Staff Investigation Committee Reports and Minutes, 1917–1918.

————. Ministry of National Service, Women's Section. Records and Correspondence, 1917–1919.

————. Ministry of Reconstruction. Women's Advisory Committee Reports, 1918–1919.

D. Books and Articles

Angell, Norman. *After All: The Autobiography of Norman Angell*. London: Hamilton Hamish, 1951.

Brittain, Vera. *Testament of Friendship: The Story of Winifred Holtby*. London: Macmillan, 1940; Virago, 1981.

————. *Testament of Youth: An Autobiographical Study of the Years 1900–1925*. London: Victor Gollancz, 1933.

Brittain, Vera, and Geoffrey Handley-Taylor, eds. *Selected Letters of Winifred Holtby and Vera Brittain, 1920–1935*. London: A. Browne and Sons, 1960.

Cook, Blanche Wiesen, ed. *Crystal Eastman on Women and Revolution*. New York: Oxford University Press, 1978.

Coward, Noël. *The Noël Coward Diaries*. Edited by Graham Payn and Sheridan Morley. Boston: Little, Brown, 1982.

Drawbell, James. *An Autobiography*. Edited by Janet Morgan. New York: Pantheon, 1964.

Holtby, Winifred. *Letters to a Friend*. Edited by Alice Holtby and Jean McWilliams. London: Collins, 1937.

————. *Truth Is Not Sober*. London: Collins, 1934.

Lejeune, Anthony. "Lady Rhondda, Founder of *Time and Tide*." *Time and Tide*, n.s. 1 (April 1985): 65–66.

Lejeune, Anthony, ed. *"Time and Tide" Anthology*. London: André Deutsch, 1956.

Martin, Kingsley. *Editor: "New Statesman" Years, 1931–1945*. Chicago: Henry Regnery, 1968.

Muggeridge, Malcolm. *Chronicle of Wasted Time*. Vol. 1, *The Green Stick*. London: Collins, 1972.

————. *Chronicle of Wasted Time*. Vol. 2, *The Infernal Grove*. London: Collins, 1973.

Pankhurst, Christabel. *Unshackled: The Story of How We Won the Vote*. London: Hutchinson, 1959.

Pankhurst, Emmeline. *My Own Story*. London: Evelyn Nash, 1914.

Pankhurst, Sylvia. *The Suffragette Movement: An Intimate Account of Persons and Ideals*. London: Longmans, Green, 1931.

Sitwell, Edith. *Selected Letters, 1919–1964*. Edited by John Lehmann and Derek Parker. New York: Vanguard, 1970.

Smith, F. E. *Judgments Delivered by Lord Chancellor Birkenhead, 1919–1922*. Edited by Roland Burrows. London: John Wiley and Sons, 1951.

Woolf, Virginia. *The Letters of Virginia Woolf, 1888–1941*. 6 vols. Edited by Nigel Nicolson. New York: Harcourt Brace Jovanovich, 1975–82.

———. *The Diary of Virginia Woolf*. Vol. 2, *1920–1924*. Edited by Anne Olivier. London: Hogarth, 1978.

———. *The Diary of Virginia Woolf*. Vol. 4, *1931–1935*. Edited by Anne Olivier. New York: Harcourt Brace Jovanovich, 1982.

———. *Three Guineas*. 1938. Reprint. London: Macmillan, 1977.

Selected Secondary Sources

Adam, Ruth. *A Woman's Place, 1910–1975*. New York: W. W. Norton, 1975.

Aldcroft, Derek H. *The Interwar Economy: Britain, 1919–1939*. New York: Columbia University Press, 1970.

Banks, Olive. *Faces of Feminism: A Study of Feminism as a Social Movement*. Oxford: Martin Robertson, 1981.

Becker, Susan D. *The Origins of the Equal Rights Amendment: American Feminism between the Wars*. Westport, Conn.: Greenwood, 1981.

Bisceglia, Louis. *Norman Angell and Liberal Internationalism in Britain, 1931–1935*. New York: Garland, 1982.

Branson, Noreen. *Britain in the Nineteen Twenties*. London: Weidenfeld and Nicolson, 1975.

Braybon, Gail. *Women Workers in the First World War: The British Experience*. London: Croom Helm, 1981.

Bromhead, P. A. *The House of Lords and Contemporary Politics, 1911–1957*. London: Routledge and Kegan Paul, 1958.

Camrose, William Ewart Berry, Viscount. *British Newspapers and Their Controllers*. London: Cassell, 1948.

Close, David. "The Collapse of Resistance to Democracy: Conservatives, Adult Suffrage, and Second Chamber Reform, 1911–1928." *Historical Journal* 20 (October 1977): 893–918.

Cook, Blanche Wiesen. "'Women Alone Stir My Imagination': Lesbianism and Cultural Tradition." *SIGNS* 4 (Summer 1978): 718–39.

Costello, John. *Virtue under Fire: How World War II Changed Our Social and Sexual Attitudes*. Boston: Little, Brown, 1985.

Davidoff, Leonore. *The Best Circles: Society, Etiquette, and the Season.* London: Croom Helm, 1973.

Delamont, Sara. "The Domestic Ideology and Women's Education." In *The Nineteenth Century Woman: Her Cultural and Physical World*, 164–187. Edited by Sara Delamont and Lorna Duffin. London: Croom Helm, 1978.

Delmar, Rosalind. Afterword to *Testament of Friendship: The Story of Winifred Holtby*, by Vera Brittain. London: Virago, 1981.

Dyhouse, Carol. *Girls Growing Up in Late Victorian and Edwardian England.* London: Routledge and Kegan Paul, 1981.

Faderman, Lillian. *Surpassing the Love of Men: Romantic Friendships and Love between Women from the Renaissance to the Present.* New York: William Morrow, 1981.

Fairbanks, A. H. M. "Women's Position in Industry." *The Englishwoman* 41 (January 1919): 1–4.

Ferguson, Neal A. "Women's Work: Employment Opportunities and Economic Roles, 1918–1939." *Albion* 7 (Spring 1975): 55–68.

Fraser, Alice. "The Persistent Peeress." *Independent Woman* (December 1948): 346–48.

Geddes, Sir Aukland. "Great Britain's Army of War Workers." *Overseas* 3 (August 1918): ix–xii.

Gilbert, Bentley Brinkerhoff. *David Lloyd George: A Political Life — The Architect of Change, 1863–1912.* Columbus: Ohio State University Press, 1987.

Gorham, Deborah. *The Victorian Girl and the Feminine Ideal.* Bloomington: Indiana University Press, 1982.

Grant, Julia Mary. *St. Leonards School, 1877–1927.* Oxford: Oxford University Press, 1927.

Harris, José. "Bureaucrats and Businessmen in British Food Control, 1916–1919." In *War and the State: The Transformation of British Government, 1914–1919*, edited by Kathleen Burk, 135–56. London: George Allen and Unwin, 1982.

———. "Political Ideas and the Debate on State Welfare." In *War and Social Change: British Society in the Second World War*, edited by Harold L. Smith, 233–63. Manchester: Manchester University Press, 1986.

Harrison, Brian. *Separate Spheres: The Opposition to Women's Suffrage in Great Britain.* London: Croom Helm, 1978.

Holton, Sandra Stanley. *Feminism and Democracy: Women's Suffrage and Reform Politics in Britain, 1900–1918.* New York: Cambridge University Press, 1986.

Hynes, Samuel. *The Edwardian Turn of Mind.* Princeton: Princeton University Press, 1968.

Iwi, Edward W. "Women and the House of Lords." In *The Future of the House of Lords*, edited by Sydney D. Bailey, 102–8. London: Hansard Society, 1954.

Jalland, Pat. *Women, Marriage, and Politics, 1860–1914.* Oxford: Clarendon, 1986.

Jeffreys, Sheila. *The Spinster and Her Enemies: Feminism and Sexuality, 1880–1930.* London: Pandora, 1985.

Jenson, Jane. "Both Friend and Foe: Women and State Welfare." In *Becoming Visible: Women in European History,* 2d ed., edited by Renate Bridenthal, Claudia Koonz, and Susan Stuard, 535–56. Boston: Houghton Mifflin, 1987.

"Ladies' Day in the Lords." *Literary Digest* 73, 8 April 1922, 24.

Lewis, Jane. "Beyond Suffrage: English Feminism in the 1920s." *Maryland Historian* 6 (1975): 1–17.

———. "In Search of Real Equality: Women Between the Wars." In *Class, Culture, and Social Change: A New View of the 1930s,* edited by Frank Gloversmith, 208–39. Sussex: Harvester, 1980.

———. *Women in England, 1870–1950: Sexual Divisions and Social Change.* Bloomington: Indiana University Press, 1984.

Liddington, Jill, and Jill Norris. *One Hand Tied behind Us: The Rise of the Women's Suffrage Movement.* London: Virago, 1978.

Lindsay, T. F., and Michael Harrington. *The Conservative Party, 1918–1970.* New York: St. Martin's, 1974.

Mackay, Jane, and Pat Thane. "The Englishwoman." In *Englishness: Politics and Culture, 1880–1920,* edited by Robert Colls and Philip Dodd, 191–229. London: Croom Helm, 1986.

MacKenzie, Midge. *Shoulder to Shoulder: A Documentary.* New York: Allen Lane, 1975.

McLaine, Ian. *Ministry of Morale: Homefront Morale and the Ministry of Information in World War II.* London: George Allen and Unwin, 1975.

Marder, Herbert. *Feminism and Art: A Study of Virginia Woolf.* Chicago: University of Chicago Press, 1968.

Marrin, Albert. *Sir Norman Angell.* Boston: Twayne, 1979.

Martin, Kingsley. *The Press the Public Wants.* London: Hogarth, 1947.

Marwick, Arthur. *The Deluge: British Society and the First World War.* New York: W.W. Norton, 1970.

Mellown, Muriel. "Lady Rhondda and the Changing Face of British Feminism." *Frontiers* 9 (1987): 7–13.

Mitchell, David. *Women on the Warpath: The Story of the Women of the First World War.* London: Jonathan Cape, 1965.

Morgan, John Vyrnwy. *Life of Viscount Rhondda.* London: H.R. Allenson, 1919.

National Union of Societies of Equal Citizenship. *Equal Rights Milestones: Presidential Addresses at the Annual Council of Meetings of the NUSEC.* London: 1929.

Nottingham, Elizabeth K. "Toward an Analysis of the Effects of Two World Wars on the Role and Status of Middle-Class Women in the English Speaking World." *American Sociological Review* 12 (1947): 666–75.

Olson, Kenneth E. *The History Makers: The Press of Europe from Its Beginnings through 1965.* Baton Rouge: Louisiana State University Press, 1966.

Open Door Council and Equal Rights Committee. *The Factories Bill: Women Wage Earners Need REAL Protection: Equal Status and Equal Safeguards.* London, 1929.

Parker, P. G. Bailey. *British Women in Business.* London: 1932.

Pederson, Joyce Senders. "The Reform of Women's Secondary and Higher Education: Institutional Change and Social Values in Mid and Late Victorian England." *History of Education Quarterly* 19 (Spring 1979): 61–91.

Political and Economic Planning. *Women in Top Jobs: Four Studies in Achievement.* Edited by Michael Fogarty. London: George Allen and Unwin, 1971.

Pugh, Martin. "Politicians and the Woman's Vote, 1914–1918." *History* 59 (October 1974): 358–74.

———. *Woman Suffrage in Britain, 1867–1928.* London: Historical Association, 1980.

Rosen, Andrew. *Rise Up Women! The Militant Campaign of the Women's Social and Political Union, 1903–1914.* London: Routledge and Kegan Paul, 1974.

Rowbotham, Sheila. *Hidden from History: 300 Years of Women's Oppression and the Fight against It.* London: Pluto, 1973.

Rubinstein, W. D. *Men of Property: The Very Wealthy in Britain since the Industrial Revolution.* New Brunswick, N.J.: Rutgers University Press, 1981.

Silverstone, Rosalie, and Audrey Ward, eds. *Careers of Professional Women.* London: Croom Helm, 1980.

Sked, Alan, and Chris Cook. *Post-War Britain: A Political History.* Sussex: Harvester, 1979.

Smith, Harold L. "The Effect of the War on the Status of Women." In *War and Social Change: British Society in the Second World War,* edited by Harold L. Smith, 208–29. Manchester: Manchester University Press, 1986.

———. "Feminism in the 1920s." In *British Feminism in the Twentieth Century,* edited by Harold L. Smith, 45–66. Amherst: University of Massachusetts Press, 1990.

———. "The Problem of 'Equal Pay for Equal Work' in Great Britain during World War II." *Journal of Modern History* 53 (December 1981): 652–71.

Spender, Dale. *Time and Tide Wait for No Man.* London: Pandora, 1984.

———. *Women of Ideas and What Men Have Done to Them: From Aphra Behn to Adrienne Rich.* London: Routledge and Kegan Paul, 1982.

Stetson, Dorothy M. *A Woman's Issue: The Politics of Family Law Reform in England.* Westport, Conn.: Greenwood, 1982.

Stevenson, John. "Myth and Realities: Britain in the 1930s." In *Crisis and Controversy: Essays in Honour of A. J. P. Taylor,* edited by Alan Sked and Chris Cook, 90–110. London: Macmillan, 1976.

———. "Planners' Moon? The Second World War and the Planning Movement." In *War and Social Change: British Society in the Second World War,* edited by Harold L. Smith, 58–77. Manchester: Manchester University Press, 1986.

Stocks, Mary D. *Eleanor Rathbone: A Biography*. London: Victor Gollancz, 1949.
Summerfield, Penny. "The Levelling of Class." In *War and Social Change: British Society in the Second World War*, edited by Harold L. Smith, 179–207. Manchester: Manchester University Press, 1986.
———. *Women Workers in the Second World War: Productivity and Patriarchy in Conflict*. London: Croom Helm, 1984.
Sweet, David. "The Domestic Scene: Parliament and People." In *Home Fires and Foreign Fields: British Social and Military Experience in the First World War*, edited by Peter H. Liddle, 9–19. London: Brassey's Defense Publishers, 1985.
Thane, Pat. "Late Victorian Women." In *Later Victorian Britain, 1867–1900*, edited by T. R. Gourvish and Alan O'Day, 175–208. New York: St. Martin's, 1988.
Thompson, Dorothy. "Women, Work, and Politics in Nineteenth-Century England: The Problem of Authority." In *Equal or Different: Women's Politics, 1800–1914*, edited by Jane Rendall, 57–81. London: Basil Blackwell, 1987.
Vicinus, Martha. "Distance and Desire: English Boarding-School Friendships." *SIGNS* 9 (Summer 1984): 600–22.
———. *Independent Women: Work and Community for Single Women, 1850–1920*. Chicago: University of Chicago Press, 1985.
Weeks, Jeffrey. *Sex, Politics, and Society: The Regulation of Sexuality since 1800*. London: Longmans, 1981.
———. *Sexuality and Its Discontents: Meanings, Myths, and Modern Sexualities*. London: Routledge and Kegan Paul, 1985.
Welch, Mary. "No Time For Tears." *Life*, 4 August 1941, 78–80.
West, Anthony. *H. G. Wells: Aspects of Life*. New York: Random House, 1984.
Wiener, Martin J. *English Culture and the Decline of the Industrial Spirit, 1850–1980*. Cambridge: Cambridge University Press, 1981.
Williams, John. *The Other Battleground: The Home Fronts—Britain, France, and Germany, 1914–1918*. Chicago, Henry Regnery, 1972.
Wilson, Elizabeth. *Only Halfway to Paradise: Women in Postwar Britain, 1945–1968*. London: Tavistock, 1980.
Wilson, Trevor. *The Myriad Faces of War: Britain and the Great War, 1914–1918*. Cambridge: Polity, 1986.
Winston, Sandra. *The Entrepreneurial Woman*. New York: Newsweek Books, 1979.
Winter, J. M. *The Great War and the British People*. Cambridge: Harvard University Press, 1986.
Worthington-Evans, Sir Leming. "The Miracle of Munitions." *Overseas* 3 (August 1918): xv–xviii.

INDEX

Abbott, Elizabeth, 79
Angell, Norman, 103–4, 126, 128, 135
Antisuffragism, 21, 27–28, 48
Archdale, Betty, 96
Archdale, Helen: and international feminism, 79, 96, 112, 123; relationship with Lady Rhondda, 107, 111–13, 114; and *Time and Tide*, 69, 112, 119, 120–21, 123
Astor, Nancy, 73, 87, 88–89, 120
Attlee, Clement, 129

Betjeman, John, 128, 131, 169n 40
Birkenhead, Lord (F. E. Smith), 84–86
Bosanquet, Theodora, 107, 113–15
Briand, Aristide, 94, 95
British Federation of Business and Professional Women, 97, 142
British Federation of University Women, 70, 97, 142
Brittain, Vera, 133; on Lady Rhondda, 28, 72, 101, 104, 109; and Six Point Group, 70, 95; on *This Was My World*, 104; and *Time and Tide*, 121, 126
Business, women in, 54–57, 60–61, 111, 159n 1
Business and University Women's Association, 61

Camrose, Lord William, vii, 118
Cat and Mouse Act, 31
Chalmers-Watson, Alexandra, 44, 119
Chesterton, G. K., 98, 107, 121

Child assault, 70, 73. *See also* Criminal Law Amendment Act
Cole, G. D. H., 129, 130
Consciousness-raising, 33, 121
Conservative Party, 71, 143–44
Consultative Committee of Women's Organizations, 87, 97
Coward, Noel, 129
Criminal Law Amendment Act (1922), 72, 73, 74
Cullis, Winifred, 107, 113
Curzon, Viscount George, 72–73

Delafield, E. M., 103, 119, 121, 126
Democratic-suffragist movement, 32, 48
Divorce, 50, 51
Domestic service, 46–47
Douglas-Pennant, Violet, 44
Drawbell, James, 124, 126

Education, women's, 8, 10, 11, 16–17, 83–84, 147
Efficiency Club, 61
The Entrepreneurial Woman (Winston), 57
Equal franchise, 88–90, 132
Equalitarian feminism, 75. *See also* Women's movement
Equal pay, 79–81
Equal Political Rights Campaign Committee, 89
Equal Rights International, 96
Equal Rights Treaty, 93, 94–96

Fawcett, Millicent Garrett, 22, 87
Franchise Act of 1928, 90, 132, 164n 94
Friendship, women's, 108, 111

Geddes, Sir Aukland, 41, 43, 44
Gordon, Helen, 31
Grant, Julia, 12

Haig, Anne Eliza, 1
Haig, Florence, 23
Haig, George Augustus, 1
Haig family, 1–2, 6
Haldane, Lord, 85, 86
Hamilton, Cicely, 27, 69, 119, 120
Herbert, Dennis, 72
Hewart, Sir Gordon, 83, 85
Holtby, Winifred: friendship with Lady Rhondda, 107, 108–111; on Lady Rhondda's personality, 58, 101; on *This Was My World*, 103; and *Time and Tide*, 121, 126, 128
House of Lords, women's exclusion from, 73, 81–88, 122, 142–43
Hunger strikes, 30, 31, 32; and force-feeding, 31

Industrial workers, women, 65–66, 67, 68
Institute of Directors, 60
International Federation of University Women, 113
International feminist movement, 90–96

Jurors, women, 73–74

League of Nations, 92, 94
League of Women Voters (USA), 91
"Leisured women," 98
Lejeune, Anthony, 127, 146
Lesbianism, 107–8
Life Peerage Act, 88

Lloyd George, David, 3–4, 38, 45, 65–66, 71
Lusitania, the, 37, 38, 128

MacDonald, Ramsey, 71
Mackworth, Humphrey, 18, 19–20, 24, 38, 49–50, 51
Mackworth family, 18, 20, 24
Macmillan, Chrystal, 19
Marion, Kitty, 26
Markham, Violet, 40, 41, 42
Marriage, 20, 27
Married women's employment, 47, 68, 73, 78–79, 81, 93, 122, 141
Married women's nationality, 93
Martin, Kingsley, vii, 128, 129
"Memorandum on Woman Power," 42
Middle class, 4, 6
Militant suffragism, 22–23, 24, 29, 31–32. *See also* Women's movement; Women's Social and Political Union
Mill, John Stuart, 27
Morrison, Herbert, 107, 129
Muggeridge, Malcolm, 128, 169n 33

National Union of Societies for Equal Citizenship (NUSEC), 75, 83
National Union of Women's Suffrage Societies (NUWSS), 22, 32, 36
National Woman's Party (USA), 77, 89, 90, 91, 94, 95
Notes on the Way, 104

Open Door Council, 79, 90, 92
Open Door International, 92–93, 95

Pankhurst, Emmeline, 22, 88–89
Paul, Alice, 90, 92, 93, 96
Pollack, Sir Ernest, 85
Pridden, Elizabeth, 13, 14, 27
Protective legislation, 75, 76, 77, 79, 91–93, 122
Provisional Club, 61
Public health, 97–98

Rambouillet, 95
Rathbone, Eleanor, 75–76
Representation of the People Act
　(1918), 49, 64, 86
Rhondda, Lady Margaret Haig
Mackworth:
　appearance, 55, 100–101
　and Helen Archdale, 111–13
　autobiography, 4, 12, 102–5
　and Theodora Bosanquet, 113–15
　and business career: activities,
　　35–36, 39; assets, 57, 58; at-
　　titudes of male colleagues, 39, 60;
　　limitations, 55, 60, 62, 63;
　　philosophy, 58–59; President of
　　Institute of Directors, 60, 61,
　　160n 28; reputation, 60, 61, 148;
　　support for women, 61
　childhood, 4–7, 10
　death, 146–47
　desire for child, 21
　divorce, 49–50
　education, 10–15, 16–17
　on education, 97
　as equalitarian feminist, 61–62,
　　76–96, 151
　and Equal Political Rights Cam-
　　paign Committee, 89
　and Equal Rights International, 96
　family background, 1–5
　female friendships, 107–16
　feminist betrayal charges, vii, 112,
　　133
　feminist influences, 27
　on foreign policy, 135–36
　on gender differences, 78
　health, 106, 136, 145
　and Winifred Holtby, 108–11
　and House of Lords, 82–88
　humanitarianism and philanthropy,
　　100, 166n 2
　and international feminism, 92–96
　on Keystone public, 118
　and Labour Party, 71, 143
　lack of personal papers, vii
　Leisured Women, 98
　lesbian rumors, 107–9

and the Lusitania, 37–38
male friendships, 106–7
marriage, 18–20
on marriage, 20, 49, 50
on married women workers, 68
on militancy, 32–33, 95
as militant suffragette, 23–33, 117,
　148, 155n 17; activities, 25–26,
　28–29; commits arson, 30; dis-
　satisfaction with press coverage,
　117; impact, 32–34; introduction
　to the cause, 23–24; prison and
　hunger strike, 30–31; with-
　drawal, 34
and "Nazi Black List," 141
Notes on the Way, 104
and Open Door Council, 79
on pacifism and peace, 135
on peacemaking role for women,
　134
personality, vii, 6–8, 27, 37,
　100–102, 105–6, 110–11, 113, 115
on "pin money" controversy, 80–81
political philosophy, 126, 132
on protective legislation, 79
and public health campaign, 97–98
on Rambouillet, 95
as reformer, 134
religion, 14, 15, 154n 51
and Julia Sandys, 12, 13
and the Season, 15–16
and Six Point Group, 69–70, 91–92,
　142
on socialism, 143
This Was My World, 102–5
and Time and Tide: assumes editor-
　ship, 123–25; contributions, 59,
　118, 120, 124–25; dissociation
　from feminism, 96; editorial
　philosophy, 125–28, 131–32, 133,
　168n 21, 169n 33; financial sup-
　port, 69, 124, 149; founder,
　117–18
on the vote, 32
on war, 131–32, 135, 136
on weekly reviews, 117–18, 127
and Win the War Centres, 45

Rhondda, Lady Margaret Haig
  Mackworth (*continued*):
  on women, 65, 74, 77–78, 133, 134
  on women in business, 56, 57, 58
  and Women's Industrial League,
    64–65
  and women's organizations, 96–97
  and women's rights, 67, 68, 72,
    76–77, 148–50
  Women's Royal Air Force inquiry,
    43–44
  "The World as I Want It," 132
  and World War I, 45–47, 49
  and World War II, 141
Rhondda Peerage Claim, 82–88
Robins, Elizabeth, 50, 69, 119, 120

St. Leonard's School, 10–11, 13, 147
Sandys, Julia, 11–13
Scott, Leslie, 87
Schreiner, Olive, 27
The Season, 15
Separate spheres ideology, 8, 13, 48
Sex Disqualification (Removal) Act,
  78, 81, 82, 83, 85, 87, 149
Shaw, George Bernard, 100, 101, 107,
  121, 125, 126, 128
Six Point Group: Black and White lists,
  72; Curzon's opposition, 72–73; for-
  mation, 69; goals, 69–70; and interna-
  tional feminism, 90, 92, 93, 95; and
  Rambouillet, 95; strategy, 70–73, 74
Social feminism, 75–76. *See also*
  Women's movement
Somerville College, 16–17
Spender, Dale, 133, 168n 17
Spurgeon, Caroline, 61
Staff Investigating Committee,
  Ministry of Munitions, 45, 46
Stevens, Doris, 90, 92, 93, 94, 95
Suffrage movement, 21–32, 36, 48–49,
  88–90. *See also* Democratic-suffragist
  movement; National Union of Wom-
  en's Suffrage Societies; Representa-
  tion of the People Act; Women's So-
  cial and Political Union

Tennant, May, 40, 41, 42
Testament of Youth (Brittain), 72, 104
This Was My World, 4, 102–4
Thomas, D. A.: business career, 3–4,
  34–35, 36, 54, 156n 7; family
  background, 2; health, 49; on militant suffragism, 24; peerage, 4, 39,
  49; political career, 3, 49; relationship with Margaret, 7, 9, 10, 35, 37;
  and World War I, 4, 36, 39
Thomas, Rachel, 2
Thomas, Samuel, 2
Thomas, Sibyl Haig, 1, 2, 6, 8–9, 16,
  34, 153n 16
Three Guineas (Woolf), 56–57, 78
Time and Tide, 69, 118–45:
  affiliation with Conservative Party,
    143, 144
  Archdale's editorship, 69, 112,
    120–23
  availability, viii, 168n 17
  board of directors, 119
  circulation, vii, 121, 128, 136, 144
  contributors, 120–21, 125–26
  demise, 171n 107
  editorial philosophy, 119–20,
    121–23, 125–28, 131, 133, 140, 143
  financial difficulties, 59, 144, 145
  and foreign affairs, 135
  on nationalism, 143
  and "Nazi Black List," 141
  non-party orientation, 119–33
  "Notes on the Way," 127
  origin, 69
  on protective legislation, 79
  rationale, 69
  readership, 129–31
  reputation, viii, 89, 129–32
  Lady Rhondda's roles, 59, 118, 120,
    129, 145
  and Six Point Group, 70, 72
  on socialism, 143, 144
  and social justice, 133
  strategies, 121–26
  and women's issues, 123, 132, 133,
    134
  and World War II, 136–39, 170n 66

Times (London), 44, 45, 50–51, 66, 87, 144, 146

Vindication of the Rights of Woman, 75

Wedgwood, Veronica, 101, 124, 128
Weekly reviews, 117, 129, 136, 144
Wells, H. G., 126, 131
West, Rebecca, 69, 111, 119, 120, 144, 146
Wiener, Martin, 59
Wilkinson, Ellen, 77, 107, 120, 125, 129
Win the War Centres, 45
Wintringham, Margaret, 73, 88
Wollstonecraft, Mary, 75
Women, social conditioning of, 8–9, 15, 19, 55–56, 121, 147
Women's Advisory Council, 46–47
Women's Army Auxiliary Corps, 40, 43
Women's Citizens' Associations, 70, 96
Women's Election Committee, 97
Women's Employment Committee, 47

Women's Industrial League, 64–68
Women's movement: attack on separate spheres ideology, 21–22; interwar movement, 74–76, 132, 152; post–World War II, 141–42, 150, 151; World War II setbacks and revival, 137–38, 139, 140. *See also* Suffrage movement
Women's Royal Air Force, 43–44
Women's Section, Ministry of National Service, 41–45
Women's Section, National Service Department, 40, 41
Women's Service Bureau, 43
Women's Social and Political Union (WSPU), 22, 25–26, 29, 31, 36. *See also* Militant suffragism
Women Workers' Charter of Economic Rights, 93
Woolf, Virginia, 56, 78, 101–2, 103, 121, 133
World War I: and Lady Rhondda, 36, 37–38; and suffrage movement, 36, 48–49; and women, 38, 40, 41–49
World War II: and Lady Rhondda, 136, 141, and *Time and Tide*, 136–41; and women, 137–39, 140–41